JUSTICE
AND
VENGEANCE

ARWEN BICKNELL

Published by Open Books

ISBN-10: 0692697969

ISBN-13: 978-0692697962

CONTENTS

Prologue: A Matter of Honor

*L*ucien Fewell breathed deeply as he watched the locomotive pull out of Bristoe Station, Virginia, and wished he had a hair of the dog to calm his nerves and steady his hands. He had ridden the train all night from Lynchburg. A whole night of restless inactivity, even if the train was lurching along at 40 miles per hour. Sitting and waiting didn't come easy for Rhoda (as his family and friends had called him since childhood). Walking the last five miles to the Brentsville Jail, over rolling hills along a dusty road, would settle his nerves. The heft of two pistols—a Navy revolver in his coat pocket and a smaller pistol in his vest—reminded him of his commitment. He nodded to the ticket agent, turned his face eastward, and began walking.

He thought about the train as he walked. It was easier than thinking about what lay before him, and it helped him

1

forget his parched throat and aching head. In 1872, Virginians were starting to take the railroad for granted again, even if snowstorms buried tracks and floods wiped out the bridges from time to time. It hadn't been like that during the war. So much fighting had centered on possession of those lines. Lucien and pretty much everybody he knew had killed in defense of those railroads; most felt a certain jealous sense of possession for each spike and tie. Then the war ended, and the Orange & Alexandria had merged with the Manassas line in 1867 to become the Orange, Alexandria, & Manassas, providing an economic boost to the town of Manassas, where the rest of Lucien's family lived. His father, William Sanford Fewell, was the depot agent there. It was this rail line that his younger sister, 16-year-old Fannie, took when she slipped off with that lying sneak Jim Clark. He still couldn't believe their father hadn't managed to catch the girl and stop her. If that had happened, today's trip wouldn't be necessary.

Lucien snorted. The girl was a blithering idiot. Bad enough she had run off with a lawyer, of all things (and one rumored to be turning Republican, at that), but of course she had chosen the one Lucien hated most. Jim, that grasping up-and-comer, had been a personal enemy ever since he'd gone to Alexandria some time ago and hauled Lucien back to Brentsville for arrest and trial after an unfortunate bout of drinking—one of many such incidents in Lucien's past. Lucien knew how to raise hell, but most people knew to stay out of his way. Not Jim; he'd made it a crusade to go after Lucien. But that was ancient history, and it had nothing to do with today, Lucien insisted to himself. His sister was a fool, but she had also been fooled, which only proved what Lucien had known all along: Clark was a bad man. Maybe Fannie had done everyone a favor, giving Lucien a reason to settle the score.

The grasshoppers and locusts were buzzing away. Even at this early hour, Lucien's skin felt damp and greasy in the humidity of late August. He walked slowly. The appointment would wait. Clark wasn't going anywhere. Lucien had put off this obligation a couple of times already. He'd planned to do this last Saturday, but dutch courage had gotten the better of him—again—and he'd had to sleep it off. And then he'd had to go to Lynchburg for work, to help install lightning rods along Orange Road.

But he was here now, ready to wrap things up.

The chatter drove him crazy. Every time he turned around, someone else was whispering gossip—or yapping right out loud—wondering why the family hadn't exacted revenge. Why? Because his father had forbidden it, that's why. But Lucien couldn't take it anymore. His father was wrong about this. It was a matter of honor, the family reputation at stake.

Lucien was approaching town now, and the sun was just clearing the trees. Sweat beaded on the back of his neck, and he could feel it pooling around his hatband. The Navy revolver, 13 inches long and more than two pounds of steel and wood, bumped against his side. He walked across the town green toward the jail with a measured, steady pace. A couple men were sitting on the porch of Kincheloe's store across the road, but they didn't call to him. Nobody approached him as he marched resolutely across the expansive strip of lawn—wider than it had been once upon a time; before the war, the county clerk's office had been next to the courthouse, but it had been destroyed in the fighting, along with countless other structures. The debris had been cleared away, but no rebuilding had occurred. Lucien strode around to the side of the jail, where he was mildly surprised to find the door open. He knew his way around the jail better than many; he'd spent enough time here on the wrong side of the law to know exactly which floorboards creaked and how loudly. His last visit had been in February, after a scrap with the Johnson boys. Getting out of that one had been expensive. He shook his head. No time to think about that. He pushed the door open and climbed the narrow stairs to the debtor's cell, where he'd heard Clark was being held.

Clark wasn't there.

But a young black boy was.

"Where's Clark?" Lucien asked brusquely, checking the other cells and finding them empty. The boy pointed back toward the stairs.

Retracing his steps, Lucien made his way back to the first floor, glancing through the grated windows of each door. Clark lay on the bed in the front cell. He looked up as Lucien approached.

Squinting a little, Lucien drew the Navy revolver from his coat pocket, aimed it through the metal grate, and pulled the trigger.

With that act, a regional scandal between two well-known local families became a national media circus, resulting in a murder trial featuring two Civil War generals, an ex-governor of the state, and an attorney who had served as a federal judge in Utah during the Mormon War of the 1850s. And yet, the slayer and his victim have essentially been forgotten, relegated to mere footnotes of a year in history that Virginia—and the nation—seems largely inclined to ignore despite the re-election of Ulysses S. Grant, the continued struggle to recover from Reconstruction, and the ongoing change in women's role in society (especially Southern society).

Chapter One: Religion, Railroads, and Rebellion

Before time and experience set them apart, James Francis Clark and Lucien Norville ("Rhoda") Fewell had more in common than not. Both were the sons of prominent men in their communities; both fought alongside their neighbors in the Civil War and survived; both returned home and achieved some degree of prosperity.

~~~~~~~

The Clarks were longtime Virginians, with a family history dating back (possibly) to the Mayflower. Elder John Clark, James' father, was born on Independence Day in 1804, to a lesser branch of the family long established on Clark's Mountain in Orange County, nestled in the Virginia Piedmont, 35 miles west of Fredericksburg. In his younger years, he worked as a millwright and studied bridge-building, working on the Chatham Bridge across the Rappahannock River at Fredericksburg in 1828, an area where people were accustomed to simply crossing by ferry. The bridge was not free; people paid for the privilege of crossing, and upon its completion, the owner, John Coalter, authorized John Clark to oversee contracts with would-be bridge users. In an announcement in the *Political Arena* newspaper, Coalter stipulated:

> I wish them to specify the number in family, including slaves, if any, who are to have the liberty to pass, or walk on the Bridge—whether they wish the use of it to carry water across, or only to walk on —whether for riding, on horse-back, in a gig, or four-wheeled carriage; or to use it for the passage of carts or wagons; so that reasonable rates in proportion unto use may be agreed upon. ... It is my wish to require no more than what may be reasonable; but all must be sensible that I have incurred great expense as well as great risk, and I hope a mutual spirit of liberality will prevail.

Coalter was not entirely unreasonable—he did give people a chance to try the bridge without charge for a couple weeks in December before enforcing tolls.

John Clark's involvement with the bridge alone would have earned him some longstanding local fame, but his true calling was a higher one. The perhaps apocryphal story goes that in repairing the aforementioned bridge a few months later, John Clark nearly died when he fell some 20 or 30 feet from the top and landed on a pile of stone. When the fall didn't kill him, he offered himself to the church; he was baptized in 1829 and ordained in 1831. Elder Clark was a diligent scholar, becoming a proficient and compelling preacher while also studying Latin, Greek, and Hebrew. In 1830, he began service as pastor of the White Oak Church in Stafford, about seven miles west of Fredericksburg. He would continue to preside there until his death in 1882.

The church, built some time between 1789 and 1835, still stands, a shabby rectangular frame structure sheathed in weatherboard. Also on the property are a woodshed, structures that used to be men's and women's outhouses, and two cemeteries. Services are still held there once a month.

By contrast, the 1830s were exciting years to be a leader in the Baptist faith. Evangelicalism was sweeping the nation. Educated and innovative ministers were encouraged by urban societies to leave the cities and traverse the backcountry and frontiers to increase their flocks—and extend their "civilized" influence.

Needless to say, this did not sit well with the native Baptist leaders who had to contend with these upstarts and saw them as a clear threat to their livelihoods. Nor did it sit well with laypeople, who began to resent the constant appeals for more money to subsidize this proselytizing. An anti-mission backlash began to develop, and lines were drawn.

As strict constructionist interpreters of Scripture, Primitive Baptists were opposed not only to missionary practices, but also to Sunday schools, temperance movements, and Bible societies. Women were expected to keep their heads covered and remain silent in church. Such reactionary stances on social and economic policy characterized the movement, with a fear of centralized authority rooted in Calvinist tenets. (The religious doctrines of John Calvin stressed predestination and that people are saved through God's grace, not their own merits.) But drawing a crude caricature from a few scant lines of understanding does a disservice to the movement. As with most people in most historical periods, the anti-missionists were not motivated by a few overwhelming social or economic factors; they were also drawing on political, cultural, and intellectual influences. Mostly, they were sussing out theological issues that had been stewing for decades, since the United States was first settled.

The faith that Elder Clark embraced had its beginnings in the early days of the republic, when the Baptists had been among the loudest to espouse religious freedom and disestablishment. This led to the ironic problem of having to compete for believers who could choose from a veritable buffet of religious options. Baptists had to contend not only with other Christian denominations, such as Methodists, but also with semi-secular doctrines, such as deism, where belief in God is based only on reason and nature.

Around 1800, the Second Great Awakening, a Protestant revival movement, was sweeping the United States. (The First Great Awakening was an evangelical and revitalization movement in both Protestant Europe and British America, especially strong in the American colonies in the 1730s and 1740s, and it left a permanent impact on American Protestantism.) At the peak of the Second Great Awakening, revivalism and religious fervor were on the rise among all Christian sects, including the Baptists, and after 1820, membership rose rapidly among Baptist and Methodist congregations, whose preachers led the movement. Mission societies, Bible societies, and theological colleges sprang up seemingly overnight, changing the shape and scope of the relationship between religion and society.

For every action, there is an equal and opposite reaction. Alarmed by these changes as they were occurring within the denomination, the Primitive Baptists arose in defense not only of "old-school" Baptist principles, but also Southern ones—the values of family, faith, and community as encompassed by the Southern definition of "honor." Elder Clark stood firmly with the traditionalists, seeking to preserve and defend their strongly Calvinist lines of thinking and practice. In 1836, he served as clerk for the Virginia Corresponding Meeting (an annual church association meeting where leaders would convene for a few days for preaching, fellowship, and discussion of where the church was heading). Held at Occoquan Church that year, six participating Virginia churches—Occoquan, White Oak, Frying Pan, Mount Pleasant, Fredericksburg, and Bethlehem—bonded together to reaffirm their opposition to the New School and their adherence to "primitive" or "original" principles.

This, then, made up the world into which James Francis Clark was born to John and Jane Frances Sleet Clark in Stafford in 1844, the sixth of seven children, and the second son. The church split even further apart that year.

In the 1800s, Baptist churches had formed national "societies" with specific mission orientations. The American Baptist Home Mission Society was organized in 1832 to raise support for missionaries in North America, mostly on the frontier, but also in Canada, Mexico, the Caribbean, and Central America. (This is distinct from, but patterned on, the older American Baptist Foreign Mission Society, formed in 1814, that supported missionaries overseas.) The society, though it declared itself neutral, in fact harbored abolitionist views and encountered resistance and challenges from its Southern members, who felt that slaveholders should be eligible for denominational offices to which the Southern associations contributed financially. Influenced by northern Baptists' opposition to slavery, the Home Mission Society declared that a slave owner could not be a missionary. The year Jim was born, Southern Baptists challenged this ruling by offering just such a nomination; when the Home Mission Society rejected it, the detractors formed the breakaway Southern Baptist Convention in Augusta, Georgia. While this schism did not affect Elder Clark directly, it did solidify his positions and support for his church. In 1853, he commenced publication of *Zion's Advocate*, which he edited for more than 28 years and which remained in circulation until 1923.

Some time in the early 1850s, Elder Clark took a tack

of his own and splintered even further from the Primitive Baptist splinter group when he began espousing what some considered "ridiculous theories, the most alarming of which was that after accepting Christ and turning 'from the love of sin to the love of holiness,' the soul was 'born again.'" Most of his contemporaries could not accept this theory, which seems much like present-day "born-again" Christianity:

> It is clear that the same identical individual that was born, is born again; that existed, exists again. ... Now to be a man he must have been born once which is of the flesh, and this is to be born the second time, or again; and it is the same man, that was born the first time, that is born the second time.

Elder Clark also got into disputes with his contemporaries on the topics of predestination and Arianism, essentially taking on fellow Primitive Baptist preacher Gilbert Beebe (among others). Beebe advocated the absolute predestination of all things; Clark averred that predestination applied to eternal salvation only, then went a step further and accused Beebe and his followers of heresy regarding the doctrine of the holy trinity (essentially, denying that Christ would return to earth—having come once and done what he set out to do, he wouldn't be back). Ultimately, Clark and a few other churches withdrew from the Virginia Corresponding Meeting and joined the Ketocton Association instead. For several years, Southeast faithful referred to themselves as "Beebe Baptists" or "Clark Baptists." While freedom of thought and going one's own way were key facets to come out of the Second Great Awakening, there were drawbacks: This rift never really got mended, and churches and associations were separated and had no fellowship for one another as a result. There was an attempt in the 1890s to reunite and heal the breach—and it seemed to work for a few years. But it did not last, and the separation continues even today, though the names have fallen away.

Today, Primitive Baptists remain strict constructionists of Scripture, holding simple services resembling those of the early churches. Approximately 72,000 Primitive Baptists are spread across about 1,000 churches worldwide. Church music is a cappella singing only, Sunday School is viewed as unscriptural, members practice only family-integrated worship and perform foot washing as a symbol of humility and service among the membership. (Men and women are separated during this ritual, in which one person washes the feet of another.) Elders are self-trained and do not attend seminaries.

But on the eve of the Civil War, politics and religion were inextricably linked, and Elder Clark used his position and publications to defend his religious and cultural paradigm. In 1860, he gained further distinction when the *Primitive Baptist*, the principal periodical of his sect, reprinted his dissertation on "The Relation of Master and Servant." It likely spoke for most Southern Primitive Baptists and probably many Northern ones as well. In a discourse before a racially mixed congregation at Stafford Courthouse, he declared himself a strict constructionist of the Bible: "What it teaches as doctrine we must receive as truth, and what it enjoins upon us in precept we are under obligation to observe; all that is not expressly commended therein is forbidden." He then proceeded to trace the institution of slavery back to Noah's curse on Canaan mentioned in Genesis[1], and declared that, "When Christ

---

[1] Sometimes referred to as the Curse of Ham, this narrative concerns Noah's drunkenness:

> And Noah began to be an husbandman, and he planted a vineyard: And he drank of the wine, and was drunken; and he was uncovered within his tent. And Ham, the father of Canaan, saw the nakedness of his father, and told his two

came ... he found the institution of slavery in existence ... yet there is no case on record where he ever protested against slaveholding as a sin, or that he ever commanded it should be abolished," though he did cite passages from Apostles urging obedience on the part of servants and kindness on the part of masters, and drew upon similarities in instructions to spouses, parents and children, and so on. "As long as these relations shall endure, which shall be as long as the world stands, or until 'time shall be no longer,' so long will there be master and servants. ... Therefore I would as soon think of laboring to abolish the conjugal and parental relation which God has established as to abolish slavery." He closed the sermon by pointing out that he had traveled in 16 states, six free and 10 slave, and observing that he never knew a Primitive Baptist "who had any standing in the Church or any character for orthodoxy, who was an abolitionist."

Jim Clark appears to have grown up influenced but unpersuaded by his father's strong positions. Education was important; the great hereafter arguably less so. After receiving "an ordinary education," young Jim was listed in the 1860 census as independent at age 16 with the occupation of farmer, although he and two older sisters

---

brethren without. And Shem and Japheth took a garment, and laid it upon both their shoulders, and went backward, and covered the nakedness of their father; and their faces were backward, and they saw not their father's nakedness. And Noah awoke from his wine, and knew what his younger son had done unto him. And he said, Cursed be Canaan; a servant of servants shall he be unto his brethren. And he said, Blessed be the Lord God of Shem; and Canaan shall be his servant. God shall enlarge Japheth, and he shall dwell in the tents of Shem; and Canaan shall be his servant."

The story's original objective was to justify the subjection of the Canaanites to the Israelites, but the narrative also has been interpreted by some as an explanation for black skin, as well as slavery.

still lived at home with their father. His older brother, Thomas, had died in 1856.

~~~~~~~

The Fewells, by contrast, led a more secular existence— and, to some extent, a more anonymous one. William Sanford Fewell hailed from a fairly wealthy family, born in 1814 to James Fewell, a farmer, and Margaret Peggy Thurman. Her family appears to have been in Virginia for several generations: Early rent roles show a Joseph Thurman residing in Prince William County in the 1750s, and Margaret's grandfather was named Joseph. William appears to have been the eldest of three children and came of age when the railroad was the way to make one's fortune. In the 1850 census, William, age 35, is listed with the occupation of engineer (probably with the Orange & Alexandria Railroad), living in Alexandria, a port city on the Potomac, with his wife, Elizabeth Norville Fewell, and three children—including five-year-old twins Lucien (or Rhoda, as friends and family called him) and William Hayden (who went by Hayden).

William Fewell was part of a wave of men seeking to capitalize on a new technology. Railroad fever ran wild in the late 1840s and early 1850s. Steam engines and all their technological promise led to rail lines connecting East Coast populations with western-grown produce and materials. In less than two decades, around 3,668 miles of track were laid.

In 1836, the Baltimore & Ohio Railroad opened a line to Winchester through Harper's Ferry, sending a frisson through merchants in Alexandria, who worried that trade would now bypass them. In 1848, the state legislature issued a charter for the Orange & Alexandria Railroad, which ran from the fields of the former to the shops of the latter. By 1850, several wealthy backers invested in the Manassas Gap Railroad, a new venture that merchants and farmers hoped would grab back the upper Shenandoah wheat trade that the Baltimore & Ohio had swiped. Rich planters and prominent business owners in the area determined its route and invested heavily in its future. Fewell's family owned land in this area, and it is probable he was involved with the line from its inception. The line, completed in three years, ran west on the Orange & Alexandria line from Tudor Hall (later called Manassas Junction), through Gainesville and the Manassas Gap, and on to Strasburg.

Giddy with success, the Manassas Gap company decided to build an independent line directly from Manassas Junction to Alexandria, thus eliminating the need to pay rail rental charges to the Orange & Alexandria. The legislature approved the plan in March 1853. By 1856, the Manassas Gap Railroad had promoted William to "transp. agent," or transportation agent.

Unfortunately, the venture did not succeed. Buying up the land and preparing it for track was expensive, and state aid was not guaranteed. The financial panic of 1857 created further problems, and by 1858, the company faced insurmountable debt amid instability and secession threats. The Civil War sounded the death knell for the line one year before it was finished; no steel rails were ever laid. Instead, the trenches and berms were used for cover in battles and as transportation routes for soldiers on both sides of the fight.

In 1858, as the railroad dreams were fading, William Fewell inherited a large portion of land in the Tudor Hall region of Prince William County from an uncle on his mother's side, Sanford Thurman. Sanford had been executor of his father's estate: Robert Thurman had been a fairly successful farmer, owning upward of ten slaves in 1810, dying in 1817. After the war, William would give up a large portion of this land for civic needs—essentially forming the town of Manassas, including an acre he would donate for a Confederate cemetery. But as war loomed in

1860, the family still lived in Alexandria, and William was still transportation agent for the rail line. Lucien and Hayden were no longer the babies of the family; they had been supplanted by two younger sisters: Margaret, born in 1851, and Frances Sanford Fewell (affectionately called Fannie), born June 29, 1856.

~~~~~~~

In 1861, war came to Virginia. After the Battle of Manassas (or Bull Run, as the Union soldiers called it), 17-year-old Jim Clark was anxious to serve his newly formed nation and signed up to fight in August. His father appears to have signed up as well, although it is unclear in what capacity Elder Clark served. He has a CSA marker beside his tombstone, and the local list of veterans includes him as having served, but no unit is listed. Given that he was 57, it is plausible he served as a unit chaplain or an honorary member of a home guard, rather than part of any fighting unit.

Jim, on the other hand, was assigned in September to Company A of the Fourth Virginia Cavalry. The Prince William Cavalry, as it was called, had come into existence in Brentsville, the county seat, in January 1860 in response to the John Brown raids at Harper's Ferry. Abolitionist John Brown and a group of 21 followers had descended on that town in the wee hours of October 17, capturing civic leaders and taking control of the federal armory and arsenal. Brown's vision was to empower and arm local slaves first, then expand to freedom fighters nationwide. He failed: The local militia held him at bay until the Marines, led by Colonel Robert E. Lee, arrived and stormed the building he was holed up in, capturing him and killing many others. Brown was quickly placed on trial and charged with treason, murder, and slave insurrection. Brown was hanged on December 2, 1859. Many Southern localities formed defense units in response to this event: If it could happen there, it could happen anywhere, and an ounce of militia was worth a pound of cure.

But with no slave uprising and no Northern invasion to date, the Fourth had seen no active service its formation. Still, as required by law, it had continued to drill once a month at Brentsville under Captain William W. Thornton. It would become a storied unit over the course of the war, although Private Clark mustered into one of the less glamorous companies. It officially formed September 4 and assembled September 19 at Sangster's Crossroads.

Much of the early enlistment was humdrum and dull, and the rations were not much to write home about, though many men did. Private John Taylor, also of Company A, described 1861 camp life in a letter to his sister: "Fresh beef but with little salt and flour cakes is all we have, a little rye coffee without sugar sometimes is our diet from month to month." But, he added, "We have some enjoyment. We have prayer meeting almost every night."

The Union troops were equally bored on their side of the lines. George Brinton McClellan, a railroad president before the war, had done a brilliant job organizing the Union Army of the Potomac, and after the disaster at Manassas, he was appointed commander of the Military Division of the Potomac, the main Union force responsible for the defense of Washington. But he was overly cautious in putting those troops to use and resisted President Abraham Lincoln's entreaties to fight, giving rise to Lincoln's oft-quoted testy telegram, "If General McClellan does not want to use the Army, I would like to borrow it for a time, provided I could see how it could be made to do something."

Another thorn in Lincoln's side was *New York Tribune* editor Horace Greeley. A strong opponent of slavery and proponent of western expansion, he founded his paper in 1841 and wielded an influence that was impossible to ignore. Thanks to alliances with political heavyweights

William H. Seward and Thurlow Weed, he served briefly in Congress in 1848 (when he also published an exposé series on congressional padding of expense accounts), which was when he first met Lincoln. Friction between the two men dated back to 1858, when Greeley had supported incumbent Stephen Douglas over Lincoln for the Senate.

But Greeley was nearly as erratic as he was eccentric. After insulting Lincoln in 1858, he reversed course as a substitute for a delegate from Oregon at the 1860 Republican National Convention, abandoning his longtime ally Seward and ultimately endorsing the Illinois lawyer for the presidential nomination.

One of the original "for it before he was against it" players, Greeley endorsed secession for the Cotton States after Lincoln's election. But not for long: By the time Lincoln was inaugurated, the *Tribune* was taking a hard line against the South, urging "no concessions to traitors." When Fort Sumter was attacked, Greeley criticized Lincoln's hesitation to respond with force. "On to Richmond" became the *Tribune*'s watchword. Partly in response to this public pressure, Lincoln gave the go-ahead for the first Battle of Manassas to be waged—but it was fought too soon, and the North was destined for defeat. Greeley went into a tailspin and hid out on his family farm in Chappaqua, returning after two weeks to take a more defeatist tone that a losing war shouldn't be fought in the first place.

On the Confederate side of the lines, Jim Clark's service was not particularly noteworthy, but he marched alongside another man whose path would cross his again after the war and whose service was far more distinguished. Benjamin Dyer Merchant—who would marry Lucien's older sister, Mary Elizabeth Fewell—was a native of Prince William County who left his father's mercantile business in Dumfries and joined the volunteer Prince William Cavalry in May 1860. On April 23, 1861, Merchant mustered into Company A of the Fourth

Virginia Cavalry as second sergeant. A month later, he captured the first Union prisoner of the war during the Battle of Fairfax Court House (really more of a skirmish) on June 1, 1861.[2] Company A participated in the first battle of Manassas the following month. In April 1862, Merchant earned a promotion to second lieutenant.

~~~~~~~

In March 1862, Lincoln was tired of inaction and removed McClellan as General-in-Chief, although he was allowed to retain command of the Army of the Potomac. McClellan devised a plan to capture Richmond and launched a campaign along the York-James Peninsula. More than 100,000 Union soldiers landed at Fort Monroe and fought up the peninsula. By mid-May, the Army of the Potomac lay on the outskirts of Richmond.

Around the same time, the Fewell twins joined the Confederate cause. Lucien and Hayden, both 17, enlisted as privates on April 6, 1862, at Orange Courthouse. They were mustered into Company H of the 17th Virginia Infantry in June and were involved in fighting almost immediately.

At least, Hayden was. Lucien got sick, and records list him as absent from fighting for the four months spanning April 30 through August 31. And less than three months after enlisting, before their 18th birthdays, Hayden would be dead, killed in The Seven Days battles, which his twin sat out.

---

[2] Officially, the first Federal prisoner listed in the Civil War was Private Manuel C. Caustin of the President's Mounted Guard, D.C. Volunteers on June 3, 1861. A Virginia raiding party crossed the Potomac at Point of Rocks, on the Virginia-Maryland border, and essentially kidnapped Causten from his brother-in-law's house in Maryland, apparently in retaliation for Fairfax Cavalrymen taken prisoner the week before.. However, the Fairfax Court House engagement took place two days earlier, lending credence to Merchant's claim. The name of his captive, a New York Dragoon of Co. D., went unrecorded, but the sword of the captured prisoner, kept in the Merchant family for a century, can be seen at the Manassas Battlefield Park Museum.

The Seven Days battles began with a Union attack in the Battle of Oak Grove on June 25, 1862, but McClellan quickly lost the initiative (not for the last time) as Robert E. Lee's tactical brilliance pushed McClellan's Army of the Potomac along for the next four days in a retreat toward the safety of the James River. McClellan left his army with no clear instructions on routes of withdrawal and without naming a second-in-command. The bulk of the Fifth Corps moved to occupy Malvern Hill, while the remaining four corps essentially operated independently in their fighting withdrawal. Most elements of the army had been able to cross White Oak Swamp Creek by noon on June 30. About one-third of the army had reached the James River, but the remainder was still marching between White Oak Swamp and Glendale, a tiny community at the intersection of the Charles City Road and the Quaker Road. Lee came up with a plan that he believed would crush his foe and, conceivably, end the conflict.

With the Union army in full retreat toward the James River in the face of Lee's offensive, the Southern army set its sights on the critical intersection at Riddle's Shop, often called Glendale and sometimes referred to as Charles City Crossroads. Most of the Union army would have to funnel through that chokepoint on its way to the river. The ensuing battle may hold the record for being known by the greatest number of names. In much the same way the Confederates called the war's first battle Manassas while the Union called it Bull Run, virtually every Confederate who fought in the next-to-last of the Seven Days battles called it the Battle of Frayser's Farm, but Union soldiers referred to it variously as Glendale, Nelson's Farm, Riddle's Shop, Charles City Crossroads, New Market Crossroads, or White Oak Swamp.

Lee ordered his Army of Northern Virginia to converge on the retreating Union forces, bottlenecked on the inadequate road network. Union forces, lacking overall command coherence, presented a discontinuous, ragged defensive line. According to plan, one Confederate division, led by Major General Benjamin Huger, would strike first in a mass attack after a three-mile march on the Charles City Road, supported by Gens. James Longstreet and A.P. Hill. Gen. Thomas "Stonewall" Jackson was ordered to press the Union rear guard at the White Oak Swamp crossing, while the largest part of Lee's army, some 45,000 men, would attack the Army of the Potomac in mid-retreat at Glendale, splitting those forces in two. Lt. Gen. Theophilus Holmes was ordered to cannonade retreating Federals near Malvern Hill.

But no plan survives contact with the enemy, and neither did Lee's. Huger missed the battle entirely, slowed by road barriers erected by Union soldiers and seeking a different approach through heavy woods but failing to arrive. At 2 p.m., as they waited in vain for sounds of Huger's expected attack, Lee, Longstreet, and visiting Confederate President Jefferson Davis came under heavy artillery fire. Longstreet attempted to silence the six batteries of Federal guns firing in his direction, but long-range artillery fire proved inadequate.

The assaults by the divisions of A.P. Hill and Longstreet, under Longstreet's overall command, turned out to be the only ones to follow Lee's order to attack the main Union concentration. They assaulted the disjointed Union line of 40,000 men, arranged in a two-mile arc north and south of the Glendale intersection, but the brunt of the fighting was centered on the position held by the Pennsylvania Reserves division of the Fifth Corps, under Brig. Gen. George McCall, just west of a farm owned by one R.H. Nelson. Formerly owned by a man named Frayser, many of the locals still referred to the property as Frayser's Farm.

Three Confederate brigades were sent forward in the assault, from north to south, including that of Brig. Gen. James Kemper. Longstreet ordered them forward in a piecemeal fashion, over several hours. Kemper's

Virginians, Hayden Fewell among them, charged through the thick woods first and emerged in front of five batteries of McCall's artillery. As Sgt. George D. Wise described it in 1870:

> We were ordered to charge a battery on the opposite hill, near the Frazier's [sic] farm mansion, and the troops moved forward briskly to the work. The guns of the enemy were abandoned, and we had possession of that portion of the field for a short time; but a terrific fire from the front and an enfilading fire from both flanks caused us to fall back; the Brigade having been unsupported, a retreat was compulsory. The vastly superior numbers of the enemy enabled them to almost surround us, causing the Brigade a severe loss in killed, wounded, and missing.

In their first combat experience, the brigade conducted an enthusiastic, albeit disorderly, assault that carried them through the guns and broke through McCall's main line with Col. Micah Jenkins' support, followed up a few hours later by Brig. Gen. Cadmus M. Wilcox's brigade of Alabamians. "Nothing could have been more chivalrously done, and nothing could have been more unfortunate, as the cheering of the men only served to direct the fire of the enemies' batteries," Kemper wrote later.

The Confederate brigades met stiff resistance in bitter hand-to-hand combat where men stabbed each other with bayonets and used rifles as clubs. Officers even took to using their (normally ornamental) swords as weapons. McCall was captured when he mistakenly rode into the Confederate picket line, looking for positions to place his rallied men.

Edgar Warfield, another private serving in the 17th, tallied up the damage:

The casualties of our regiment in this battle were 18 killed and 23 wounded. **** In addition, 73 were taken prisoner, making the total loss 114. After the fight the usual details were made for bringing in the wounded, burying the dead, and assisting the surgeons at the field hospital. This hospital was located behind several large stacks of hay on the battlefield, just in rear of where our regiment fought.

Warfield, who like the Fewells was in the same company as his brother, then underwent another experience typical to Civil War soldiers wandering in the confusion after a battle.

I had been assigned to look after the slightly wounded. I came upon a Union soldier with a scalp wound and while I was dressing it my attention was attracted to the cap he had with him. I recognized it by the name cut on the visor as the property of my brother. I asked him how he came in possession of it and he answered that he had lost his own and had taken this one from a dead Confederate soldier lying near him. I questioned him closely as to whether the owner was really dead but he was positive, saying that they had both fallen within arm's reach of each other.

This was the first information I had of my brother's death. Although he had been missing, I had been buoyed up with the hope that he might have been numbered among the prisoners captured by the enemy. When we had started on this charge he was about thirty yards on my right, in line, and was fighting in his shirt sleeves. As I afterward learned, he fell, shot through the breast, and was bayonetted in the stomach after he fell. He was killed at the most advanced point reached by our regiment.

I hurried through my work on the prisoner and started in search of my brother's body, hoping to find it before darkness came. It was then about sundown. After wandering over the field, strewn with hundreds of dead and dying of both armies, I failed to find it but I finally came up with the burial detail. With the aid of torches of burning wood they had just finished their work of burying all of the regiment's dead that they could find and were returning. One surgeon, Dr. Harold Snowden, who was in charge of the detail, told me that he had just finished burying my brother. He was buried with three others of the regiment, all in one shallow grave, near where he fell. The others were Daniel Lee and Conrad Johnson of Company A and Hayden Fewell of Company H.

Hayden was dead, the cause recorded as "vulnus sclopeticum"—a gunshot wound.

The battle was tactically inconclusive, and Lee failed to achieve his objective of preventing the Federal escape and demolishing McClellan's army. Confederate casualties totaled 3,673 (638 killed, 2,814 wounded, and 221 missing). Longstreet lost more than a quarter of his division. Often identified as one of the Confederate army's greatest lost opportunities, the campaign was perceived as disastrous on both sides. McClellan's huge mass of troops was forced to abandon its bid to seize Richmond and retreat to the safety of Washington. Having completely lost confidence in McClellan, Lincoln named Henry Halleck as General-in-Chief of the army, and the Army of the Potomac was given to General John Pope.

After the battle, Lee wrote, "Could the other commands have cooperated in this action, the result would have proved most disastrous to the enemy." Eppa Hunton, a colonel of the Eighth Virginia Infantry (who would go on to become a brigadier general and play an important role in Lucien's later life), referred to Frayser's Farm in his autobiography as "the best-planned battle of the war." Even if he was right, it is doubtful the Fewells would have agreed. The South's best chance was squandered, and Hayden was gone. His family received $87.16 for his service, about $2,000 today. A tally sheet of his effects at time of death lists the boy as "17, gray eyes, brown hair, 5 feet 8 inches tall; student." A statue honoring war dead at the intersection of Prince and South Washington streets in Alexandria, Virginia, bears his name.

It is hard to say, a century and a half removed, what shapes a man's personality. It is safe to assume the war had a severe and lasting impact on Lucien. There is no record of what malady laid him up for those four months, if he embellished his symptoms upon learning of his brother's death, or if he suffered some sort of guilt-ridden breakdown. It is certainly safe to say that the death of his twin affected Lucien in negative ways that manifested for years to come.

As the war continued, Lucien returned to his company in September 1862. The same month, after the Union defeat at the battle of Second Manassas, McClellan was once again leading the army that had such strong affection for him, and the Army of the Potomac moved to counter Lee's invasion of Maryland. After a series of skirmishes along the Blue Ridge mountains, the two armies clashed at Antietam on September 17, the single bloodiest day of the war. Battle weary and bloodied, the Confederate Army retreated back into Virginia under the cover of darkness. When McClellan failed to pursue Lee aggressively, Lincoln ordered that he be removed from command on November 5, 1862.

After the failure of the Peninsula Campaign, a letter Greeley had written to Lincoln was reprinted in the *Tribune* as the "Prayer of Twenty Millions," demanding action on emancipation. Lincoln's much more famous response: "My paramount object in this struggle is to save the Union, and is not either to save or to destroy slavery. If I could save the Union without freeing any slave, I would do it, and if I could save it by freeing all the slaves I would do it; and if I could save it by freeing some and leaving others alone I would also do that."

On the home front, Elder Clark's church was playing a key role. In November 1862, it became the center of a Union camp with 20,000 soldiers for seven months, serving as a military hospital, U.S. Christian Commission station, and a photography studio.

~~~~~~~

While McClellan and Halleck were busy in Virginia, a Union general from Galena, Illinois, named Ulysses S. Grant was tearing up Tennessee, capturing Fort Henry and Fort Donelson in February and earning the moniker "Unconditional Surrender Grant" in the newspapers. In April, the Battle of Shiloh was the bloodiest battle of the war—until Gettysburg, a year later. Advancing into Mississippi, Grant began laying the groundwork for his siege of Vicksburg, an operation that lasted several months, ending in a 47-day siege and capture on July 4, 1863. The fall of Vicksburg essentially split the Confederacy in half.

Lucien began 1863 away from his regiment once again. After having spent only four months with them, he was detailed with an ordnance train. It is possible he ate better than his company. Warfield described the rations as dwindling:

> As the war progressed, failure to issue any at all was no uncommon occurrence in the Army of Northern Virginia. Even when the issue was made the soldier might be told that in lieu of tea he would get coffee, and that to the amount of seven

grains per man per day, 21 grains being counted out for three days. Every old soldier will remember as part of his experience that more than once he had to rely on the commissary of the enemy for his next meal.

By 1863, the fresh beef mildly complained of in 1861 was a delicacy. On May 2, Sgt. Lawson Morrissett of the Fourth Virginia Cavalry's Company B recorded another day of hunger: "Nothing for ourselves or horses since April 29."

In October of that year, Merchant was promoted to first lieutenant and later wounded. But the glory didn't last long. In December, Merchant was given leave from his duties and immediately headed off to visit his sweetheart, Lucien's older sister Mary Elizabeth, who was staying with her mother's family, Benoni Harris and his wife, Catherine Norville Harris, at their La Grange estate near Haymarket. He almost made it. Just a few miles from his destination, he was surprised by Union troops and captured in the cemetery of Antioch Baptist Church.[3] After being bounced from prison to prison, he wound up at Fort Delaware on Pea Patch Island in the Delaware River.

~~~~~~~~

Grant was having unprecedented success in 1864, and with his rise, the South truly began to collapse. After resisting congressional entreaties, Lincoln finally capitulated and named Grant supreme commander of the Union armies in March. Grant immediately began a campaign to destroy troops rather than capture cities. Unlike other generals, he fought a war of numbers; realizing he had more resources than his opponents, he was not deterred by heavy losses in battle and splashed through a series of bloody clashes in

---

[3] The La Grange estate remains standing today, and is home to one of the better wineries in the area. The owners renovated the manor and welcome guests daily.

the Wilderness, Spotsylvania, and Cold Harbor battles.

Lincoln's support of Grant mirrored Greeley's support of Lincoln: grudging and belated. Greely did not initially support Lincoln for re-election in 1864, writing in the *Tribune* in February that Lincoln could not be elected to a second term. When Lincoln was nominated in June, the *Tribune* gave muted praise. Once the Union captured Atlanta in September, Greeley became a fervent supporter of Lincoln, hailing Lincoln's re-election and continued Union victories.

Unlike Lucien Fewell's now-you-see-me-now-you-don't military record, Jim Clark appears to have served with the Fourth Virginia Cavalry without interruption. From March through April 1864, shortly before the Battle of Yellow Tavern, records indicate he scouted for field officer William C. Wickham. The rest of Jim's tenure in the military was relatively unremarkable; there is no record of further distinguishing action on his part. Later news accounts mention his being shot in the lungs at some point—and while it is possible this happened and he recovered enough to return to his company, there is no military record of it.

All this time, the Confederacy was suffering. Resources were scarce, and expensive. Food was foremost in the minds of most soldiers, including Warfield:

> When the campaign in northern Virginia began in May 1864, the commanding general reported only two days' rations on hand in Richmond for the army. On June 23, he reported 13 days rations on hand and on December 5, rations for nine days.
>
> Because of the high prices in Confederate money the civilian population shared to a certain extent in these privations ... A breakfast of coffee, bread, and bacon and eggs cost ten dollars, dinner [the largest meal of the day] at the lowest was fifty-seven dollars and supper could not be had

for less than seven dollars and a half, so that the guest of the Ballard Hotel found himself faced with a bill of not less than $74 per day. The bill of fare was as follows:

Ham and eggs: $5
Ham and cabbage $5
Potatoes $5
Roast beef $5
Shad $5
One-half dozen fried oysters $7
Milk toast $3
Butter $1
Eggs, plain, $3
Onions $4
Chicken $20
Raw oysters $5
Coffee or tea $3
Corn bread $3

On the market, apples were selling for $3 per dozen, tomatoes $1 each, onions $1 each, and potatoes $4 per quart. At the same time, the soldiers' pay was $16 per month, Confederate money.

Things for the Clark and Fewell families at home were no less expensive and painful. Manassas Junction was left in ruins after the withdrawal of Confederate forces in March 1862. Controlled by Union forces since then, the area was ravaged. In April 1863, Major General Joseph Hooker shifted the focus of Union operations to the Prince William County area. On October 14 of that year, a portion of Lee's army under General A.P. Hill suffered a bloody repulse at Bristoe Station, followed by skirmishes at Brentsville Courthouse on November 26 and 29, 1863, with little result.

Throughout 1863 and 1864, Confederate forces under the command of John Singleton Mosby conducted a series of raids on Union supply lines. Mosby and his Rangers, granted permission to operate behind enemy lines, were the most effective partisan group of the war. In March 1864, Mosby's Rangers attempted to interrupt the Union supply line at Bristoe Station. A military action commenced April 15, when three members of Mosby's command ambushed the Union pickets of the 13th Pennsylvania Cavalry above the station on Broad Run, killing one Union soldier.

Early in the summer of 1864, Lucien and his company were stationed on the Howlett Line, a critical earthworks dug during the Bermuda Hundred Campaign, named for the Howlett House that stood at the north end of the line. On the way there, the command passed over the old battlefield of Frazier's Farm on June 13. Warfield "took advantage of the opportunity to mark afresh the grave of my brother, who had been killed and buried there two years before." He does not mention whether Lucien visited Hayden at the same time.

On July 30, 1864, the same day the siege of Petersburg blew up in the Battle of the Crater ("the explosion was heard distinctly on our part of the line and it waked me from a sound sleep," Warfield reported), Lucien was captured in ignominious fashion.

During nonfighting hours, a certain amount of fraternizing took place with the enemy, with trading in newspapers, tobacco, and other such luxuries. An order issued July 26 prohibited this fraternization, but did not prevent it. The procedure developed that a man from one side would go into no-man's-land, lay down newspapers and other materials, and depart. Then someone from the other side would go out, collect the bounty, put down their side's donations, and depart. The first man would then return to collect what had been left.

So began business as usual on July 30, when Lucien

went between the lines for an exchange of newspapers, placed his paper down, and returned without event. The enemy picket then went out and left one for him. But when Lucien went out the second time to retrieve the paper, he was captured and taken before General Benjamin Butler to be questioned.

Butler was even more of a *persona non grata* than most Northern commanders. Following the Battle of New Orleans in 1862, he had established himself as military commander of that city. Many of the city's inhabitants were strongly hostile to the Federal government, and many women in particular expressed this contempt by insulting Union troops. Accordingly, on May 15, Butler issued an order to the effect that any woman insulting or showing contempt for any Union officer or soldier should be treated as if she were soliciting prostitution. The order had no sexual connotation; rather, it permitted soldiers to not treat women performing such acts as ladies. If a woman punched a soldier, for example, he could punch her back. Needless to say, this raised a terrible controversy, as women throughout New Orleans interpreted it as Butler legalizing rape. Butler came to be known as The Beast. The general dislike over his order went so far as people printing his portrait on the bottom of chamber pots, and contributed to Butler's removal from command of New Orleans on December 16, 1862.

This, then, was the man in charge of Lucien's fate. Actually, Butler felt the capture a dirty trick and wanted the private returned to his lines, and he sent over a flag of truce to arrange the matter and express his regrets. The receiving Confederate commander has escaped identification. The official story is that he would have nothing to do with Butler's offer, lest it imply a formal recognition of the general. Given later records of Lucien's contempt for authority and his belligerent personality, the Confederate commander may have viewed this as a win-win situation. Regardless, it marked the end of active duty for Lucien.

His family didn't know what became of him for months. An ad in the October 20 *Richmond Daily Enquirer & Examiner* sought information about his whereabouts.

> "Lucien N. Fewell, Company H, 17th Va infantry, Corses's brigade, Pickett's division, was captured in front of Bermuda Hundreds about the last of July, since which time his friends have heard nothing from him; he is supposed to be at some of the Northern Prison camps. Any information concerning him through the New York Daily News or other Northern newspapers and the Richmond Enquirer will be gratefully received by his parents."

As it turned out, Lucien was imprisoned at Point Lookout Prison in Maryland on August 5 and sent to Elmira Prison in New York on August 8. Presumably, news of his whereabouts did reach his family at some point before his release on June 19, 1865.

~~~~~~~

The Fourth Cavalry had taken part in surrender activities at Appomattox two months earlier, in April 1865, but Jim wasn't there. He had been captured and was paroled at Ashland on April 28, 1865. His discharge listed his occupation as "school teacher."

But Benjamin Merchant had the most harrowing experience. Detained at Fort Delaware, he was one of 600 prisoners moved in August 1864 into harm's way in Charleston Harbor—a Union retaliation for 600 Union prisoners put into the same position by Confederate officers. Union officials made the voyage on the Crescent City as abominable as possible, with three tiers of six-foot bunks occupied by four Confederates each. Fresh water was in short supply; seasickness abundant. The trip took the better part of ten days, including a delay when the crew ran the ship aground off the coast of South Carolina. Finally, the vessel reached Charleston Harbor and was anchored directly in the line of Confederate battery fire. Seven days later, the prisoners were marched up the eastern shore of Morris Island and placed in a stockade, again in the line of Confederate fire, to serve as "human shields" for the Union-held strip of land. As soon as the prisoners—who came to be known as the Immortal 600— were in place, Union ships bombarded Charleston. Confederate batteries returned the fire. This kept up for a month, until Union generals learned the Federal prisoners had been taken to Columbia, S.C. (although the Confederates on Morris Island were held an additional 15 days in their position). After this ordeal, Merchant was sent to Fort Pulaski, Ga., where conditions were, if not as dangerous, every bit as dreadful, with close living quarters and short rations of spoiled food. After 65 days, the prisoners were sent back to Fort Delaware. Some were offered parole, but most rejected the offer as a point of honor—Merchant and his remaining 200 compatriots refused to take the oath until after they heard of Lee's surrender. Merchant swore his allegiance on June 12, 1865, and was at last sent home.

Chapter Two: The Lightning-Rod
Man and the Lawyer

$\mathcal{T}$he shooting ended in 1865, but the war didn't, really. Southerners had put down their guns, but they didn't have much left to pick up. Their economy, their resources, and virtually any way of making a living were wiped out. The future was bleak. The men of Virginia who had survived the war responded to these new conditions in different ways. A few dropped everything and headed west to begin again with a blank slate. At the other end of the spectrum were men like Lucien Fewell, who dug in and refused to let the old ways go, fighting and resisting change every inch of the way.

A month after Lee's surrender, President Andrew Johnson named Francis H. Pierpont Virginia's provisional governor. Congress submitted the Fourteenth Amendment (protecting the rights of freedmen) to the states for ratification the next year, but the Virginia General Assembly voted against it on January 9, 1867. The South was chafing under economic desolation, bruised egos, unclear directives from their Northern conquerers—in a word, Reconstruction.

No other Southern state suffered anywhere near the colossal amount of war devastation that Virginia did. More than 40,000 of her residents had died, most in military service, and thousands more were injured. Even where battles had not raged, the land was stomped to bits, ground into dust by troops, horses, and cannons. The state had served as both campground and parade ground for two huge armies for four years, and the area from Washington, D.C., to Richmond, out west to the Blue Ridge, was a dry carcass, picked clean by the armies for provisions, fodder, and wood.

John T. Trowbridge, a Northerner who visited Virginia at that time, described the area from Alexandria to Manassas as showing "no sign of human industry, save here and there a sickly, half-cultivated cornfield ... The country for the most part consisted of fenceless fields abandoned to weeds, stump lots and undergrowth."

This was the world to which men like Benjamin Merchant, Jim Clark, and Lucien Fewell returned. It was doubtless a bewildering time for all involved: Not only were the men who returned scarcely recognizable as the boys they had been when they had marched off to war, but the home they came back to bore little, if any, resemblance to the lush, prosperous land they had left. After five years of exhausting war effort, there was little rest or comfort to be had: They now had to figure out how to survive in a wasteland, under the galling yoke of Northern control.

In the North, Grant was publicly riding a wave of popularity, writhing with discomfort in private. Deeply involved with Reconstruction policy, Grant was named General of the Army of the United States in 1866 by President Andrew Johnson. But Johnson favored a light touch when it came to Reconstruction, and Grant found himself increasingly at odds with his commander in chief.

He played a difficult game of attempting to appear loyal to the president without alienating the Radical Republicans in Congress. Things went from bad to worse as Johnson continued to harass Congress and Grant remained in the middle. The situation came to a head in 1867, when Johnson ousted Secretary of War Edwin Stanton, a Lincoln appointee who sympathized with Congressional Reconstruction, and named Grant an interim appointee during a Senate recess. When Congress reconvened and reinstituted Stanton, Grant immediately stepped aside, incurring the wrath of Johnson. The battle went public, with both sides publishing scathing letters in the newspapers, severing all relations between the two and increasing Grant's popularity with the Radical Republicans. Grant sat out Johnson's resulting impeachment and acquittal in 1868 but was preparing the ground for his own presidential run. He cruised to election over New York Governor Horatio Seymour.

The hijinks in the White House did not stop Congress from running the country, of course. Radical Republicans were irritated with Johnson and with the foot-dragging of the Southern states to admit defeat and fall in line. On March 2, 1867, the U.S. Congress placed the South under military administration. Virginia was designated Military District Number One.

During this time, in yet another about-face, Horace Greeley proved a surprising ally to the South. He urged magnanimity to the rebels, and upon the capture of fugitive Confederate president Jefferson Davis, advocated that "punishment be meted out in accord with a just verdict." He lobbied that Davis, being held at Fortress Monroe, should either be set free or put on trial, and in May 1867, he was among those who signed Davis's bail bond after a Richmond judge set bail for the former Confederate president at $100,000.

Greeley also flip-flopped on Johnson and Congress, ultimately coming to side with the Radical Republicans over the president. He ran for Congress in 1866—losing spectacularly—and then for the Senate in 1867 and for governor in 1868, only to lose both times to Roscoe Conkling. Greeley supported Grant for president in 1868.

~~~~~~~

By 1867, Jim Clark had been home for two years. Based on his discharge papers, one assumes his original plan was to teach school, but it appears he went into law almost immediately, instead. An ad in the June 17 *Virginia Herald* lists him as "attorney at law, near Fredericksburg, will practice in the courts of the adjoining counties." Later newspaper accounts described his courtroom style as "a fair lawyer, though more noted for shrewdness than depth."

No records remain on what Lucien Fewell did for the first two years after he returned home. At the age of 20, he probably lived with his family and worked the farm, as best the land could be worked. But on May 27, 1867, the 22-year-old Lucien married Sarah Brawner, a widow 20 years his senior who had two sons, James and Charles, who were a mere four and five years younger than Lucien.

But Jim and Lucien were doing better than most. Many Virginians were still struggling to repair their losses. Led by the example of Robert E. Lee, moderates supported much of Reconstruction, though they opposed Republican efforts to give freed slaves the vote while stripping ex-Confederates of the same right. Republicans, meanwhile, couldn't quite get their act together. Generally united in a desire for black suffrage and new social order, the party couldn't agree on how to arrive at that point. The blacks in the party were, reasonably enough, pushing for equality of rights, opportunity, and access to education and jobs; bolstered by white supporters, the braver members of this group also lobbied for confiscation of land from the defeated rebels. Others in the party, less interested in black rights and property redistribution, were inclined to move more slowly and forgive ex-Confederates.

State voter registration reflected huge demographic changes wrought by Confederate defeat. Nearly 106,000 blacks were registered in Virginia, which was only 14,000 fewer than the number of whites, while about 20,000 ex-Confederates were denied the ballot. More of them dug in and boycotted. In October 1867, this new electorate approved a constitutional convention and elected delegates that reflected the new voter makeup. As a result, Republicans—radical Republicans, at that—ran the show. Of the 104 delegates, more than half were Republican: Among those 68 delegates, 24 were black, 23 were from the North or overseas, and 21 were "scalawags"— the contemptuous name for native white Virginians with Republican loyalties. Most of the 36 conservatives who managed to get elected were, unsurprisingly, Confederate veterans.

The state constitutional convention met in Richmond from December 3, 1867, to April 17, 1868. It was a bumpy road. Led by John C. Underwood, an abolitionist "carpetbagger" and federal judge,[4] the resulting Underwood Constitution (as it came to be called) was, for the most part, generally agreed upon. In the end, it established voting rights for blacks, instituted a written secret ballot, called for creation of the state's first public schools, granted the governor veto and pardoning power, established a homestead exemption from debt collection, and limited the state's power to contract debts. It did not call for confiscation of Confederate property or for school integration.

---

[4] In the tradition of bitter losers, conservatives heaped abuse on their vanquishers. The term "carpetbaggers" was a pejorative that allegedly referred to opportunistic Northerners who had moved South after the war to profit from the instability and power vacuum (so named for the fashionable luggage they toted with them). But many painted with that brush had, in fact, lived in Virginia for years.

Stopping there, the terms of the new constitution seemed a reasonable middle ground. But the Underwood Constitution was entirely unacceptable to conservative whites, for two reasons. First, it granted "universal" suffrage to all men over the age of 21 "without limitations," except for "idiots and lunatics," those convicted of embezzling or treason, those convicted of dueling—and those who had been disfranchised under the Reconstruction acts. So, not only did the document include all black men among the voting public, it also excluded anyone who had served in the Confederate army or government, which was a sizable chunk of the white, male, native population—including Benjamin Merchant, Lucien Fewell, and Jim Clark. (Suffrage for women, of course, remained beyond the pale; it did not even merit a mention at the convention, although Underwood had proposed it initially.) Further, no man who had aided or engaged in the "rebellion" would be eligible for election to public office. The other clause that stuck in conservatives' craw was the "ironclad" oath clause, which required any man elected to public office to affirm that they had never voluntarily borne arms against the United States.

Conservatives were understandably angered by this and had to figure out how to respond. Some simply sat the whole thing out, hoping Northern sympathy might carry the day and restore their rights. But a larger group took action, forming a new Conservative Party, largely constituted not of the old aristocracy, but of practical, forward-thinking businessmen and attorneys who, although Confederate in loyalty and values, envisioned their state rebuilt on finance and manufacturing.

~~~~~~~

In terms of reaction to the war, Benjamin Merchant was part of that large group in the middle of the bell curve— men who were sure they had been on the right side of things, who resented the outcome and consequences of their position, but who also realized they had lost, it was time to move on, and they had to find the best way to go about it. When Benjamin returned to Virginia as one of the Immortal 600 (those prisoners who survived the nightmare of Charleston Harbor), he rejoined the family's mercantile business and branched out with a new Merchant & Son hardware business in Manassas. In 1867, the same year Jim was practicing law near Fredericksburg, Benjamin married Mary Elizabeth Fewell, Lucien's older sister, three weeks before Lucien married Sarah Brawner.

Not all men took this reasonable approach, of course. Some turned to terror. But it is interesting to note that the extremist faction of hatred that bloomed in other parts of the South largely died on the vine in Virginia. The newly formed Ku Klux Klan did spread across the state in 1868 with posters, costumes, and reports of assaults, but its influence was apparently limited to an outnumbered, if vocal, minority. In 1860, slaves had made up 28 percent of the population in Prince William County. In this new world, where the former ruling majority lived in real, if not legitimate, fear of retribution under a rising oppressed class, there would be a certain appeal in an organization endorsing nothing more than "purely defensive" "protection of the white race."

And deplorable acts certainly occurred. Even Virginia historian Virginius Dabney—a rock-ribbed, old-school Southern Democrat if ever there was one—included examples in his sprawling account of the period. During the Underwood Convention, the Klan threatened to hang the Rev. James Hunnicutt (a slave-owning secessionist before the war who reversed course in dramatic fashion and endorsed wholesale black enfranchisement) from the tail of Washington's horse in the Capitol Square, and to clip the "superfluous tongue and ears" of Dr. Thomas Bayne, an eloquent black delegate from Norfolk. In Appomattox, the group's main goal was to frighten blacks away from the polls. A woman in the Yorktown-Williamsburg region related how the Klan had been active in her neighborhood: "One of them held out a skull to one of our men [a Negro] and asked him to please to hold it while he fixed his backbone! Another in some way disposed of a whole bucket full of water; our Aleck ... asked how anyone could drink so much, and the 'sperit' cried aloud 'wait til you've been in hell for a year!'"

Reports like this appear to have left a bad taste in at least some Virginians' mouths, however; the KKK's presence in the state seems to have dissipated by the end of 1868. This is not at all to say that Virginia was a bastion of civil rights and progressive thinking; merely that it appears that many white men in positions of power in the Old Dominion were more focused on rebuilding their businesses than on parading around with masks and torches (at least, for the moment). And Virginia was only slightly ahead of the curve: The original version of the Klan was essentially wiped out by 1872—broken up by President Ulysses S. Grant, Attorney General (and former Confederate General) Amos Akerman, and the U.S. Army, operating under the Civil Rights Act of 1871 (also known as the Ku Klux Klan Act).[5]

---

[5] The Invisible Empire emerged at three distinct periods of U.S. history: from 1865 to the 1870s, from 1915 to 1944, and from the 1950s to the present. The second Klan gained much from the romanticized legacy of the first, portraying Klan members as chivalric defenders of civilization and gentility, expounded in popular culture, such as the film *Birth of a Nation*.

This version of the Klan persisted in Virginia through the Depression, shifting in focus from anti-Catholicism to "patriotic" anti-Communism, often donating flags to schools—including the one in Brentsville—during the early 1940s. In 1944, the U.S. Treasury sued the national Klan for unpaid back taxes; the Klan settled the case by disbanding. The organization was revived in the 1950s and 1960s to fight desegregation of public spaces and to block African Americans' increased efforts to gain full civil rights. Between 1949 and 1952, a number of cross-burnings occurred in Nansemond and Suffolk counties. The Klan exists today, but it is scattered and disorganized. In 2012, the Southern Poverty Law Center, which tracks extremism in the United States, identified active klaverns in

The Underwoood Constitution was supposed to be voted on in July 1868, but the state had no money to stage a popular election and the federal government did not step up, so the election was canceled. That fall, Ulysses S. Grant was elected president, which led to a softening of feeling for the South in the nation's capital. Meanwhile, factions were splintering in Virginia, as well. By April 1869, the U.S. Congress had every reason to believe the Underwood Constitution would be rejected by Virginia voters. So, lawmakers created a loophole, passing a bill saying Virginia should vote on its constitution, but providing the president with discretionary powers as to the timing of the election and the ability to set aside such clauses as he deemed should be voted on separately from the rest of the document.

~~~~~~~

It is a recurring theme in history that social change follows economic and political upheaval. For women in the postbellum South, their entire reality was virtually turned on its head, and they had to find a way to cope. With no slave labor, a decimated male population, and precious few practical skills, women had nonetheless survived the war and were exploring ways to survive the peace. Those born after 1820 were largely responsible for altering and expanding feminine power and influence after the war. Women born between 1820 and 1849—especially upper-middle-class women like Sarah—had adult memories not only of the war but of what preceded it, and some were naturally a bit wistful and anxious to hold on to what they could of better times gone by, albeit with some concessions. About half of war widows remarried, with age the biggest indicator: Nearly all widows under 25

Abingdon, Powhatan, Martinsville, and Dungannon.

remarried; about half of those between ages 26 and 30 did. (After age 30, the percentages drop precipitously.) Those who did remarry tended to end up with men either much older or somewhat younger than they—matches that would not have been acceptable before the war but were worth settling for in the new circumstances. And despite the age disparity, Lucien wasn't a total write-off; he was from a good family, and accounts describe him as fairly good-looking: Like his brother, he was 5-foot-8, but he had auburn hair and hazel eyes. Sarah Brawner was a social equal of the Fewells; her late husband, William, had been a prosperous farmer before his death in 1861 (whether by war or illness is unclear). Her son Charles attended the local Clover Hill School with Lucien's youngest sister, Fannie; in the fall of 1866, Charles had written an essay extolling the virtues of winter:

The gay season is fast approaching, which is my estimation of winter. Excuse me kind reader if you think I am wrong, but I sincerely think that winter is much more gay than Spring or Summer.

It is true that Spring always brings with it pretty flowers and mild warm days, but we cannot have any fun, no enjoyment to be had only in hard labor, for Spring always brings plenty of work with it. No, I enjoy the cold storms and blasts of winter much more. For generally, the gay dances for which we are all so fond, come off during the season of winter. And then the sport we have in hunting: what amusement do we have in spring or summer that can equal that of chasing the rabbit or fox!

What music is sweeter than that of a pack of hounds as they go yelling over the hills and valleys and ... then away we run home to relate the details of the chase and rejoice over our Victory. Then why is it, we all dread the approach of Winter so much?

In Winter we have the snow which affords so much fun for the young people. They can jump into the sleigh and away they go gliding over the smooth surface mingling their gay laughter with the music of the sleigh bells.

When is the old farmer happier than in a snow storm when he knows all his stock is under shelter with plenty to eat. He lights his pipe, crosses his legs, and sits back in the arm chair to enjoy his ease and read the news.

Well my fellow writers, some of you have sung about the beauties of Spring, the pleasures of Summer, the delights of Autumn, but when you come to the real true enjoyment, give me the usually dreaded season of winter.

It is possible Charles became less fond of winter with his new stepfather in the picture; with less work to do and more time to drink, Lucien does not appear to have been the relaxed, pipe-smoking type.

~~~~~~~

It took several months, but Virginia voters were presented with two state constitutional measures on July 6, 1869: the main body of the document, which passed, and a separate ballot item on the disfranchisement and ironclad clauses, which was defeated. On October 8, 1869, Virginia voted to ratify the Fourteenth and Fifteenth Amendments as part of the requirement for rejoining the Union. The act readmitting Virginia to the Union and its representatives into Congress was signed by Grant on January 26, 1870. Military District Number One was no more; representatives were allowed back in the U.S. Senate and House of Representatives. The federal garrison was withdrawn and Governor Gilbert C. Walker and his government were given complete control of the state.

This ended the era of Reconstruction in Virginia, a period that was relatively brief and somewhat less oppressive than other regions in the South. But it was not an easy peace. Outwardly, many blamed carpetbaggers and federal tyranny, but interracial democracy was the real sticking point. And that experiment failed dismally for the next century—white Southerners worked hard to suppress it and white Northerners gave it up for a bad job.

Where Reconstruction was fairly quick, actual recovery would take much longer. Virginia was back in the Union, but thousands of her men were dead, and those who survived were impoverished. The consequences would last for generations.

With the conservatives back in the driver's seat, the major issue was the state's public debt, which had reached $45 million, while income was scarce with West Virginia gone and huge losses accrued in freed slaves and worthless land. Despite this impossible situation, conservatives insisted the full debt must be paid with interest, as a matter of honor. Some disagreed, pointing out that the vast majority of Virginians had suffered colossal and irreparable losses and that it was hardly fair to expect them to be left holding the bag for the state's pre-war obligations, especially considering most of those bonds were held in the North or in England. If an individual could legally take out bankruptcy, this group suggested, why was it so outrageous for a state to take comparable action when its economy was wrecked, its currency worthless, and its land devastated by the very people who held the bill? This was an argument that would go on for years.

Conservatives in favor of paying the full amount drew much of their support from areas that were, six years after the war, in relatively good shape—in particular, the upper Piedmont and northern Virginia (including Prince William County), where crops were more diversified and the larger towns and cities served as agricultural marketplaces and railroad centers. Competition for control of rail lines and markets was fierce, and several unsavory scandals occurred, reflective of the cronyism and corruption for which the Grant years were infamous.

Perhaps the most infamous corruption scandal was the Credit Mobilier incident. On the eve of the 1872 election, it came to light that major stockholders in the Union Pacific railroad had formed a company, the Credit Mobilier of America, and given it contracts to build the railroad. The stockholders offered shares to congressmen, who in turn approved federal subsidies for construction, enabling railroad builders to make large profits and improve the value of their stock. Ultimately, two lawmakers—Oakes Ames of Connecticut and James Brooks of New York— were censured. Also implicated were outgoing vice president Schuyler Colfax, incoming vice president Henry Wilson, and Rep. James A. Garfield, who denied the charges and was ultimately elected president eight years later.

~~~~~~~

In the South, such schemes and sums were the stuff of dreams. Virginia's new aristocracy, shabbier than it had been, was reconciled to a reconstructed Union but committed to preserving old codes of honor and maintaining social structures and a firm hold on its storied past.

Ladies associations were a large part of this effort. While planning her wedding to Lucien in 1867, Sarah Brawner, as befitted a woman of her age and station, was also busy organizing the Ladies Memorial Association of Manassas, with the goal of "collecting and suitably interring the remains of the gallant men who fell fighting gloriously for you and yours on this ever memorable field." The Association was officially organized May 25, two days before Sarah's wedding, with Sarah as president (and already listed as Sarah Fewell) and her new sister-in-law, Mary Fewell Merchant, as vice president.

Such associations were springing up all over the South, in unabashed glorification of the Lost Cause, and providing women with a public voice—often allowing them to express views that men couldn't, by law: "The object of the society being to care for the Confederate Dead and to instruct children as to the sacred duty of remembering and caring for the graves of the loved and lost—of the land we love; and the duty of each officer, or any one who might hereafter become a member, should be, to urge others to become members."

More than this, the associations were also social organizations, designed to draw all manner of membership. On July 1, 1868, the pupils of Clover Hill School, including young Charles Brawner and Fannie Fewell, gave an entertainment and turned $30.00 over to the Manassas Ladies; the scholars were made "Life Members."

The ladies of Manassas were further assisted by William Sanford Fewell: On November 2, 1868, he donated an acre of land that had been bequeathed to him by his uncle, Sanford Thurman (although it is unclear how much of a sacrifice this was—land prices were still tanked compared with before the war). The Confederate Cemetery established on this land is still maintained today by the United Daughters of the Confederacy, a group that organized 30 years after the Ladies got the ball rolling.

Although the Daughters receive much of the credit, it was, in fact, the Ladies who did all the work of acquiring the grounds, seeing that remains were relocated, and keeping sites beautiful in those early years. It was this group of middle- and upper-class white women who sought to maintain the gentility of the Old South, to create rituals for its memory, and to boost the egos of their surviving veterans. They planned Memorial Days, which were elaborate annual events calling on participants to remember and honor Southern heroes alive and dead, and seeking to instill a sense of history and loyalty to younger generations. When the Manassas Ladies invited General Robert E. Lee to attend such an event, they received a letter of thanks for his "Honorary Membership," but he also sent his regrets: He stayed away from all such festivities, claiming it sent a negative message to the North and undermined the idea of reunification. He was not entirely wrong; the Ladies might very well have readily acknowledged this as a motive.

It is possible that Lucien Fewell smiled upon these exertions by his family, but it is doubtful. There is no mention of him in any of the Association's records, nor the records of any charitable or social organization in town, nor is there any record of him misbehaving before his marriage to Sarah. In June 1867, however, an altercation with resident Israel Jones left Lucien accountable to the county courts for keeping the peace for one year or having to pay $100 for breaking it, with a similar penalty imposed on his father intending for William Sanford Fewell to keep his son in line.

There is no way to know if Lucien was a hard character before going to war; what remains is the record of who he was after he returned—and that person, by all accounts, was difficult to get along with. He had signed the oath of allegiance, but that didn't mean he was sincere. It was one of those empty, largely unenforceable promises like, "I'll never lie again," or "I'll never touch another drop of alcohol." Among his own people, Lucien was apt to get away with quite a bit. By 1868, he was busy burnishing his own reputation—as a Yankee-baiting hellraiser. In February, he was again before a magistrate, accused in a January 30 incident of assaulting Thomas and George Jones, a father and son—the latter also the constable. George described how Lucien was striking and kicking me in the face in a violent and angry manner, to the effusion of my blood that left wounds that were painful and seriously interfering with my business, to my loss. He also threatened to skin me and my father "and all the Dammed Yankees about." From his threats and known character I have reason to fear that he will assassinate me.

Thomas' affidavit reiterates all this and goes on to declare, "I have good reason to believe that my life and property are insecure, and from past experience I have no confidence that the Civil Authorities as at present constituted will punish the said Fewell, or attempt to restrain him from further outrages." Jones was right: This case, prosecuted by Commonwealth's Attorney Aylett Nicol, was dismissed in September and the defendant charged with court costs of $16.51.

Tragedy struck the Fewells the following month, when matriarch Elizabeth Norville Fewell died on March 2; no records remain regarding the circumstances. Lucien's home life was apparently no haven of repose: Two weeks after his mother's death, a complaint was sworn out against him for beating his stepson, James, and William Hynson (possibly a friend of young Brawner, but perhaps a family friend who sought to intervene). Records indicate Lucien appeared in court in May, July, August, and September, although it is unclear whether these were continuances of the Jones and Brawner incidents or other brawls.

It's hard to say what drove Lucien. Was he hard-wired to be hateful, or did he come home broken after the war? There's no way to tell. Plenty of veterans went on to lead violence-free lives, but plenty of others didn't. Or perhaps Lucien was just a mean drunk: Heavy drinking was a longstanding masculine tradition in Southern society; it is a safe assumption that alcohol consumption increased during the years immediately following the war due to trauma and stress. Plenty of men like Lucien found themselves in jail thanks to inebriation and emotional outbursts.

And yet, the man clearly had his good points. The fact that he wasn't locked up permanently is indicative not only of a family willing to bail him out on a constant basis, but also of some community sympathy and fondness for him, whether it was a shared dislike of Northerners or simple affability for the man when he was not on a tear. And he apparently did make exceptions in his refusal to traffic with Yankees when it suited him, to the point of compassion and generosity. In July 1869, he placed ads in the New York papers seeking owners of a sword he had picked up during the war.

> July 9, New York Herald: TO THE HEIRS OF THE LATE LIEUTENANT COLONEL J. FRED PIERSON.—L. N. Fewell, of Manassas Post Office, Virginia, has sent a letter to a gentleman of this city, stating that he is the custodian of the sword of the late Lieutenant Colonel J. Fred Pierson, of the First regiment of New York Volunteers. Mr. Fewell states that the sword was captured at the battle of Manassas Junction, and that Colonel Pierson was fatally wounded while gallantly directing his command in action.

Henry Lewis Pierson, Jr., brother of J. Fred Pierson, saw the advertisement and arranged for recovery of the sword, upon which he received the following letter:

Manassas, Va. July 12, 1869

Henry L. Pierson, Esq.

Dear Sir:

Your communications of 9th and 10th inst at hand and contents noted. I am gratified to know that you are the brother of Lieut. Col. J. Fred Pierson whom I supposed was killed as the person that I took the sword off was dead and evidently an officer. The officer that wore it had severed the head of a Lieut in one of the Companies in my regiment and was in the act of piercing the heart of another private when Sergeant Deavers and myself killed him by shooting at him. He would not have lost his life if he had have surrendered but he swore he would die before he would surrender. I don't charge anything for keeping the sword but if you feel disposed you can send me an ordinary double barrel shot gun as a present which I would prize very highly.

Excuse the paper being in two pieces but after I have finished my letter the ink stand turned over the letter and made a portion of it illegible. I forwarded the sword by Express to H. M. Leman and Bros 116 William Street New York Importers and dealers in H. M. Lemans celebrated steel pens and Lead Pencils. You can get the sword by calling on him. Any thing or any information I can furnish you will be done with pleasure. Let me hear from you if you receive the sword.

Vry Respectfully
L. N. Fewell
Manassas

Henry Pierson sent Lucien a double-barreled shotgun—a kind gesture, although one that was probably not very reassuring for Lucien's fellow townsmen.

In May 1869, Lucien drew the ire of new Commonwealth's Attorney George C. Round, a New Yorker who fought for the Union but fell in love with

Virginia during his time in battle and moved to Manassas after the war. Round was aware of Lucien, but apparently had no cause to move upon him until a noted temperance speaker, the Rev. Lewis Leonidas Allen, put in an appearance in the Presbyterian Church in Manassas. Lucien showed up at the event and created havoc. Court action was deferred until Round could present the case to a grand jury. In October, despite Round's best efforts (and despite the fact that Lucien had gotten into at least one more altercation in the intervening months), two grand juries returned rulings of "not a true bill" in the Allen case. This stuck in Round's craw, as indicated in testimony he made before the House Reconstruction Committee in December of that year regarding the general state of affairs in Prince William County, the outlook of the Republican Party there, and whether the atmosphere was such that granting the state readmission to the Union would not be a mistake.

> Soon after I settled at Manassas, I found that a young man, formerly one of Mosby's band, had been in the habit of making indiscriminate assaults upon the community, the Northerners especially appearing to be the objects of his reckless malice. The farce of putting him under bonds to keep the peace was occasionally gone through with, but no fine or imprisonment had ever been meted out to him. Soon after my appointment as Commonwealth's Attorney, an old gentleman from Ohio named Leonidas L. Allen came to Manassas to deliver a Temperance Address, at the instance of a Lodge of Good Templars mostly composed of Northern citizens. He had with him the most flattering testimonials from Presidents Lincoln, Johnson, and Grant; also from Generals Sherman, Howard, and other distinguished soldiers and statesmen. During the course of his

Address, which was made in the Presbyterian Church, the young man referred to, supposing that some remark made by the speaker was intended to refer to him, walked out doors, picked up a long club, and walked up the aisle, raised it over the gray head of the old man, saying, "Damn you, chaw[?] your words," and other language to the same effect. A general commotion ensued; the women and children ran screaming from the church; some of the men rushed forward in time to prevent an actual battery; and when the young man saw he was meeting with opposition, he withdrew. Such a terror was he in the community that no one dare, or at least no one did, make any complaint before a magistrate. Our newspapers made no mention of the affair. Mr. Allen went to Richmond and laid the occurrence before Gen. Canby, who said the civil authorities must attend to it. I summoned the witnesses before the next Grand Jury, but they returned my indictment endorsed "not a true bill." Two months afterward I summoned the same witnesses before another Grand Jury, with the same result, and this gross outrage to the public, and assault on a gray-headed citizen of the Nation, within the sacred precinct of a Church, of God, goes today unpunished.

Even the notoriety of being mentioned before Congress didn't slow Lucien down. On January 3, 1870, Lucien was back in court again for disturbing the peace; this time he was found guilty and fined $5 plus the cost of this prosecution—$1 per juror.

In 1870, Lucien was 25. His younger stepson, Charles Brawner, was now 19 and an express agent, possibly working with Lucien's father in the Manassas depot. An express agent's job was to ship packages, but these men were also often on the payroll of the local railroad, especially in smaller communities, serving as ticket agents or telegraph operators, among other tasks. No occupation is listed for Lucien or for his older stepson, James (now 21); Lucien apparently had plenty of free time to terrorize the town. In December of that year, Elijah B. Georgia hauled Lucien and another man (a hotelier named Harvey B. Varnes) up on charges of assault with intent to kill, "and did then and there unlawfully beat, wound, and ill treat" Georgia, and "in the presence of his family did profanely curse and swear and declare that he would kill him." The defendants were released on $300 bail apiece.

A side note of some interest is that the justice of the peace who arbitrated this case is Wilmer McLean, a man of some renown for having the alpha and omega of the Civil War occur on his property. McClean's farm, the Yorkshire Plantation, was the site of the initial engagement of the war—First Manassas, or First Bull Run, depending which side you were fighting for—on July 21, 1861. Union artillery fired at McLean's house, being used as a headquarters for Confederate General. P. T. Beauregard, and his kitchen was destroyed. Beauregard made light of the incident, referring to the destruction of his dinner as a "comical event," but it's doubtful McLean shared his levity. McLean, who was too old to fight, made a nice living during the war as a sugar broker supplying the Confederate States Army, and moved his operations to Appomattox County, partly because his commercial activities were centered mostly in southern Virginia and partly to protect his family from a repetition of their combat experience. On April 8, 1865, a messenger knocked on McLean's door, requesting the use of his home as a meeting place for Confederate General Robert E. Lee, to surrender to Union General Ulysses S. Grant. McLean reluctantly agreed, and saw much of his house carried off as souvenirs after the fact. In 1869, bankruptcy forced the family back to the farm in Manassas, during which time he served as justice of the peace. He secured a job under Grant working as a tax collector in 1873 and moved his family to Alexandria, transferring to the U. S. Bureau of Customs in 1876, where he worked until 1880. He died June 5, 1882.

~~~~~~~

All of Lucien's time in and out of trouble with the law apparently gave him some keen insight into making the judicial system work for him. A document from 1871 indicates that Lucien represented himself in getting Sarah's dower—the late William Brawner's land—signed over to him. Brawner had died intestate, and noted local attorney Eppa Hunton had been named trustee of the land, with another relative, Basel Brawner, named as administrator. (Technically, Virginia did not grant married women the right to own property in their own names until 1877—the last state in the Union to do so.) Under the law, Sarah was allotted a dower portion of about 13 acres of the 42-acre plot. In a stunning display of dense legalese, Lucien petitioned for Sarah's land to be signed over to him— successfully, as it turned out. All involved parties— Hunton, both Brawner sons, and Basel Brawner—declined to contest the bill of complaint and Sarah signed her 13 acres over to Lucien. George Round notarized the document; with phrases like "being examined by me privately and apart her husband and having the writing aforesaid fully explained her," it is hard to tell whether Round was using simple boilerplate or providing a record of his disapproval of the whole affair.

This acquisition appears to have calmed Lucien down a bit; his name is absent from court records for more than a year. But he was back to mixing it up and in jail in February 1872, when the stakes rose considerably from the $100 for breaking his peace from three years before. This time, bail was set at $1,000, "for keeping the peace toward all citizens of this county and especially toward George W. Johnson and Jos. D. Johnson." A February 16 account from the Washington, D.C., *Evening Star* explains why:

> It is understood that a young man named Rhoda
> Fewell, while under the influence of liquor,
> created a disturbance at a public exhibition of
> tableaux in that village, night before last, which
> broke up the entertainment and occasioned so
> much alarm among the ladies present that several
> of them fainted, and that the excitement for a time
> was intense. After considerable difficulty, in which
> several of those assisting the constable were hurt,
> Fewell was arrested and taken before a magistrate,
> who bound him over to keep the peace in the sum
> of $1,000, but being unable to furnish that security
> he was sent off under guard to the jail at
> Brentsville. On his way to Brentsville he escaped
> from the guard, and though shot at by Constable
> Cannon, succeeded in reaching the railroad track
> in time to take the morning train for [Alexandria].
> Constable Cannon reached here yesterday evening
> in his pursuit and last night Fewell was arrested
> and kept in jail until this morning, when he was
> taken back to Manassas.

Before his daring escape, Lucien had filed a petition
protesting his bail, stating that his "estate is very
inconsiderable, and that the bail required of him ... is very
excessive" and requested a writ of habeas corpus. As the
commonwealth's attorney at that time, Jim Clark would
have been the one prosecuting the case, and it was under
his writ that Cannon retrieved Lucien from Alexandria and
hauled him to jail.

Jail in those days was not the vast industrial institution
of today. The Brentsville jail was built some time between
1820 and 1822 and was a small, two-story affair with six
cells (two on the first floor and four on the second)—and
that was larger than most. In the early days, prisoners were

provided meals from a neighboring tavern, but by 1872, the jail had its own kitchen, although it is unclear who did the cooking because all bills were paid to the jailer, who may have employed a family member, an ex-slave, or some other third party. Maintenance was funded through local taxes, as well as fees that prisoners paid. County record books list several orders for items such as locks, buckets, blankets, beds, and stoves. The Civil War left the jail in bad repair: It was the most-used structure in town during the fighting, since Union soldiers would lock up Confederates while they controlled the region, and then Confederate soldiers would turn the tables when they were in control.

By March 1872, Lucien was free again, and involved in what might have been a new racket or his first stab at gainful employment: selling lightning rods. An ad that month in the *Alexandria Gazette* directs parties interested in this "absolute safeguard against atmospheric and ground electricity" to contact Lucien as subagent to the installer, a man unfortunately named Joseph Ash. Listed among the references for the product are two familiar names: C.L. Hynson (half-brother to the William Hynson beaten by Lucien in 1869), and George Round, who by now was a member of the Republican State Committee.

The history of the lightning rod man is a spotted one, and his tarnished image is one that has largely fallen by the wayside of popular culture. Modern Americans consider lightning in terms of Ben Franklin's quaint experiments and of temporary power outages. It is not viewed as a mortal peril, so, while lightning rods are still with us, their hard-charging salesmen are not. They were to the 1800s what aluminum siding salesmen are today: selling a possibly legitimate product while capitalizing on fear and uncertainty. A large number of them were rightly categorized as con men, thus the need for references from upstanding community members to boost sales. Critic John Phin took an especially dim view of the business:

"Next to the substitution of sawdust packages for counterfeit money ... the business of putting up lightning rods is a favorite field for the operations of the swindling fraternity."

Before the 1850s, those who had lightning rods generally either made their own or hired a blacksmith or mechanic. But for every market, a supplier will come, and an industry was born. As the century progressed, some manufacturers sold their products through mail order or the general store, but most companies preferred door-to-door salesmen. Some were shysters. Others were simply ignorant, selling and installing protection against a force of nature they didn't entirely understand. As a population, they were almost universally disdained. A short story written by Herman Melville in 1856 uses the job and stereotypical reputation of a lightning rod man to serve as an allegory between good and evil: "But spite of my treatment, and spite of my dissuasive talk of him to my neighbors, the Lightning-rod man still dwells in the land; still travels in storm-time, and drives a brave trade with the fears of man."

In 1860, there were 20 establishments in the country manufacturing lightning rods, turning out a product valued at $182,750. One decade later, the number of companies had risen to 25, but the value of the products had skyrocketed to $1,374,631. Most systems cost between $65 and $200—5 to 10 percent of what it cost to build a medium-priced house.

Thus, lightning rod men had to be persuasive. The faithful were already converted and, generally speaking, there were no follow-up sales. Those whose property had been recently hit were not particularly susceptible either, being likely to cite the adage that lightning never strikes the same place twice.

Lightning rod men also had to be credible. Given that homeowners could obtain and install lightning rods with relative ease on their own, companies realized that what they were really selling was expertise, or peace of mind. They provided pamphlets, samples, and warranties.

> These pamphlets are a formulaic compendium of various kinds of authority. They typically include a lengthy technical discussion of the nature of lightning and lightning conduction, testimonials from famous or authoritative men—typically scientists, heads of schools, and government officials—and quotes from books and articles about lightning. At least some salesmen also carried elaborately illustrated books detailing the decorative elements that could be added to a system, thereby reinforcing the decorative side of the sales pitch.

In any event, it was a living in 1872, and the role of subagent appears to have worked well for Lucien; he was still at it a few months later when his youngest sister, Fannie, threw the family into chaos.

~~~~~~~

Fannie, like her older brother, was a petted and indulged child, although she was part of a larger household that held far more-moderate attitudes. At some point after 1868, the Fewells and Merchants had merged households. It is unclear whether this happened before or after Elizabeth Fewell died, but by 1870, patriarch William and all his daughters, including young Fannie, were living with the Merchants, who had two young children of their own. When William remarried in July 1871, Fannie chose to remain with her sister, rather than move in with her father and new stepmother, Virginia G. "Maggie" Mankin.

So, Fannie's existence was on an almost entirely different plane from that of Lucien's. Holding only a child's view of the war, Fannie was part of a younger generation of women struggling, not to come to terms with a new social structure in the South, but to shape and mold that structure to their postwar paradigm. While women like Sarah Fewell and Mary Merchant were keeping the glorious past alive with their memorial associations and hired cooks and servants, girls Fannie's age were experimenting with different visions of womanhood. Society balls, the pinnacle of antebellum courtship, were now overtaken by dramatic plays and jousting tournaments.[6] The wartime press had also promoted different images of heroines and female role models: spies, nurses, clever women who guarded their homes and families in the absence of male protectors. The ideal of womanhood was coming to feature a more active and outspoken character. Where upper-class white women would only have practiced the art of ornamental sewing before the war, one of the most-advertised items in postwar newspapers was sewing machines, which these young women used to create whole wardrobes.

But even the relatively forward Fannie would have been scandalized by a woman who was making a splash on the New York scene at the time. Victoria Canning Woodhull lived up (or down) to every shocking observation one could make about a Yankee woman in the late nineteenth century.

Born in 1838 in rural Homer, Ohio, Victoria California Claflin was born into dirt-poor conditions. Her father was a con man, but so bad at his calling that when he burned down his own house for the insurance, he was discovered

---

[6] While the postwar North was much taken with the sport of baseball, the most popular athletic activity among Virginia spectators was sculling, with jousting a close second. At the tournaments, young gentleman "knights" riding horseback and carrying lances sought to spear rings along a track of about 80 feet. The knight who collared the most rings got to crown a queen and the couple would be featured at a ball that followed. Tournaments gradually fell out of fashion, supplanted by football and basketball in the 1890s.

and chased out of town. Her mother was an illiterate adherent to the Spiritualist movement. The seventh of ten children, Victoria showed the most ambition by far, and took her shot at escaping when she was 15 by marrying a doctor 13 years her senior. Canning Woodhull did not have a medical license (one was not needed to practice in Ohio in those days) and his healing skills were questionable. He was, however, very good at self-medicating: An alcoholic womanizer, he often disappeared for days, leaving Victoria to fend for herself and their two children as best she could.

In her own youth, one of the ways Victoria and one of her sisters, Tennessee Celeste "Tennie" Claflin, had been exploited by their parents was to be presented to the public as clairvoyant healers. Victoria, who was indisputably gifted in oratory and holding an audience (and, perhaps, with a photographic memory), claimed she could talk to spirits and channel their wisdom. Spiritualism, a belief that spirits of the dead have both the ability and the inclination to communicate with the living, first gained traction in the 1840s in upstate New York (where earlier religious movements had emerged during the Second Great Awakening). This particular flavor of religion is largely traced back to the Fox sisters, who claimed to communicate with spirits through knocking on tables, which made it possible for onlookers to observe. The Fox sisters developed an immense following: Even the irascible Horace Greeley proclaimed they were on the level. Greeley's wife, Mary, sought their help in contacting one of her deceased children.

The Greeleys did not have a happy marriage. Horace took a back seat in running the house and avoided the place as much as he could. When he was around, however, he did a good job of keeping Mary almost constantly pregnant. She suffered several miscarriages, and of the seven children she did carry to term, five died young. Mary Greeley, who appears to have had some legitimate mental problems, desperately sought communications from beyond with one son, Arthur (called Pickie by his family), after his death at the age of five. She hired a Fox sister, Kate, to live at the Greeley house and contact him.[7]

The Fox sisters ultimately confessed to being frauds, and the movement was rife with charlatans. Still, Spiritualism had become a mania. It offered more than last-ditch efforts for grieving parents and a new religious fad for the fashionably up-to-date—it also offered a view of the afterlife that was not all fire and brimstone, which appealed to many progressive Americans. Further, it provided a forum for women, as it embraced women's rights and viewed women as equal participants.

The hard-scrabble Claflin family sought to cash in on this movement while it was still going strong. With Victoria gone and married, Tennie was declared the one with the strongest gift, and she brought in the majority of the family income. They ran into trouble in Illinois when one of Tennie's patients came forward shortly before dying to say the Claflin cancer treatment was worse than the disease. Tennie was charged with murder, and the Claflins went on the lam to evade the charges. They did not stop their racket, however.

Victoria, who had shed her alcoholic husband and was now linked with a Civil War hero and free-love proponent named James Harvey Blood, reunited with her family near the end of the Civil War. In 1868, Victoria claimed that her

---

[7] Another famous mother also notoriously turned to Spiritualism in her grief. While in the White House, Mary Todd Lincoln used the services of mediums and spiritualists to try to contact her dead sons, Willie and Tad. Interestingly, Confederate first lady Varina Davis took in a show by Margaretta Fox some time in the mid-1850s and declared she felt "humbugged." Varina had her share of family tragedy in and out of the Confederate White House. Her first son, Samuel, died in 1852 when he was about a year old; five-year-old Joseph died falling off a third-story balcony in 1864; her youngest son, William, was born weak during the war and died of diphtheria in 1871 at the age of 11. Still, there is no record of her turning to Spiritualism for answers.

spiritual mentor, the Greek orator Demosthenes, had told her to move to New York, and soon the whole clan had relocated.

With this kind of desperate background, Victoria and Tennie had an outsized ambition—not just to be free of their sordid past and trashy families, but to be free altogether: not dependent on male family members for their survival. The two took New York by storm. Their combination of bravado, progressive attitude, and flat-out circus atmosphere combined to ensure they were famous (and infamous) in their time. Shortly after their arrival in New York, the sisters claimed the spotlight (in matching outfits, of course) as the first female stockbrokers on Wall Street (with assistance from Cornelius Vanderbilt) in 1870, then turning around quickly and using the funds to found a newspaper, *Woodhull & Claflin's Weekly,* the same year. The sisters were ardent feminists and used this pulpit—which lasted six years—to espouse a "free love" philosophy; i.e., freedom to marry, divorce, and bear children as they saw fit, rather than having those life changes dictated to them by men. And the sisters wouldn't stop there.

But most women, even in the North, were not this progressive, and women in the South were generally appalled by such talk. The Southern ideal of womanhood reflected in popular culture at this time was several steps away from Woodhull's emancipated embrace of the orgasm. Southern female authors in the 1870s presented heroines who sought fulfilling, useful lives, preferably including marriage to a supportive man. In Frances Christine Fisher's 1870 work *Mabel Lee,* Mabel is a delicate, lighthearted girl who winds up getting abducted by a creepy suitor who tries to hypnotize her. In what constituted racy passages full of innuendo and imagery, Mabel bravely and staunchly defends her virtue and resists the villain—which, in an irritating twist for modern readers, renders her insane. But she is rescued, the villain dies, and after a year in Europe, she miraculously regains her senses (who wouldn't, after a relaxing vacation abroad?), and looks toward a happily ever after with a far more suitable young man.

Such material had every bit as much impact on young girls in those days as young adult fiction and YouTube have on them today. It is not likely that Fannie wanted to *be* Mabel; the popular literature simply provided glimpses of a lifestyle that appeared to fit better with postwar reality than the rules and modes preached by stodgy elders. Fannie was a clever girl, and a flirt. Her life seems to have involved a busy social calendar and far more freedom of movement than would have been enjoyed by heavily chaperoned antebellum belles. Had she been more strictly supervised, it is unlikely she would have been at liberty to fraternize much with Jim Clark when he came on the scene.

~~~~~~~

While Jim's law business was successful, he also apparently dabbled in newspapers. This is not as odd as it sounds; lawyering in 1870s Virginia was not the lucrative avocation it is today, and many augmented their income by other means. In January 1868, the Luray *Page Valley Courier*'s front page boasted James F. Clark & Co. as publishers and proprietors, with the strongly Democratic paper's motto ("The White Man's Organ, Now and Forever") endorsing the primacy of white citizenship over that of recently emancipated blacks. Jim had moved on by October, however; a masthead from that time lists the editor as F.M. Perry, who was also an elder at the local Broad Street Baptist Church (and, as an old-school Baptist, almost certainly a friend of Jim's father).

Jim also had a rather active social life and was considered a bit of a ladies' man. Although he was not much to look at for modern eyes and a bit on the small side (he was somewhere just around five feet tall), he had "deep blue eyes, light hair, and fair skin; a frank countenance, pleasant address, and agreeable manners." On October 24, 1868, at the age of 24, he married 16-year-old Mary Elizabeth Lee, the eldest daughter of William Lee of Stafford, in a "runaway marriage" held "in opposition to the wishes of her father's family," according to later accounts. The wedding was held at Jim's residence in Washington City, but was conducted by the Rev. J. M. Charlton of the Methodist Protestant church. It is unclear whether Elder Clark also disapproved of the union, or if his influence simply did not extend to his daughter-in-law.

William Lee was a farmer in Stafford County whose family had been rooted in Virginia for three generations, arriving from Ireland some time in the 1720s or '30s. Coming from Ireland, it is unlikely that they were related to the more famous Lees of Virginia. Still, William Lee was prosperous enough that in 1840 he owned six slaves. In 1860 he owned a farm worth $10,000.

On July 5, 1869, the day after Elder Clark's birthday, Jim and Mary were proud to announce the birth of their daughter, Laura Lee, and Jim was again in the newspaper business, this time with his father. Elder Clark, who had been editor of the religious publication *Zion's Advocate* since 1854, branched into the secular print world when "James Trout, John Clark & son" established the Democratic-leaning *Warren Sentinel*, with the first issue published April 9 and yearly subscriptions selling for $2.50 (about $30 today).

It is unclear how long the young family stayed in Washington City, but they lived in Brentsville by the time daughter Laura was born, with one black domestic servant, Deliler Strother. (Slave records are difficult to trace and it is unclear if she was hired after the marriage or if she knew Jim or his wife from childhood.) Jim's law practice spanned Stafford and Prince William counties, but most legal activity centered on Brentsville, the county seat for

Prince William (and the place where Lucien Fewell had spent so much time incarcerated and in front of judges).

Like Lucien, Jim was a popular and affable fellow—and more consistently so, without the bouts of violence. The January 1 *Alexandria Gazette and Virginia Advertiser* reports that Jim rounded out 1869 at a high-spirited social event, delivering the charge "in a very eloquent and impressive manner" at a jousting tournament held at his father's White Oak Church. "An hour after the tilt, the coronation took place in the yard of the meeting house ... Clark delivered a beautiful ... address and placed the wreaths on ... the selected ladies. The day passed off pleasantly—all hands in the evening peacably and in order retired to their respective homes." An ad in the same paper proclaims that "James F. Clark, Attorney at law, Brentsville, Prince William County, Va.; Will attend promptly to any business in the Courts of Prince William, Fairfax, and Stafford Counties." Jim was well known and respected enough to be elected commonwealth's attorney for the county later that year. Things were going swimmingly—and then he moved to Manassas.

Chapter Three: Two Towns and Party Politics

*J*im Clark's star was clearly on the rise. An ambitious man, he was anxious to be where the action was. For a lawyer in Prince William County in 1870, that meant Brentsville.

To look at it now, it is hard to believe Brentsville was ever a bustling center of anything. Eight miles west of Manassas, it is a small, sleepy span of a couple miles along a winding two-lane rural highway cutting through rolling hills, largely undeveloped farmland dotted with small houses. The most notable feature is the Brentsville Courthouse Historic Centre, featuring a restored section including a church, schoolhouse, courthouse, jail, and log cabin from different periods of the town's history. But in 1870, it had been the county seat for 50 years. It was a thriving community with hotels and stores, and on market days and court dates, hundreds of people would throng the public green surrounding the courthouse and jail.

The town was established on 50 acres in 1820 to

become Prince William's fourth county seat. As residents had moved farther west for better farm land, the old county seat of Dumfries lost its claim to being a centrally convenient location. Dumfries was a town in decline. At the extreme east end of the county, it had once been a center of trade, but tobacco cultivation had silted in Quantico Creek, eliminating the port traffic. The third strike for Dumfries was that many interested parties had already invested in land around what would become Brentsville, which was centrally located along the present-day Bristow Road, at that time the major east/west passage from Dumfries to the Shenandoah Valley. The courthouse, jail, clerk of court's office, and tavern were completed in 1822, although the jail was notoriously problematic; several escapes were reported over the years.

But some of the escapees were actually to be rooted for. One of the less pleasant aspects of Brentsville's history is its association with the National Underground Railroad Network to Freedom as a site of arrest and jailing of runaway slaves and abolitionists. Prince William County before the war was an ardently pro-slavery region, although wheat, rather than tobacco, was the cash crop, and dairy and livestock farms were common. An influx of Northern farmers seeking cheap farmland did not expand the use of slavery but did exacerbate it, as these men rented slave labor from local plantations.

In 1833, a free black man from Ohio named William Hyden was traveling through Virginia to Washington, D.C. Lacking the papers required by Virginia law verifying his emancipation, he was arrested on suspicion of being an escaped slave and offered for sale. As was the custom, Hyden remained incarcerated while awaiting the transaction. An 1835 petition indicates that deputy sheriff Basil Brawner (who apparently used his position to his advantage by doing a little slave trading on the side whenever black inmates went unclaimed by white owners) sold Hyden to an agent for an unnamed buyer, who then refused to pay Brawner. Seeking to cut his losses, Brawner tried several more times to sell Hyden, but local traders would not take him, "alledging [sic] that his colour [sic] was too light and that he could by reason thereof too easily escape from slavery and pass himself for a free man." After a year of this, Hyden escaped. Efforts to track him were unsuccessful. (Some speculate Brawner just didn't bother to pursue him, finding him too much of a financial drain.)

Other tales were even more sordid. In 1850, a slave named Agnes was hanged on the gallows at the back corner of the courthouse lot after killing her master, Gerard Mason. Mason, the son of founding father George Mason, was a notoriously ruthless man who had been imprisoned himself five years earlier for killing one of his slaves without provocation. Investigators contended that Agnes, who had been ordered whipped by Mason (who was disabled) a few weeks before, killed her master with an ax while he was sleeping. Agnes claimed self-defense; she said Mason had asked her to bring in the ax, threatened her with rape when it was not sharp enough, threatened her with a gun when she resisted, and then struggled with her over the ax when she got the gun away from him. When she got the ax away from him, she struck him, but realized she had gone too far and then decided to finish him off. She was imprisoned immediately, convicted, and sentenced to death, but claimed she was five weeks pregnant. (Virginia law forbade execution of pregnant women.) Medical examinations were inconclusive, and the court, under public pressure, delayed for two months, during which time she remained imprisoned. She was examined again July 10, and when the doctor found her "not to be in that condition," she was hanged July 16.

Somewhere around 13 people were sentenced to execution at the Brentsville gallows. Of these, all but one were African-American; all but one of those were slaves.[8] The last execution that took place at Brentsville was on March 19, 1875; a freedman named Jesse Fouks.[9]

As the nation girded for war, the Brentsville courthouse

---

[8] It is unclear how many of those sentences were commuted or overturned. As far as can be determined, James Burgess, a highwayman, was the first person to be charged and tried there for murder, and was the only white person hanged there. Described as a white male laborer, Burgess was convicted of the murder of Charles Gollyhorn in 1824 and hanged August 8, 1825. "He was hardened to the last," according to the New York *Telescope* of August 13. "While religious exercises were performing at the gallows, he seemed to be totally ignorant of, and indifferent to, the subject and sat, during the entire time, marking in the dust on his coffin with the end of the rope which was tied around his neck."

[9] Jesse Fouks was a former slave and worker for wealthy landowner Jeremiah Herndon. Fouks was said to have argued with Herndon over a piece of meat that Herndon claimed he stole. On the morning of December 4, 1874, Herndon's son found both his parents and their live-in servant, Addison Russell, near death, having been brutally attacked with an ax. Bloody fingerprints were found on the Herndons' money box, which was empty. The Herndons, who were mortally wounded in the attack, later regained consciousness, both stating that they did not know who attacked them, but Mr. Herndon, who had been found lying in his field, remembered the spat with Fouks. Jesse claimed he was innocent and implicated a man named Willis Tibbs. Yet another alternative scenario posits that Herndon's son committed the crime and framed Jesse. Evidence was largely circumstantial except for the deathbed testimony, but the missing money was allegedly later found at the home of Fouks' sister. Fouks was found guilty of first-degree murder on January 14, 1875, and sentenced to hang March 19. On January 30, Jesse escaped, but was found two days later hiding in a bale of straw and returned to custody. An interesting side note to this is that Fouks' defender, James Williams, was in the process of writing Fouks's appeal when he was found dead February 25. He had spent the better part of the evening of February 24 at a tavern, departing somewhat the worse for wear around 8 p.m. He was last seen alive holding onto a fence rail on the edge of town in a seeming "bewildered condition." From the marks on the ground and his missing clothing at the scene of his death, the inquest concluded that Williams attempted to drag himself toward a farm house from the road. His death was deemed due to "intemperance" and "exposure." Still, some speculated he may have been ambushed on the road, given the timing of his death in relation to Fouks' escape and the impending execution.

was where citizens voted on secession and, later, where they enlisted. March 3, 1862, was the last Court Day in Prince William County until the end of the war, which was not kind to Brentsville. As mentioned, the jail was in constant use, but the county clerk's office was torn down and its bricks used for camp chimneys. County records were destroyed or taken by soldiers as souvenirs.

Confederate partisan units operated in Brentsville throughout the war, but the Battle of Bristoe Station, fought three miles west on October 14, 1863, brought actual combat within shouting distance of town. Federal General John Buford was posted there during the battle, tasked with protecting the Federal supply train.

Despite the ravages of war, Brentsville limped on as the county seat during peace time. Court Days continued to draw crowds of onlookers, and the County Board of Supervisors met in the courthouse. Lacking the necessary funds and manpower to restore itself to the condition it was in before the war, Brentsville nonetheless maintained its position of influence, and several relatively wealthy citizens remained in residence there. The first school for white children was formed in 1871.

But the village of Manassas was rising in popularity and affluence, and by 1872, it was on the verge of incorporation. A place of indeterminate origin and mass contradictions, not even its name was original to its locale; the place was called Tudor Hall until the railroad arrived. The town that came after was named for the railroad's Manassas Junction, because that was where the line that ran to Manassas Gap in the Shenandoah Valley connected with the Orange & Alexandria. And the war events for which Manassas is best known also essentially wiped the place off the map. When the war came, the railroads were worse than abandoned; they were targets. Along with the repeated and vicious damage wrought to all Virginia railroads, the Manassas Gap ran the gamut of railroad involvement in the war: It was the first railroad used to transport soldiers into battle when Confederate troops were taken from Delaplane to the Battle of First Manassas; and in September 1862 in the Second Battle of Manassas/Bull Run, General Stonewall Jackson used a portion of abandoned and defunct roadbed as a defensive earthworks to hold off superior Union forces. Manassas Junction, a critical strategic location between Washington and Richmond, was the oft-traded prize in a tug of war between North and South.

But after the war, the railroad, such as it had survived, was for the people's use once more. The Baltimore & Ohio Railroad gained control of the Orange & Alexandria in 1865 and of the Manassas Gap Railroad in 1867, merging them to form the Orange, Alexandria & Manassas Railroad. The damaged portions of each were repaired, and new construction resumed up the Shenandoah Valley from Mount Jackson, reaching Harrisonburg in 1868. Next to public debt, the issue of railroads was the most discussed in the state legislature for the next several years.

Working with what he had and with his eyes on the future, William Sanford Fewell laid out the first section of the future town of Manassas in 1865, going on to sell his land for community growth. The earliest deed firmly establishing the town's existence is dated September 11,1865, when Fewell sold a lot to Sumner Fitts of New York. Fitts built a number of residences in town, as well as the first hotel, the Eureka House, which was located on the east side of Main Street next to the railroad tracks and also used as a ticket and telegraph office—and which Benjamin Merchant was running by 1869, offering "meals at all hours." Surrounded by farmland, it was a thriving little village. A tract dated 1869 indicates the area was home to a school, churches, and two hotels. The railroad (William Fewell was depot agent) provided transportation for area residents and their goods. Several stores had sprung up, catering to residents, railroad workers, and travelers.

And the people were generally focused on rebuilding and industry. George Round, in his address to Congress in December 1869, explicitly reported on this general sense of good will:

> Lest I may be misunderstood, permit me here to say that Prince William is and has been one of the most quiet and orderly counties in the entire State. This results partly from its proximity to the National Capital, partly from the presence of about 300 Northern families, which have settled in our county; partly from a well-organized and determined Union Republican organization which has existed in the county since the war; and partly from the existence of a large element of "poor whites," so-called, who are and have been growing restive under the domination of the slave-holding aristocracy.

The year 1872 began (and ended) on a Sunday. Manassas was an up-and-coming area, with the railroad chugging life into the town and a cadre of motivated landowners seeking to incorporate. The up-and-coming Jim Clark doubtless viewed the fresh energy (and rising income) of Manassas as a good foundation on which to build his future success, and he relocated his family there in early January.

In March, the *Raleigh News* reported that "Mr. James F. Clark has become editor of the Prince William (Va.) Gazette, in place of Mr. H. M. Waters, who resigned." (In actuality, this was the *Manassas Gazette*.[10] Jim was daily

---

[10] The *Manassas Gazette* would have been an invaluable resource for this book, if an archive still existed. Unfortunately, a devastating fire in 1905 that destroyed a large portion of the city's commercial center took the entire newspaper with it. What few copies remain for public use have been donated to the RELIC room at the Bull Run Regional Library.

growing in popularity and influence, and between his law practice and his editorial reach, he was also expanding his political ambitions. He was warmly supported in convention by the county for the nomination of state senator for the first district, although the seat ultimately went to someone else. In those days, as in safe districts today, winning the party nomination was pretty much the same thing as winning the seat. Jim's wife Betty had another daughter, Bertha. To all who saw them, they seemed a happy and secure family. But a scant three months later, Jim's world would be collapsing around his ears.

It began with the struggle over the county seat. Manassas felt it was the new nerve center of the region and lobbied to have the county seat moved there. As western residents had pushed for the courthouse to move from Dumfries to Brentsville in the early 1800s as a matter of convenience, so they now lobbied for removal to Manassas, with its railroads, wealthy businessmen, and fresh look, leaving behind the still unrepaired damage Brentsville had incurred during the war.

Prospects looked good, at first. On March 12, 1872, the General Assembly issued a bill putting the matter to a vote the following May by qualified residents and outlining further arrangements:

> If from such returns and abstracts of votes so cast upon the question of the removal of the courthouse of Prince William county it shall appear that a majority of the votes were "For Manassas," the said village of Manassas shall be, to all intents and purposes, the place of holding courts in the said county of Prince William, and for conducting the business incident there or so soon as suitable buildings may be erected for that purpose; provided, that the people of Manassas shall furnish the necessary lot of ground, enclosed,

and erect thereon, without expense to the people of the county, as good or better courthouse, jail and clerk's offices than those in present use, and shall convey, by proper legal conveyance, the title to the said lot and buildings thereon to the said county, the funds for the purchase of said lot and erection of said buildings to be received by Benjamin D. Merchant, Charles L. Hynson, and William S. Fewell, who shall constitute in connection with the Board of Supervisors, a building committee to erect the courthouse and other necessary buildings; and it shall be the duty of the Board of Supervisors of the county of Prince William, to sell the public buildings at Brentsville upon such terms as they shall deem best, and appropriate the proceeds of said sale towards the erecting of the necessary public buildings at Manassas aforesaid; and the Board of Supervisors of said county shall select a lot on which said public buildings shall be erected; and further provided, said removal of the said courthouse shall not take place before the year 1873.

Voting on the county seat was not the only political issue facing Prince William voters in 1872. It was a presidential election year; and most Southerners, even those willing to look ahead and keep their bitterness in check, were not terribly thrilled with President Grant. Democrats were regrouping and regaining their control of state and local governments; they were waxing enthusiastic about their prospects at the federal level. How they ended up with Horace Greeley, arguably one of the worst presidential contenders in history, would be a comedy of errors had the stakes not been so high, nor the consequences so tragic.

Greeley's candidacy did not begin with the Democrats.

It began with a faction of disgruntled Republicans unhappy with Grant's unsteady leadership, corrupt Cabinet, and soft-pedaling on Southern reform. This Liberal Republican group—led by influential newspaper editors, politicians, and special interests—was a loose gathering of strange bedfellows. Opinions ran the gamut on everything, including strident support and opposition to free trade, as well as stances for civil reform that ranged from "none" to "total." The only thing they really agreed on was that Grant was a stiff and reform was of the essence.

It was of primary importance, then, to select a leader who would galvanize the party. A number of likely candidates had already dropped out of consideration: Chief Justice Salmon P. Chase couldn't find the base of support. Massachusetts Sen. Charles Sumner, famed for being beaten for his antislavery stance on the floor of the Senate, was deemed too abrasive and erratic. Kingmaker Carl Schurz, the main force behind the Liberal Republicans, was ineligible, having been born in Germany. Greeley, still in the running, was not a primary contender; it was doubted he'd even be able to carry his own New York delegation. He was considered a secondary player in the ranks of Missouri Gov. Gratz Brown, notorious for endorsing hare-brained schemes and being a bit of a lush. The three major candidates were Sen. Lyman Trumbull of Illinois, Charles Francis Adams of Massachusetts, and David Davis, an Illinois friend of President Lincoln. Trumbull had an illustrious congressional career to his credit; he had worked on the slavery-abolishing 13th Amendment and the Civil Rights Act of 1866. But he'd also cast one of seven votes that exonerated Andrew Johnson from impeachment. Trumbull knew he had political shortcomings, and what's more, he hated campaigning. He was not terribly enthusiastic about a candidacy. Adams, who had served as minister to Britain during the war, had the statesmanlike views expected of a diplomat and the third generation of a presidential dynasty; his grandfather and father were John Adams and John Quincy Adams, respectively. But he, too, had shortcomings. Too patrician and Yankee for many tastes, he did not embody the reform movement and (like Trumbull) he disliked the dirty and exhausting business of campaigning. The front-runner was, in fact, the least-remembered Davis, a Supreme Court Justice backed by a number of congressional Democrats with apparently strong support in the South and Midwest. Davis also had problems with his candidacy, but the greatest of them was self-inflicted: His supporters at the convention became so obnoxious in their grasping for delegates that they cast themselves as a common enemy, creating so much dislike for Davis among the rest of the party that the various factions came together to defeat him. Four newspaper editors banded together to attack Davis from different angles, with all editorials published together in the *Cincinnati Commercial.*

The Liberal Republican convention opened May 1 in Cincinnati and began with the task of creating a platform. The document required to gain support from all in attendance was by necessity a rather bland version of liberal conventional wisdom calling for economical government, fair taxation, and a one-term presidency. The delegates adopted it unanimously.

Then the fun began. With time running short, the delegates skipped nominating speeches and went directly to balloting. On the first ballot, Adams led with 205, Greeley had a surprising 147, Trumbull had 110, Brown had 95, and Davis was sunk with 92. The editors' blow had struck home. But since 358 votes were required for the nomination, a second round of balloting was required.

And a third. And a fourth. And a fifth. With each round, delegates became more frenzied, and Greeley picked up strength, draining votes from Trumbull and Adams. Momentum begot momentum, and more states jumped on the Greeley bandwagon. In the final, sixth round of balloting, Greeley won 482 votes and Adams was left with 187. With no particular opposition, Brown was named Greeley's running mate.

When the adrenaline wore off and the hangover kicked in, most of the nation was baffled, if not appalled, by the outcome. Newspapers across the country published head-shaking editorials of disbelief, distilled in a May 18 *Harper's Weekly* column: "If there is one quality which is indispensable in a president, it is sound judgment. If there is one public man who is totally destitute of it, it is Horace Greeley." Grant supporter and famed diarist George Templeton Strong was blunter in his assessment: "This is the most preposterous and ludicrous nomination to the presidency ever made on this continent. He is so conceited, fussy, and foolish that he damages every cause he wants to support." Speculation abounded regarding whether the Democrats would endorse Greeley or a three-party election would transpire—and just what the result of that might be. Nonetheless, Greeley accepted the Liberal Republican nomination on May 20 and promptly rewrote the platform in such a way as to make it more palatable for Democrats.

On May 10, an even more bizarre convention took place in New York, yielding a platform with even less chance of success than Greeley's. Victoria Woodhull, the colorful character who rose from dirt-poor circumstances in Ohio to glittering celebrity in New York, became the first woman to be nominated for president after a long string of female firsts.

Woodhull had actually been campaigning since 1870, when otherworldly spirits had told her she should run for the nation's top office. The weekly paper she and her sister had founded served largely as a platform for her presidential run, although it published a wide-ranging variety of articles espousing such horrific notions as defense of the eight-hour workday and vegetarianism; it is now noted for printing the first English version of Karl Marx's Communist Manifesto. Woodhull and Claflin were living large. In a mansion on East 38th Street, they formed a sort of salon that included politicians, financiers, artists, and radicals. Raising eyebrows as they went, the sisters staged a frontal assault on Washington in 1871; Woodhull used connections with Benjamin Butler (he of Lucien Fewell's 1864 military capture) to wrangle an audience with the House Judiciary Committee. Her argument was simple: Women already had the right to vote because the Fourteenth and Fifteenth Amendments guaranteed the protection of that right for all citizens.

This argument was not exclusive to Woodhull: Suffrage leaders were in fact in Washington at that very moment for the National Woman Suffrage Association's third annual convention. But Susan B. Anthony, Elizabeth Cady Stanton, and Isabella Beecher Hooker quickly recognized that Woodhull was something they badly needed: a charismatic figure capable of grabbing and holding the public's attention.

With the power of her first public appearance as a woman's rights advocate, Woodhull moved to the leadership circle of the suffrage movement. Although her constitutional argument was not original, she focused unprecedented public attention on suffrage—and she was the first woman ever to petition Congress in person.

The suffrage sisters went on in relative peace with a common goal for the next year. But in 1872, Woodhull incurred Anthony's wrath when Anthony insisted on backing whichever major party supported women's suffrage and Woodhull instead established the Equal Rights Party in support of an array of reforms almost as dazzling as that of the Liberal Republicans: pro-labor, pro-free love, pro-Spiritualism, and pro-racial and sexual equality.

The clash came to a head on May 9, when Woodhull essentially hijacked Anthony's meeting of the National

Women's Suffrage Association and declared a convening of the Equal Rights Party the next morning. The session was packed, and Woodhull delivered an impassioned hour-long stem-winder calling for revolution. The crowd went wild, and the session ended with Woodhull claiming the party's nomination for president. Frederick Douglass was nominated as her running mate, along with a Sicangu Lakota Indian named Spotted Tail. Another delegate said if Douglass didn't accept, they should nominate "a heathen Chinese."

Douglass never did respond. He'd never expressed interest in joining the radical group, but when the nominations were ratified, he was also contending with the fact that his house had been burned to the ground—and all his research along with it. But his lack of participation didn't really matter. Woodhull, along with being a woman, was also only 34 years old, one year shy of the constitutional age requirement to be president.

In Virginia, little attention was paid to Woodhull and her wacky notions of free love, female politicians, and short skirts. (A reprint in the January 22 *Alexandria Gazette* tweaks Woodhull, who "in one of her recent harangues in Washington, availed herself of the occasion to make an argument in behalf of Spiritualism and claimed that she spoke under the inspiration of Demosthenes. The Star thinks, from this specimen, that the Athenian orator has been greatly overrated, or, perhaps, that he was affected by the prevailing influenza.") The vote on the county seat, an issue of greater importance to local residents with far more-relevant consequences, was held Monday, May 27. Both sides had pulled out all the stops, and the result was a squeaker: Brentsville won by 49 votes.

Immediately, the losers decried the outcome. A petition was circulated alleging the decision was rendered under protest and that it was "wholly wrong and erroneous." The petitioners, mostly Manassas luminaries (including several familiar names, such as Merchant, Hynson, Round, and

Harvey Varnes), provided a litany of reasons for challenging the decision: It was made on the wrong day, a quorum was not present, two Commissioners who did meet were not properly sworn in, and poll-books were left unsealed. By June 4, 1872, the Board of County Supervisors and Commissioners of Elections for Prince William County published in the *Manassas Gazette* that they would contest the election. The July 1 *Alexandria Gazette* reported the outcome:

> The contested matter relative to the county seat was taken up, Judge Smith of Fauquier County on the bench, and the case finally dismissed for want of jurisdiction. The legal points were argued by Mr. Forbes, of Fauquier County, on behalf of Manassas, and Mr. Brooks, of the same county, for Brentsville. The latter place remains the county seat.

The courthouse and county seat remained in Brentsville for another 20 years.

~~~~~~~

After all the other political excitement of the year, the Republican Party's two-day convention in Philadelphia, held June 5 and 6, was a virtual anticlimax, resulting in a fairly low-key and utterly unsurprising renomination of Grant. There was little to do beyond the obvious and probably could have been accomplished in a day, but for obligations to hotel-keepers for rooms reserved. The renomination speech was 79 words long, the vote unanimous. The only question that was not predetermined was that of who would be the vice presidential candidate: a toss-up between incumbent Schuyler Colfax of Indiana and Sen. Henry Wilson of Massachusetts. Colfax, who had irritated Grant by intimating he'd run for president if

Grant did not, garnered 321 votes in the first round to 364 for Wilson, an antislavery veteran and former shoe manufacturer supposed to be strong with labor and black votes. The Virginia delegation threw its support to Wilson on the second vote, and Colfax's political career was over. Grant accepted the nomination on June 21, and the ticket was cemented.

All this had left the Democrats in an unusual position. They were gaining control in border states and throughout the South and consolidating power in northern urban strongholds. It made sense, then, that joining forces with the Liberal Republicans would bolster their ranks and swell their numbers above those of the GOP. But Greeley was a bitter pill. He had been against slavery before he had been for it. He was famed for the comment, "All Democrats may not be rascals, but all rascals are Democrats." Despite the appeal of bigger numbers, many Democrats urged party leaders to stick with their own men in selecting a candidate for president. It was a lackluster group that convened in Baltimore for the convention in early July. Wisconsin Sen. James Doolittle, the convention chairman, advised delegates to ratify the Liberal Republican platform, which they did with scarcely a whimper. Dissident Democrats claimed only 62 votes against the platform, which claimed 670 votes of support. Greeley and Brown received 686 and 713 votes, respectively. Their work completed and their mood glum, Democrats fled Baltimore after a mere six hours of work.

The public response to this appeared to be resignation. Nobody appeared overjoyed at the outset, but most seemed inclined to pinch their noses and go along with it. Looking for a bright spot, the May 10 *Cincinnati Gazette* pointed to an advantage Greeley had over Grant in the cronyism department: "Greeley has but one brother-in-law, no father, and his nephews are all nieces."

In the midst of all this election-year politicking, in what probably was not a coincidence, Congress summarily shut down the Freedmen's Bureau, which had been established in 1865 to assist the newly freed slave population. Technically named The Bureau of Refugees, Freedmen, and Abandoned Lands, it provided an array of services intended to assist blacks in their transition to freedom, including programs to reunite families, improve literacy, and assist blacks with their new role as "labor" when negotiating contracts with landowner "management." The Bureau had suffered obstacles thrown up by Andrew Johnson during his presidency (Johnson claimed federal efforts to assist blacks were an unconstitutional imposition on states), and it had not received much support from other political leaders, either. While the bureau can be credited with several successes in education (hundreds of new black schools were built—including one in Manassas in 1868—and black universities received much-needed funding), its other efforts were pretty much categorical failures. Nobody in a position of influence supported the idea that land should be redistributed among blacks and whites; blacks could not receive due process in Southern courts, and even the personal safety of blacks could not be adequately protected. Congress, which had severely curtailed staffing with the passage of time, recognized this as low-hanging fruit in an election year and pulled the plug that June, much to the satisfaction of hostile Southerners.

~~~~~~~

In a similarly futile position, Jim Clark had known since the beginning of June that he was essentially undone. He had backed the wrong horse in the county seat dispute (and likely incurred the ill will of the Brentsville elite in the process), and despite his conservative credentials, rumors were floating around that he would stump for Grant, and rumors of that nature were entirely sufficient to make him very unpopular in highly conservative Prince William County. He was also apparently facing a significant amount of debt, and he began taking steps to reduce his holdings and presence. He packed up his wife and two small daughters and delivered them to live with her father near Fredericksburg, then came back to Manassas alone to wrap things up.

But resigning as editor of the *Manassas Gazette*, selling off his law library, and transferring his legal cases only took so many hours in a day. He apparently still found time to attend parties and dances, and with his wife away, indulged his reputation as a flirt and a ladies' man. Fannie Fewell was only one of many who shared his attentions—but she would do the most with what she got.

It is safe to assume that young Fannie Fewell was unfazed by the goings-on in her town. The outcome of the county seat vote was a distant disappointment—something more upsetting to the men of her family than to her. The presidential election was even less relevant: Fannie had lived almost her entire life under a Republican shadow at the national level; this election was shaping up to be business as usual as far as she was concerned. The more pressing matter, for Fannie, involved courtship and making a good match. The idea of a woman running for president was probably anathema to Fannie, who appears to have maintained her family's conservative views. While she certainly had more independence than her mother and sisters had enjoyed, it appears she used this independence largely as means to achieve fairly traditional ends: a husband and children. Marriageable men were a scarcer commodity in her time than they had been in years past; a girl had to be resourceful in securing her future. If having an able-bodied husband required accepting a previous marriage that ended in divorce, so be it. She would spend the months of June and July pursuing that end.

Chapter Four: Manassas to Missouri—and Back

On the night of Saturday, August 24, 1872, Fannie Fewell perched on the edge of her hotel bed and fretted, twisting a handkerchief in her hands. She had always been able to charm and smile her way out of scrapes before, but even if she had any smiles or charm left in her at this point, she couldn't see a way out of the mess she was in. She felt for all the world like the fictional heroine, Mabel Lee, torn asunder from her family by a wicked man. But unlike Mabel, Fannie had been a willing accomplice—at least, at first.

Having just turned 16 on June 29, Fannie was the baby of the Fewell family, petted and spoiled. She had been four when the war came to her doorstep in Virginia; she had been 11 when her mother died. When her older sister, Noonie, had married Benjamin Dyer Merchant, Fannie had moved in with them and was well cared for. By the time she was 15, she came and went as she pleased; nobody appeared to mind much whether she was home embroidering or out picking raspberries with friends.

This was not entirely unusual for girls Fannie's age. Although Reconstruction was officially over for Virginia, things were still in social flux and domestic upheaval. Elite women were still figuring out how to deal with emancipated servants who theoretically could quit any time, cookstoves instead of giant fireplaces, and different approaches to housework.

Fannie does not appear to have been particularly interested in becoming one of the new generation of domestically inclined and modern women. Her family seems to have raised her to be the feminine ideal, although this definition was increasingly split between the traditional belle and the emancipated new woman. From all appearances, Fannie seemed to hew to the belle side of things, more focused on etiquette and social standing than on practical applications of running a household — although belles in Fannie's day were incredibly brazen based on the standards set by their antebellum grandmothers. Like Sarah Brawner Fewell, even women who argued for traditional female roles were also claiming new positions for themselves in charitable societies. And others turned toward women's rights and politics. While the actions of women like Victoria Woodhull tended to generate disgust, the war had nonetheless built up images of heroines who spied, nursed, or protected their homes and valuables through clever and intrepid means. In her clandestine romance with Jim Clark, Fannie no doubt fancied herself as clever and intrepid as any Confederate spy in crinolines, such as Belle Boyd or Laura Ratcliffe.

At first, she hadn't paid much attention to him; she had met him when he moved to town, but he was older, married, with two babies—not the sort of man to hold her attention at all. Their first prolonged encounter was at a fishing party in May—one of those large affairs with several people, which made it easy for him to get her alone for stretches of time. She flirted back, but not seriously; Fannie saw nothing to gain from expending her efforts on a married man.

Everything changed a month later. When Betty Clark left town to live with her father and took the two babies with her, Fannie assumed the marriage was over; that was what she'd heard, anyway, and it seemed to fit her observations. Around the same time, she received a note from Jim asking her to meet him at the house of Georgianna Weedon Hynson, his niece and an old friend of Fannie's family. Fannie went willingly, and the discussion was candid: Jim said he wanted to see more of her and she agreed. The next day she received a note from him asking if she would consider going away to Washington with him to be married. "On being assured that he was divorced I agreed to this," she said later. "I did not feel that it was morally wrong for Mr. Clark to pay his addresses to me under the circumstances; it did not occur to me that I should not go to Washington and be married when I had every assurance that he was an unmarried man."

From there, it was a whirlwind, if somewhat secretive, romance. Jim flirted harder with her, and she saw no reason not to respond in kind, though propriety apparently ruled in all their meetings. They met at picnics, danced at parties, and chatted in these social situations—seemingly innocent encounters that could easily be explained away. She looked forward to seeing him, wore her hair in ways she thought he would like, memorized clever things to say to him. She understood him; she accepted his view of things.

She found him charming and funny—and, perhaps most attractive of all, a bit dangerous. The Fewells, while friendly with Elder Clark, were no fans of Clark the younger. He had earned their ill will when he dragged Lucien back from Alexandria to face charges for drinking a while back. Her father and Benjamin refused to allow the man in their homes and had warned her once to stay away from Jim at social events, then never said another word about him. Fannie was sure they just didn't understand. Jim had been having a rough time since the fight over the county seat. He talked about plans to leave town; there was no future for him here. Fannie was gracious and sympathetic. He told her he had not lived happily with his wife.

And so they began an affair, kept secret from her family. He was anxious to leave and start anew somewhere else. Jim warned her about her family's disapproval and worried about her. But it sounded terribly exciting to Fannie. It would mean cutting all ties, she knew. But she fancied herself courageous and resourceful, like the women in the popular novels, and being with him would be enough. They would be married. It would be wild and romantic.

So Fannie plotted her departure, but hesitantly. It would be another month before she actually took the plunge. Still, she wrote impassioned notes assuring him she would not fail him.

> I have only time to write a short note. It will be a day or two before I can decide positively at what time I can leave. But don't think I have given it out, for I would not for the world; I will write you a long letter by Tuesday's mail, telling you when I can go. — How short the time seems last night when we were together. You cannot imagine how delighted I was yesterday when I saw you on the picnic grounds. Can you remain until Sunday? Do by all means. I want you to go down to Church; Lizzie and I are going.[11]

Fannie, knowing how much trouble she would be in if her family caught her in this illicit romance, was careful to destroy all of Jim's letters to her. This fear was not enough

---

[11] All correspondence in this chapter was reprinted in the *Alexandria Gazette*, November 8, 1872. According to Fannie's court testimony, Lizzie is a code name for Georgianna Hynson. "Mr. Clark and I called her Lizzie; he addressed his letters to me in care of Lizzie Twyman, a name he gave Mrs. Hynson."

to prevent her from planning their rendezvous, however. And like all lovers, they had their moments of misunderstanding, jealousy, and hurt feelings.

> What shall I say to convince you that I am not mad with you; and why you have taken up such an idea, I can't imagine; have I ever acted in any way to cause you to believe me angry? If I have, I assure you I was unconscious of it, and I have never heard that you said anything respectful or disrespectful about me. ... I do not hesitate to trust you in anything, and indeed, I have already trusted you a great extent. In regard to fishing, I can go at any time, whenever convenient to you. I will be ready, and your company on the creek will be perfectly agreeable. I have never heard that any one ever suspected us, but for fear that this might get lost. I had rather you would destroy it immediately. Don't stay longer in Fredericksburg.

Jim proceeded apace with his plans for relocation and for finding new work. He traveled frequently, and Fannie scouted and schemed ways to evade her family and go with him. She turned 16 on June 29, and her secret plans made her feel very grown up, indeed. Mrs. Hynson kept her apprised of Jim's movements. Plans to run away began to solidify, as the deception of her family grew deeper.

> I can't leave Monday as I expected, but will go after the fourth of July. Mrs. H. tells me you expect to leave for [Baltimore] tomorrow. But, darling, try and put your trip off until the first of next week. We think of having a dance tomorrow night. I expect by all means to be there. Don't think my seeming negligence is an indication that my feelings towards you are changed, but you become dearer to me every day, and I agree with

you in the arrangements you have made for me to leave with you, and hope it will not be long before we can be together to be separated no more. Do, for my sake, defer your trip until the last of the week. Goodbye, darling. Yours until death. Destroy at once. No signature and no date.

By July, their plans were almost complete.

July 2, 1872 — My own darling: According to promise I seat myself this morning, not at home — but you can guess— to ask you if you don't think it best to come back once more before we leave; you have left many things which I think you will need, and I would like to make some arrangements in regard to getting my clothes away; but if you think it impossible for you to return, don't you think it best that I should express them to you? I can do it with safety. I have considered the matter, that is, about leaving Friday, and think that will be rather soon after your departure. It might cause suspicion, and I had rather wait a little longer. I can let you know this week at what time I will be ready to leave. Now darling, don't be angry, for I assure you I am doing this for the best. I am anxious for the time to arrive when we shall be together, as much as you are but don't think it prudent that I should leave Friday. The time has weighed heavily since you left; the days have seemed weeks. I would like for you to be here tomorrow night any how. Everybody expects you back, and come if you possibly can. Lizzie wants to know what is to be done with all your clothes you have left here. ... I find that I can leave either on the passenger or the freight without any one finding me out, but tell me which you think will be the best. If you can't come up tomorrow, write a long letter to Lizzie telling me what to do. I will have to stop writing and go home immediately. Lizzie joins me in love to my little darling.

Jim appears to have been coming and going as he pleased, and he was gone again in mid-July. There is no telling whether he meant it to be for the last time, but that was how it turned out. The July 20 *Alexandria Gazette* ran a short item:

The Manassas correspondent of the Virginia Star says that James F. Clark, recent editor of the Manassas Gazette, has gone South on a prospecting tour, and that Mr. D.W. Whiting, editor and proprietor of the Fairfax News, has resumed the editorial chair of the Gazette. Mr. W. was the original founder of the Gazette.

Two days later, the newspaper ran an item about another departure:

A young lady residing at Manassas, got on the freight train which passed that station last Saturday night, and though her father, who, it appears, was on the qui vive, searched the cars for her, concealed herself so successfully that she escaped detection and reached the city in safety. At the depot here she was met by a young man with a hack, and the two started off immediately for Washington, where, it is supposed, they were made one in a short time.

So, the plan for Fannie's escape went off, not without a few hitches.[12] Jim had sent her $50 and told her to watch for a man named Hartman; he would help her get on a train out of town. She had already paid for her ticket, and kept the $50 in her trunk. On Friday, July 18, she watched from her window, fascinated, as an old man she'd never seen before stumbled into the Eureka House hotel near the depot, then crossed the street and headed for the saloon, staggering a little. Had Jim sent her a drunkard for an escort? Fannie stole out onto her porch and had a whispered conversation with the man, who appeared to be loitering in front of her house on the way to the saloon. It was Hartman; he was doing a practice run, only pretending to be drunk so nobody would suspect his real intentions.

On Sunday night, a freight train arrived in Manassas at midnight. As it pulled in, Fannie tiptoed past the door to Benjamin Merchant's room.

"Where are you going?" he called to her. Fannie was startled. She hadn't really expected anyone to be awake. But she was prepared for all contingencies. Her trunk had been stashed behind the house since Friday.

"I'm ill," she told him. "I'm going to the privy."

"Is it serious?"

"No, no. I'll just be a little while."

Benjamin considered. She looked all right. The moon was bright outside his window. Little harm should come to her.

"Take the maid," he finally said. Fannie nodded obediently and headed down the hall.

She practically danced out through the door, gesturing wildly to Hartman, who loaded her luggage on to his

---

[12] The events depicted from here on in this chapter are from testimony at the trial of Lucien Fewell, as recounted in the *Alexandria Gazette*, November 6-12, 1872.

handtruck. The two of them hurried to catch the train. Fannie had a moment of panic when she saw her father watching them. But he didn't come toward them, and she hurried aboard as soon as he turned his back. Hartman took care of her trunk, then they both settled themselves inside the car. They did not speak; Fannie had no idea what to say. She breathed a sigh of relief and excitement when she finally heard the shriek of the steel wheels and felt the lurch of the car. She was free and on her way. It was 12:39 a.m.

She didn't get far. A few miles down the track, the train chugged to a halt. Throwing a panicked look at Hartman, she fled for the water closet and locked herself in. It was a lame hope she wouldn't be discovered, but the only hiding place to be had.

She heard men talking through the door, and recognized her father's voice. Though the words were muffled, she understood that Benjamin had gone looking for her and roused her father, the Colonel, when she couldn't be found in the village. The Colonel had stopped the train and they began at the caboose and worked their way along. But they didn't search the water closet, and with their fruitless search concluded, they disembarked and the train began moving again.

Fannie couldn't believe her luck. She had really pulled it off! She stayed hidden away for what felt like several more miles before she felt confident they weren't going to come looking for her again. She'd only just settled herself into her seat across from the old man when the conductor walked up to her.

"Aren't you Miss Fewell?" he asked.

"Yes," she replied gaily. "I'm off to Washington to be married. A man named Lee," she lied easily.

"How old are you, miss?"

"I'm 16."

The conductor gave her a kind yet reproving look, the sort of expression that can only be achieved after years of patient dealing with the public. "Miss," he said. "I am much older than you, and if you ask me, you'd best return to your father."

Fannie was in too good a mood to feel patronized. This man was just trying to help, and she should respond graciously. "I thank you," she replied. "But I have fully made up my mind to go."

"Miss, I really feel I must insist that you go back."

At that, Fannie flared up at him. "I will not go back; I am going to get married. And if you take me back against my will, it won't matter, I'll just run away again the first chance I get and find him." The conductor must have seen that she meant it, for he said he wouldn't trouble her anymore.

When the conductor left, Hartman looked over at her. "The Lieutenant will not stop in Washington," he said, referring to Jim. Fannie was surprised, but Hartman went on to explain they would debark at the first station beyond, in Alexandria, where Jim would be waiting with a hack. Hartman wasn't sure where they would go from there.

For the first time, Fannie felt a twinge that this might have been a bad idea. Up to this point she had buried all misgivings, suppressed the idea that there might be consequences to writing off her family and running away. Now, in the dark, on a train to who knows where, worry crept into the corners of her mind. What if Jim wasn't there? What if he had been lying? What if she had misunderstood? Where would she go? What would she do? She swallowed hard. It was absurd. Of course Jim would be there. He was clever. He probably had a plan she just didn't understand.

The train pulled into Alexandria at 3:30 a.m. The kindly conductor escorted her to a hack that was waiting while the old man again handled her luggage. And there was Jim, wonderful Jim, so handsome and smiling, and she had been so stupid to doubt him. She wanted to throw her arms around him in relief, but with all these strange men around, she merely gave him a salute, which he returned. He then helped her into the hack and got in with her, as did the old man.

When they were settled and the horses were clopping along, Fannie didn't notice at first that Jim seemed uneasy. Rather, she assumed he did not want to converse with her while Hartman was sitting there. They rode in silence for what seemed like a long time. When the hack finally stopped and Jim got out, they were at another train depot. Fannie was bewildered.

"Is this Washington?"

"No, Bladensburg."

Fannie had heard of Bladensburg, but had only a dim idea where it was and guessed it must be part of the Washington suburbs.[13] Jim was walking toward the depot.

"What? But you said we would be married in Washington!"

Jim fixed her with a smile that would have been patronizing on anyone else's face. "It's too early to get married. It's not even light out."

Fannie froze. She did not know what to do. Again, she felt a surge of panic that things were not going the way they should, but she had no idea what to do about it. "Jim?" her voice quavered a little.

He turned back to her. "What?"

"You are going to marry me, aren't you?"

"I told you; it's too early. You don't want to roll some poor preacher out of bed at this hour, do you? Come on. We need to catch the train." He put his arm around her and ushered her into the station. Fannie felt reassured. Surely if he was going to throw her over, he wouldn't have picked her up in Alexandria. She swallowed her misgivings and tried to be cheerful on the next leg of their travels,

---

[13] Bladensburg is actually in Maryland, on the other side of Washington, D.C., and 15 miles northeast of Alexandria.

which, she learned, would take them to Baltimore. They arrived around 6 a.m. and drove to the Rennert House, where they registered as Mr. Green and wife and spent the day together.

For all his faults, Jim could not be accused of bad taste. The Rennert House—on Fayette Street and adjoining the U.S. courthouse on the west—had been built the year before by Robert Rennert and featured a European style. The main entrance led to the first floor, but another entrance immediately off the street took one into the basement-level bar and eating counter, which extended about one-third the length of the building. The clerk's office and desks adjoined this, and behind them were suites of dining rooms. The kitchens were in the very back of the basement. In the rear of the clerk's office, a hall gave way to a wide stairwell to the first floor, which featured handsome hotel parlors in front, with bedrooms in the rear. The upper stories were also used for the accommodations of guests. One of the most popular eating houses in Baltimore, Rennert House was famous for featuring 13 oysters to the dozen, deep dish oyster pie, toasted soft shell crabs, and terrapin à la Marylande, a sort of buttery turtle stew with liberal doses of sherry, served in a chafing dish and garnished with hard-boiled eggs.[14] The couple dined well.

When the meal was over and they were in her room, Fannie felt secure enough to ask again when they would be married.

James took his time in answering. "We aren't," he

---

[14] Robert Rennert, a German-American, sold the Rennert House property to the U.S. government in 1881 for use as a post office. In 1885, the building was demolished and the city took 15 years to erect a Renaissance Revival edifice to house both the post office and the courthouse. Rennert went on to found Hotel Rennert, a spot that became so renowned that its story now appears on a new historical marker installed on Charles Street. His genius with food persisted as well; the Hotel Rennert was reportedly H.L. Mencken's favorite dining room.

finally said.

"What?" Fannie felt the blood rush from her face.

"It's impossible," he said simply. "I'm a married man, and it would be bigamy. You know what bigamy is, right?"

Fannie nodded, stricken.

"Well, bigamy is a penitentiary offense; it's not going to happen."

Fannie burst into tears. She expected Jim to say he was joking, to console her, at least tell her to stop crying. Instead, he rose and left the room. Fannie cried even harder.

He didn't come back until much later. Fannie was still in tears. He sat down with her.

"Look," he said. "You might as well resign yourself to this. We are together."

"I gave up everything for you!"

He shrugged. "If you made a sacrifice in leaving home with me, you should remember I also made sacrifices."

"If you do not intend to marry me, I'll go home."

"You're not going home," he said, seriously. "Our fates are linked irrevocably. You have taken a step you cannot recall. Your family would not receive you, the world would not believe you faultless." His face grew a little harder. "Besides," he added, "if you try, I will leave you to it. Without your family and without me, you will have no protector."

Fannie had no tears left, and no strength. She knew he was right. She made a helpless gesture. Something in her appearance must have touched him, for he comforted her then. They couldn't be man and wife, but they could live like it, he told her.

Next morning, he said he had business to attend to and left their room at 8. Fannie, with no idea of what else to do, looked listlessly out the window until he returned. Nothing had worked out the way she expected, and she was out of options. She may have thought dimly of the heroine Mabel Lee, and wondered if she would perhaps go insane herself. It seemed possible. But by the time Jim returned, she was resolute, ready to be his wife in spirit, if not under the letter of the law.

Jim was traveling on business and financial matters, but it was as good as a honeymoon for Fannie. From Baltimore they went to Rochester, N.Y., for two or three days, then on to a night in Detroit before leaving at 7 a.m. the next morning for Chicago, arriving at 9 p.m. Saturday and registering as Mr. and Mrs. Paxton. On Sunday, they skipped church and Fannie delighted in a drive around Lincoln Park. The area was still recovering after the Great Fire the previous year, but to a girl who had grown up amid war's devastation, construction and temporary wooden structures were commonplace, while the lakefront views and manicured green swards were completely new to her and breathtakingly beautiful.

~~~~~~~

While Jim and Fannie were taking in the sights of the greater United States, another, more famous pair of explorers were calling it quits after a year together. The Scottish explorer David Livingstone had undertaken his third expedition to Africa in 1866, hoping to find the source of the Nile. Instead, he wound up witness to a massacre in the village of Nyangwe, where Arabic slave traders killed hundreds of people. Due to his extended absence, the *London Daily Telegraph* and *New York Herald* threw in together and sent English journalist Henry Stanley to find him. Stanley did, in Ujiji in late 1871. There is some debate whether he actually said the well-known words, "Dr. Livingstone, I presume?" (an utterly facetious comment; Livingstone was the only other white man around for hundreds of miles), but the phrase is used in one of the first published summaries of Stanley's letters, printed July 2, 1872, in the *New York Times*.

Stanley beseeched Livingstone to return with him to

civilization, but Livingstone demurred and the two parted ways in 1872. Many found Livingstone's refusal to return unfathomable but some took a lighter view: On July 9, the *Charlotte* (N.C.) *Democrat* reported that

> Stanley says he found Dr. Livingstone clothed *au naturel*, sitting in a large watermellon [sic], eating bananas, and had a long conversation with him. The doctor, of course, asked all the news, and at first determined to return, but on hearing that Gen. Grant was still President of the U.S. and that a horrible new fashion had been introduced in the shape of the Dolley Varden, said he didn't think he could stand civilization under such circumstances, but thought he could just take a short trip up the country, about four or five thousand miles, and thus amuse himself until spring, when both Grant and the Dolley Varden will have gone out."[15]

Livingstone did not last long after that. He died of dysentery and malaria in 1873 in what is now Zambia. Stanley continued exploring, served in Parliament, was knighted, and died in 1904. He has been somewhat vilified, probably not incorrectly, for the way he conducted his expeditions, with charges of indiscriminate cruelty against Africans.

~~~~~~~

---

[15] The Dolley Varden, named for a character in Charles Dickens' *Barnaby Rudge*, was a fashion craze in the early 1870s, doubtless embraced by Fannie along with thousands of other girls. It consisted of a brightly patterned, usually flowered, gown with a cutaway, draped, and swagged overskirt made of printed cotton or chintz, worn over a revealed underskirt or petticoat. A matching Dolley Varden hat was a flat number decorated with ribbons and flowers. Full of flounces and layers, it was an incredibly fussy look.

At the beginning of August 1872, Jim and Fannie were heading for what would turn out to be the last stop on their adventure together. From Chicago, they headed south to Missouri; first Palmyra, then Hannibal, where they remained several more days. From there, they continued south to the city of Louisiana, where they spent an afternoon admiring the Mississippi River, then headed 50 miles west to the town of Mexico, where they registered at the Ringo House as John R. Lee and wife. Fannie was tired of trying to remember new names at every stop.

"I know we aren't married, but what's to stop us from registering under your name? Nobody here knows you or whether you're married."

"Not so," Jim answered. "I have a friend named Dudley living near here." Jim did not point out that many newspapers published the names of hotel guests, which would have made them easier to track.

"Well, what of it?"

Jim explained patiently. "I don't want him to find out where we are living because he might have a likeness of Betty. It would go badly if he were to learn you aren't what we purport you to be."

Much like the Rennert House, the Ringo House was a famous and fancy hotel for its time and place, with a stellar dining room. Mexico was hardly New York City, but the Ringo House, built in 1866, did a large and prosperous business. Built at a cost of $65,000, it was an impressive three stories, all brick, and could accommodate 60 guests. In many ways it was ahead of its time, offering meeting halls for local groups, as well as a ballroom and a billiards parlor. Like many modern upscale hotels, the ground floor was rimmed with shops offering such things as clothing and barber services—anything travelers and residents alike might need.[16]

---

[16] A.R. Ringo took an active part in Mexico's recovery from the war and made

They had been in Mexico a few days when Jim burst into Fannie's room in a dither. He had been out conducting business when he had run into Dudley on the street.

"He just kept walking with me. I couldn't shake him," Jim said. "He's in the saloon; I told him to wait and we'd meet him."

"What are we to do?" Fannie asked.

"Best I could come up with is I'll introduce you as my wife, and if Dudley realizes you aren't, we'll just pass it off as a joke," Jim said. "I'll say you're a cousin traveling with me." Fannie was dubious, but she didn't have any better ideas, so she went along.

Dudley suspected nothing. Buoyed by this success, Jim invited a real cousin, a Miss Patten, to call. Fannie reveled in being introduced to one and all as Mrs. Clark at last.

After two weeks in Mexico, Jim was low on funds. He said he wanted to go on to St. Louis, where some friends owed him money. He would not take Fannie with him for this trip, and she gave him the $50 she had held onto since he had left it for her with Mrs. Hynson back in Manassas. It never occurred to Fannie that this might be a misstep.

Jim had been in St. Louis a day when he wrote to Fannie telling her their plans were in disarray and she should meet him in Cincinnati.

Fannie was at a loss. She had given Jim all of the money, and the hotel bill was unpaid. How was she supposed to leave the hotel and get on a train? She asked

personal and business loans from his own pockets. In 1861, he established the Mexico Savings Bank, which continued as a fixture for many years. The Ringo Hotel went on to become the favorite meeting place of local horsemen in Mexico, early days of becoming "the Saddle Horse Capital of the World." It was also invaluable to them as a place to "put up in style" clients who came to town on horse-buying visits. These often were people of great wealth or of importance far beyond the horse world. A few who are on record as visiting Mexico are Teddy Roosevelt, Buffalo Bill Cody, William McKinley, William Jennings Bryan, and William Howard Taft.

the hotel clerk what she ought to do. To her embarrassment, he sent for the father of the cousin she had met. Mr. Patten and the hotel proprietor, Mr. Ringo, worked out an arrangement for her. They bought her a ticket to Cincinnati, but Ringo kept her clothes as security against his bill. One can only imagine what Mr. Patten must have thought of his cousin running off and leaving his wife with debts and no money.

Furthermore, although 1872 was a time of increasing liberation for women, most did not travel without a male escort. At her age, Fannie had probably never traveled far beyond the limits of her home town, much less done so without a more-experienced adult in control of the situation, and she was probably so terrified that embarrassment over this lack of propriety was the least of her concerns. She arrived in Cincinnati at six in the morning and waited for Jim in the ladies' sitting-room of the depot until nearly lunchtime, to no avail, getting more and more upset. As she sat, biting her lip and trying to keep the tears at bay, a policeman approached.

"Are you all right, miss?" he asked, kindly. "I'm Officer Kinney. Do you need anything?"

Fannie had no idea if she was all right or not, but she knew if anyone could help her, he could. She told him her tale of woe—how she was supposed to meet Jim, about the hotel, and how he had left her with no money and no way to get home.

"It sounds to me as if you were abandoned," the policeman was saying, when the conductor of the train Fannie had ridden from Missouri stepped up.

"This poor woman," he declared. "She must be my guest. Madam, my name is Marsh. I will take you to a hotel and cover your bills. What has happened to you is criminal, and no mistake."

Fannie could have wept with relief at the offer, but something in Officer Kinney's face made her pause. "Will you excuse us?" the officer asked the conductor, in a tone that made clear he was not really asking. He drew Fannie aside. "Look, ma'am, you are, of course, free to do as you like. But it would be wrong of me not to warn you. Marsh is a single man, and you should really have nothing to do with him. There's no telling what he might feel was owed him. Why don't you come with me and let my wife take care of you instead? I'd feel better if you'd accept." Fannie did, gratefully.

Mrs. Kinney was a gracious hostess. Fannie spent the night with the policeman and his wife, who were explaining to Fannie next morning that her safest option was probably to go to the Home of the Friendless, when the telegraph operator sent a message saying Jim had been at the office and dispatched a money order for $31 to Mexico, and that Fannie could get the money by calling upon the operator. She went immediately, but Jim was not there; the operator said he had just left.

While she was out, Fannie picked up a local newspaper and was horrified to read a notice that a man by the name of Clark had deserted his wife, and that she was without money or friends in that city. That was it for Fannie. She wanted to go home.

Mrs. Kinney helped her get a ticket back east, and Fannie arrived in Washington about 10 p.m. on Sunday, August 18, exhausted and despondent. She knew no one in town, but remembered Jim talking about a friend who was a clerk at Boyle's Hotel. Hoping against hope that this friend would extend her some kindness, she made her way there with the help of a policeman.

It wasn't a long walk; Boyle's Hotel, at 52 and 54 C St. NW, stood opposite the Baltimore & Orange railroad depot. But the clerk at the desk had never heard of Jim, and Fannie was not sure of her next move, when a thought struck her.

"There isn't a John Lee registered here, is there?"

The clerk looked surprised. "As a matter of fact, there is." Fannie asked the clerk to tell Mr. Lee that she was there. The clerk stepped away, but returned quickly.

"He's not in his room," the clerk reported. "He's probably left the city."

Fannie decided to wait him out. After all, she had no way to get anywhere else. She signed in and the clerk showed her up to Room 37. Fannie flopped on the bed. Her mind was spinning. Should she try to contact her father? Would Jim come back to the hotel? Suddenly, there was a knock at the door. It was the clerk.

"Apologies, ma'am. I mistook the wrong room for Mr. Lee's—he is still in town; in fact, he just walked into the hotel."

"Please bring him to me," was all Fannie replied. She sat primly on a chair, waiting. Jim came through the door, curious at first, then astonished.

"My God, how did you manage to get here?" he asked.

Fannie poured out her entire story. She was too tired to be upset or angry. Jim assured her it had all been a huge misunderstanding. For the first night since leaving Missouri, Jim spent the night with Fannie.

In the morning, he asked her to repeat her story. When she told him about the newspaper article, he grew livid.

"Abandoned! In destitute condition!" he fumed.

"Oh, what does it matter?" Fannie asked. "I'm not, not anymore, right? So it's just a silly article."

"It's not," Jim insisted. "Your family might see this. They already hate me, and if they see this they'll think I've done wrong by you and step up their search for you." He paced the small room. "I need to get to Fredericksburg," he said. "Some people there owe me money. I'll get it and come right back for you." His mind thus made up, there was no stopping him, although Fannie was dismayed at again being left alone with no money. "There's no helping it," he insisted. "You must continue to pass as Mrs. Lee, and I'll be back as soon as I can."

And with that, he left. Fannie would never see him again.

Confined to the hotel as she was, Fannie made friends with the hotel clerk, Mr. Gale. The next day, Tuesday, he appeared at her door with a grave look. What he had to tell her generated another frenzied letter to Jim.

> Washington, D.C., August 22—Oh, my darling! For God's sake come back as soon as possible, there is a great long piece in the Baltimore paper, and it says you ran off with the agent's daughter from Manassas, and that you have a wife and three children.[17] Oh God, what are we to do? Come to me at once. I am cast off from them all at home; you are all that I have to look to and don't leave, but come right back to me. Mr. Gale came up here and told me of it just now. He says he heard some one making remarks about it, and told them it was another man. Please darling come back to me tomorrow. I am so nervous I can scarcely hold the pen. Don't fail to come right away. Yours, I hope forever, F.___

But there was no response. Fannie had no choice but to wait for him to come back. She spent the week pacing and fretting, wondering what was to become of her.

On Saturday afternoon, August 24, as Fannie sat twisting her handkerchief on the edge of the bed, wondering for the thousandth time when Jim might return, there was a knock at the door. She flew to open it, hoping for a letter, a telegram, anything. Instead, she saw three men she didn't recognize. They were holding badges. For a moment, Fannie wondered if she were under arrest.

"Benjamin Merchant sent us," the first man said. "Will you come with us, please?"

---

[17] Jim only had two children; the news account had gotten it wrong.

Families

Photo courtesy of Jane Shreshley

James, Mary, and Laura Clark, 1872

Originally in Biographical History of Primitive or Old School Baptist Ministers, R.H. Pittman, ed., 1909

Elder John Clark

Photo courtesy of the Manassas Museum System, Manassas, Virginia

Benjamin Dyer Merchant,
brother-in-law of Fannie and Lucien Fewell

Presidential candidates

Ulysses S. Grant

Horace Greeley

Victoria Woodhull

Prosecution team

Henry A. Wise

Charles E. Sinclair

Used by permission, Utah State Historical Society

Defense attorneys

Eppa Hunton

William Fitzhugh Payne

Henry Wirtz Thomas

Locations

The Ringo House, where James Clark left
Fannie Fewell, pictured here about 1900.
The building burned down in 1918.

The courthouse and jail where Lucien Fewell
was held and tried are now part of the
Brentsville Courthouse Historic Centre,
open for tours from spring through fall.

Locations

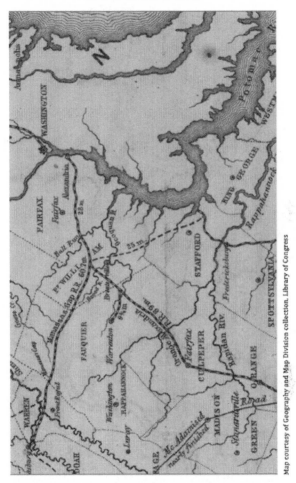

Map of northern Virginia, circa 1852,
showing Brentsville and Fredericksburg. Mansassas,
not incorporated until 1873, is eight miles northeast
of Brentsville, where the Orange Alexandria and
Manassas Gap railroad lines converge.

Chapter Five: The Lawyer, on the Wrong Side of the Law

Benjamin Merchant adored his wife, but there had to be times he wished he had married an orphan instead of a woman with siblings like the Fewells. His beloved Betty was a gem, for sure, but her brother, Lucien, was constantly in trouble and having to be bailed out. And her baby sister, Fannie, lived with them. While generally a sweet girl, Fannie was very pretty and clever, and got away with far more than she should have—much like her brother, though on a significantly less violent scale. Within the family, she was the petted youngest child, and with her mother dead, she was rather spoiled, allowed to do as she pleased with little accountability. And now she had repaid their kindness by running off on the night train to who knew where.

Benjamin may have had his suspicions that Fannie was not entirely blameless in this escapade, but the last thing he would have wanted was any increase in scandal. When the

113

family is in trouble, you circle the wagons. William Fewell had been hysterical since his daughter had vanished, and had nearly gone out of his mind when he learned she was probably with Jim Clark.

The night Fannie left, Benjamin had realized fairly quickly that something was amiss. When she took much too long to return from the privy, he and Betty searched the house and yard; when it was clear Fannie was gone, Benjamin sought out William and they searched the freight train together. Not finding her, they searched the village. When she didn't turn up, Benjamin took the next train for Alexandria and traced her steps as far as Baltimore. The description he got from the railroad agent there convinced him Fannie was with Jim, and he returned home.[18]

It is virtually impossible in today's world to fathom the isolation and lag time involved in the circulation of information in the 1870s. Even with the advent of the telegraph, newspapers were still the primary source of information, and they copied stories from each other verbatim in a sort of domino effect. With no telephones, much less Internet, it was fairly easy to disappear if one wished to do so. So when Fannie vanished, tracking her down was an expensive and time-consuming prospect.

Several anxious days passed. Benjamin was more angry and concerned for his understandably frantic wife than anything; the worry this child was putting his family through largely eclipsed his concern for her directly, which allowed him to focus more clearly on action to effect her return. He sent out inquiries, scoured the newspapers, took all the steps he could think of. Benjamin learned that Jim had given out that he had gone to Memphis and had ordered his letters to be sent there. On writing to the postmaster at that place, it was learned that he had not

---

[18] The sequence of events in this chapter is taken from lengthy accounts in the *Fredericksburg Ledger*, August 27, 1872, and the *New York Herald*, October 8, 1872.

been there at all, but had ordered his letters to be forwarded to Alton, Illinois. Other details were coming out, too. Neighbors had been involved. Benjamin and William were irate; had they been privy to half the information that the neighbors apparently were, Fannie's disappearance could have been prevented.

So when Benjamin saw a piece in the *Lynchburg Republican*, taken from the *Cincinnati Enquirer*, talking about a young woman whose husband had left her unattended, he sent out more inquiries. Nothing came of it for a few days.

But then, news arrived. Fannie was at Boyle's Hotel. William and Benjamin conferred on what to do. Surmising that Jim would leave Fannie in Washington and go see his wife and children, they sent a telegram of inquiry to Fredericksburg and received an answer that he was, indeed, there—but they were rebuffed in their request for his being placed under arrest. The two men immediately prepared to head south and make their accusations in person.

They arrived in Fredericksburg at 11 a.m. August 23. As soon as they were off the train, William set about having Jim arrested. After consultation with Commonwealth's Attorney C. Wistar Wallace, they met with a justice of the peace, Recorder J.B. Sener, and obtained a warrant for Jim's arrest, on the charge of abduction of Fannie Fewell.

But Jim wasn't in town. He'd hired a horse from Thomas Haydon's livery stable and departed for Stafford, where his wife and two children were staying with her father, William Lee. The party set out for Stafford immediately. William was in a fury, swearing he would shoot Jim on sight. Benjamin couldn't get him calmed down, and neither could Sgt. Charles Edrington, the lawman charged with handling the case. William was in such a state, in fact, that Jim, though assuring no trouble and agreeing to come along quietly for his arrest, refused to come out until William had been bound over to keep the peace. Perhaps he found the father's behavior a bit too reminiscent of the ne'er-do-well son.

It was an uncomfortable ride back to Fredericksburg. William had subsided into a seething fury; Edrington (a Civil War veteran who had been wounded in the same battle at Frayser's Farm that had killed Hayden Fewell) tried to make polite conversation to ease the tension. Jim, on the other hand, took every chance he could to firmly assert his innocence, addressing himself more to William and Benjamin than the lawman in whose custody he rode, as if he knew where the greater danger lay.

Upon arriving, Jim was arraigned that afternoon before Justice of the Peace Sener. As his counsel, Jim had retained John L. Marye, Jr., and Charles Herndon; Wallace appeared for the prosecution. Immediately, the proceedings snagged. Wallace requested a delay, saying he "did not wish to proceed with the case until ... procuring certain necessary witnesses"—specifically, Fannie.

Marye countered that the only examination that could now be had was one determining whether to send Jim back to Prince William County, where the alleged offense had occurred. "The proceedings here would be widely disseminated," he said. "Mr. Clark pronounces the reports of this affair a most unfounded aspersion of his character. He assures me, distinctly and unequivocally, that he had no connection whatever with the disappearance of the young lady," and that he had no knowledge of her during his travels west, where he had simply been looking for a new place for himself and his family to live. "As soon as he heard of the rumors connecting his name with this affair," Marye continued, "he had turned from his business in the west and started home to face his accusers in Prince William, and is ready to go now, this moment, with the officers and these gentlemen."

Wallace and William Fewell were in agreement that this was all they wanted. With everyone on board, Sener then heard William's and Benjamin's accounts of the girl's disappearance and how they had tracked Jim down, then waived the examination and ordered Jim to appear before a magistrate of Prince William County within 30 days. Bail was set at $600, and five days provided to furnish it; meanwhile, Jim was remanded to jail for transport to Prince William County.

Plans were made to take the night mail train to Manassas. But all that changed at about 9 p.m. The group was at the Exchange Hotel,[19] awaiting the hour of departure, when reports came in that an angry mob had assembled at the Manassas depot, with all the rage and promise of violence that such mobs usually entail. Jim was no fool; he knew he'd be better off where he was than facing the angry throng in Manassas. He applied for a writ of habeas corpus, which was awarded, the hearing set for the next morning. Jim was then taken to jail in Fredericksburg and locked up for the night.

Judge John Goolrick took his seat promptly at the hour of 10 a.m. on August 24, and Jim was brought before him. Officer Edrington showed the warrant for Jim and Sener's affidavit stating Jim's agreement to go to Prince William. Herndon made a strong appeal for the accused, reiterating Jim's emphatic denials and pointing out again that due to a lack of evidence, Jim would have been discharged the day before if he hadn't offered on his own to go to Prince William County, and that he had reconsidered this plan

---

[19] The Exchange Hotel had been in operation before the war, but burned down in 1857 and took so long to rebuild that between construction and the war, it did not reopen until 1868. The building, however, was not entirely deserted during the war. The *Richmond Examiner* reported on September 19, 1862, that it was "turned into negro quarters, and from five to fifteen hundred negroes were generally loitering around. When they got too thick they were sent off, but continued accessions kept up the supply to the full capacity of the respective buildings." The building changed owners and names, but remained a hotel until 1973. The ground floor is now commercial space, including a restaurant and a clothing boutique.

only because of a well-founded fear for his life. Goolrick considered all this and basically upheld Sener's ruling: Jim must appear before a magistrate of Prince William within 30 days, and bail was set at $600, with five days to furnish it. He remanded Jim to custody.

Jim may have figured he was home free. In fact, he had run out of time.

As the order was being entered into the official record, there was a flurry of activity; a messenger arrived stating that Fannie had been found in Washington and her story cast serious doubt on Jim's—and more, that evidence of his guilt would be supplied Monday. The judge accordingly reconsidered his order for bail and determined to rehear the application. Jim went back to jail without bail, and William Fewell returned home to Manassas.

~~~~~~~

While Jim was facing William Fewell in court, Benjamin Merchant was in Washington, tracking down his sister-in-law. He had left Fredericksburg on the night train and arrived in Washington at an unsociably early hour, so he went to the Baltimore & Ohio railroad depot and stayed there until 5 a.m.

As soon as it began to get light, Benjamin walked over to Boyle's Hotel, where he had been told Fannie was staying in Room 37. It was still very early, but he asked at the front desk about the party in that room. The man behind the counter, who looked like a porter, told Benjamin that he could not give out this information, and that the clerk was out. Frustrated, Benjamin went back to the depot and double-checked his information; reassured that she was at the hotel, he went back there and ate breakfast. Going to pay the bill, Benjamin saw the clerk was in, and asked if the lady who occupied Room 37 was in. The clerk was evasive, but replied she was not, that there was no lady in the hotel who had been left unattended. Benjamin was not one to be deterred. Rather than pick a fight, he went to the police.

A detective by the name of George McElfresh took the matter in hand and deputized two policemen to go back to Boyle's Hotel.[20] This time, Fannie was found to be in residence. She accompanied them to the office of the chief of police, where Benjamin was waiting. He did not speak, at first; he listened closely as the police asked her questions.

Fannie said she had married Jim in Washington, but could not tell them the name of the minister or place where the ceremony was performed. When they checked her story, there was no record of her name or Jim's on the marriage record in the office of the clerk of court. The harder they pressed, the more tearful and incoherent Fannie got.

After an hour or so of this, Merchant finally spoke.

"Are you willing to go home with me?"

"Yes," the girl replied. "I'm willing to go with you." And she burst into tears again. She cried all afternoon. She was for all the world like the hysterical Mabel Lee upon being rescued—if only she could have suffered amnesia; it would have been a mercy!

They took the 7 p.m. train to Manassas. Fannie looked exhausted, but—for all her guilt and hysteria—relieved to be home. Her family sent for her doctor, Emlyn H. Marstellar, who declared her in a fragile and hysterical state and prescribed rest.

She didn't get much. Next morning, she was in a hack on her way to Occoquan to catch the train for Fredericksburg, accompanied by her father, her sister, her brother-in-law, Dr. Marstellar, and Commonwealth's Attorney Charles Sinclair—the man who had been

---

[20] McElfresh had been part of President Lincoln's security detail in 1864. Nine years after handling Fannie's case, he was one of three officers who escorted Charles Guiteau to jail after the assassination of President James A. Garfield.

appointed to Jim's job when he gave it up. Upon arriving in Fredericksburg, the family decamped in the Farmers' Hotel.

Court gaveled in promptly at 4:30 p.m., but the prosecution and defense both requested a delay and the case was postponed until 8 p.m.

Even with the delay, however, Fannie could not pull herself together. Dr. Marstellar affirmed she was not capable of a public examination, and by consent of counsel it was determined to take her affidavit from her rooms. Her voice quavered like the gaslight as she spoke for the record:

> My name is Fannie S. Fewell; born on the 29th of June, 1856. I am the daughter of W. S. Fewell, a resident of Manassas, Prince William County, Virginia. I first became acquainted with Mr. James F. Clark early this summer at the residence of Mr. Hynson at Manassas. I met him often at Mr. Hynson's. His wife and children were with him when I first made his acquaintance. I don't know how long this was before the removal of his family to King George County; he paid me no particular attention until after his wife left. I received a note inviting me to Mrs. Hynson's. Mrs. Hynson said he had left his wife forever. The next day I received another note from Mr. Clark, in which he stated that he had separated from his wife, or rather that his wife had left him, and that he intended settling in the West; from that time up to the time I left I received notes from him, these notes urging me to come with him. I then wanted to know if he and his wife had really separated; he told me that they had positively. I then made up my mind to go with him; that is, I was urged to go with him. He promised to marry me when I got to Washington.

At this point Fannie collapsed, and Dr. Marstellar refused to allow her to continue. It was just as well, the family felt, given the involvement of other good families in Manassas.

When court resumed that evening, Benjamin was sworn in. After recounting the activities of the past month, from the time of Fannie's disappearance until he brought her home, he then revealed that Fannie had given him a damning letter Jim had sent to her at the hotel:

MY DEAR LITTLE GIRL — I got here this morning about a half hour ago and shall go out to Mr. Wroe's to-day to see if papa is out in that country anywhere. I am immensely warm and know you are almost melted without thin clothes to wear. You do not know darling how much I have missed you, and how much more I shall miss you before we again meet, which I hope is not far distant. Everything looks dreary here. I've only met one man I knew and he was a mere passing acquaintance. You must try my precious little girl to be contented while I am gone and keep as quiet as possible. I will be back in a day or two, perhaps before the time I appointed. I can't tell yet whether I will take the train here or come up through Prince William. It depends upon what I hear from papa and others, I don't apprehend any difficulty though and you must not be uneasy in the least. I shall expect you to write to me so I can get the letter Saturday without fail, and a long letter, for I shall be anxious to hear from you, and whether short absence has made you forget one who like yourself, has made sacrifice of the past. Don't make any exposure of yourself in any way for fear some one will find out where you are and get you away from me. I am writing this letter very badly I know, but I can't help it. My hands are wet with perspiration and I can't put them on the paper without soiling it. I hope your clothes will have come by the time I get back, and that you will be a little more comfortable. You need not be afraid I will forget you darling while I am gone, for you are too dearly impressed upon my heart in the most solemn and deep manner for me to lose sight of you. Bless your dear little heart, don't forget me and be sure to write. I declare I am nearly melted. It is scandalously warm now, and everybody is just sweating away. I shall write again so it will leave here by Saturday's mail. Don't fail to write, and don't forget me and be a good little girl in every way. As bad a little flirt as you are I am not afraid to trust you. God bless you darling and preserve you in quiet and safety for me.

Ever and fondly yours, James
Fredericksburg, August 22, 1872

Dr. Marstellar was called to the stand after Benjamin stepped down and testified to Fannie's condition, referring to her "nervous symptoms, having just recovered from hysterical spasms," but offered tentative agreement that she could "undergo examination tomorrow, though ... the paroxysm might occur at any time."

At the end of the evening, the judge delivered his opinion. Upon a writ of habeas corpus, James Clark was legally held in custody, and would remain thus. Jim was then remanded to the custody of the sergeant to be carried to Prince William County, without bail. He did reassure the prisoner that he had it on good authority that no violence was anticipated, but if Jim did apprehend danger from anyone, that person would be arrested. Further, he ordered the sergeant to provide a sufficient guard for the trip.

Once again, Jim was on his way back to his former home, this time with an entourage of Sgt. Edrington and five guards— C. A. Gore, C. D. Cole, J. A. Tayloe, A. B. Rowe, and R. W. Gravvott—all armed with revolvers. They set out for Brentsville on the night mail train.

The train arrived in Alexandria at 4 a.m. on August 27. As would be the case today, a throng of reporters greeted them as they debarked and made for the City Hotel to await their connection. It was the hour the city began to stir; many men were beginning their usual morning routines of going to market, and soon the hotel lobby and all the public rooms on the lower floor were filled with people anxious for a glimpse at the Don Juan. He wasn't much to look at—the days had taken their toll and he was haggard, dressed in a blue cap and pants, with a black alpaca sack coat covering a soiled shirt with no collar.

That didn't stop the surge of onlookers, some of whom had once been his friends.

"How did you come to get in such a scrape?" one asked.

Jim replied he had acted "without thinking of the consequences" but that he "was not the only one to blame in the transaction."

Upon reaching the dining room, Jim sat at the first table he came to and ate heartily, still surrounded by people, answering questions between bites. The crowd did not disperse until the prisoner and his party left for the depot, and even then, many hangers-on followed the party to the train.

Before they could get on their connecting train, a few men pulled Edrington aside and warned him that he would not be able to carry Jim through Manassas alive.

Edrington took the warning to heart. Just before reaching Manassas, he positioned his men in protective positions on the car and told Jim to lower himself in his seat, with his head sunk below the window. Jim, already on edge and fearing for his life, needed no second urging. But it turned out not to be necessary; a crowd was at the depot, but the only threats made were that if Jim escaped conviction, he would certainly be held to account by the family. The train pulled out of Manassas without incident and proceeded to Bristoe. It was early, and there was no ride awaiting them, so after the extremely long day and night already behind them, the prisoner and his guard detail had to wait for a wagon to take them the last five miles to Brentsville as the sun rose. Upon arrival, Jim was delivered to Justice P. G. Weedon. Jim waived an examination and was committed for his appearance at an examination to be held the following Saturday, August 31. He would have to remain in jail until then—Weedon would not allow him to post bail. Jim was then taken to Brentsville jail. He entered his cell, exhausted and anxious for rest.

~~~~~~~

Brentsville was hardly a maximum-security facility. There was one jailer. The cells were not like cells you see in the movies; they were not cages of iron bars. They were regular rooms, with thick walls and, unless there were more prisoners than cells, some privacy. There were iron grates over the windows (but no glass; bored prisoners were too prone to such easy vandalism) and secure doors consisting of a full-length inner iron grate and an outer two-part dutch door of thick wood. There was no guard posted outside Jim's cell, and the wooden door was left wide open. Jim even could have shimmied up the fireplace chimney, if he were really desperate. Still, even with all those gaps, Jim felt a lot safer in jail than he did out on the street, where every doorway was cover for some angry relative of Fannie's or some disgruntled former convict.

And his circumstances, while meager, were not entirely unpleasant. He was being kept in the debtor's cell, a room about ten feet square on the second floor, with an iron grating over an ordinary sized single window opening to the south with a view of the Episcopal Church. It allowed for an occasional breeze through the room, even in the stifling August heat. His sleeping arrangements were an iron bedstead with a cornshuck mattress and comforter, and a discarded shawl for a pillow.[21] The room's furnishings were rounded out by a table and two chairs, although one had only three legs and had to be kept in a corner to prop it up. He was provided with paper and envelopes, pen and ink, and he was fed well, with a blackened tin wash basin and a chamber pot housed under the bed. He did have to share the room with some discarded parts of a wooden bedstead, and the walls needed whitewashing, but it could have been far worse.

Still, Jim was in a fix. Being a lawyer, he knew how this game was played, and that talking to the press was his best chance to sway public opinion. The newspapers weren't going to get any points of his defense; that was for the trial. But there were plenty of other things he could say, and he was indignant enough now to say them. He was finishing breakfast when the first reporter, Dr Harold Snowden from the *Alexandria Gazette*,[22] arrived. Jim gave him the one good chair and took the bed for himself. Reclining there in his shirtsleeves, he talked easily and at

---

[21] A cornshuck mattress may have been more comfortable than it sounds. According to *The New England Economical Housekeeper and Family Receipt Book*, "It is not just any old husks tossed into a bag: The husks are gathered as soon as they are ripe, and on a clean, dry day. The outer husks are rejected, and the softer, inner ones are collected and dried in the shade, and when dry, the hard ends, that were attached to the cob, are cut off. They are then drawn through a hatchel or comb, so as to cut them into narrow slips. These, enclosed in a sack, or formed into a mattress like prepared hair, will be found almost equal to the best moss or hair mattresses, and are so durable that, with any ordinary care, they will last from five to ten years."

[22] In a strange coincidence, this is the same Doctor Snowden who buried Hayden Fewell and Edgar Warfield's brother after the battle of Frayser's Farm. He went on to become editor of the *Alexandria Gazette* in 1876 and remained in the job until his death in 1901.

length with Snowden; the interview lasted nearly an hour. The only moment he felt a brush of unease was when Snowden asked if he was worried about retribution. Not from the law, he replied—then, as if to reassure himself about family vengeance, he added that the jailer had promised not to admit anyone into the jail at night. Jim averred he had no interest in escaping: "You see there is no guard around the jail, there is but one jailer, my door and the outside door are open, or this, the chimney, out of which I could crawl were I so disposed."

When the interview was wrapping up, Jim said he would like to write a notice to the paper and asked Snowden if he would deliver it and have it published. Snowden agreed, and withdrew, giving Jim time to think and write.

Jim's mind was undoubtedly still reeling from the events of the past few days, if not weeks. He tried to put things in order, to sum them up as if he were writing a brief. How had he wound up here?

He had not promised Miss Fewell that he would marry her. He had not seduced her; he had never seduced any girl. And he was confident he would be acquitted.

Did it really all begin with the parties? But he hadn't hosted any parties after he had sent Betty and the girls to her father. He had attended them, and of course he had danced with the girls; he enjoyed it. People could think whatever they chose, but there was no harm in dancing, and he would continue to jig and reel as long as he liked. And he certainly hadn't danced every set with Miss Fewell. Why, the only time he had ever been seen with her alone was one buggy ride, and even then they were accompanied by another couple. He had flirted, but he flirted with everyone. It was in his nature to flirt, and it was just good business to pay deference to the daughter of one of the most influential men in town.

He hadn't skulked around with her after hours. Frankly, he had been too busy with his own affairs to notice the girl, for the most part. He'd seen her at a dancing party at his cousin's house last winter, and Fannie was always hanging around Georgianna's. It was true they had spent a pleasant time chatting at that fishing party to Milford Mills last spring — but so had half the town. And once he had moved Betty back in with her father, his evenings were not spent chasing young women around town — in fact, he had spent most of his time at Georgianna's, taking supper with them and conversing until late in the evening. With only a couple of exceptions, he'd left there every night, gone back to his own place, and stayed up late catching up on work. Everything was strictly above board.

No, this was a smear campaign. This was people getting even with him for pushing to move the courthouse to Manassas, which was why he'd been trying to get out of the county in the first place. That was why he had been charged with radicalism, and that was how that silly story had gotten started about him being paid $1,000 to stump Tennessee for Grant, but these charges, like that of abduction, were groundless. He had never been to Tennessee, and what grounds were there for abduction? Certainly Fannie had eluded her family—but his explanation of why, how, and for whom would divulge his line of defense.

Jim knew that being at odds with the Fewells—and by extension, the Merchants—was an unpleasant, if not downright dangerous, situation. That was part of why he had been so careful with Fannie; he did not want to create further tension with her family. He had never intended to marry the girl, but he hadn't been able to figure out a way to let her down gently. William and Lucien had been hostile toward him for months already, ever since he'd had to send Constable Cannon to Alexandria to get that drunken hothead arrested and brought back to Prince William for disturbing the peace. Lucien was notorious for that kind of thing. Jim had heard that even last Saturday, Lucien had been talking about coming up to shoot him, but instead had gotten so drunk that he had to sleep it off—and after that, had been obliged to go up the road and help install lightning rods, keeping him too busy to carry out his act of vengeance.

Jim shifted uneasily at that thought and looked around his room. The jailer had promised he would admit no one into the jail at night, but Lucien could be extremely charming when he wanted to get his way—and very intimidating when charm didn't work. It would be a very easy matter for him to assassinate Jim here, with no escape and no arms of his own. And then what? His wife would be left alone. His two baby girls would have no daddy.

That was the one thing Jim did feel sorry about. Poor Betty. And Betty's father, poor soul, who had even volunteered to pay his bail. And his own father, for that matter. He would cut off both his arms if it would have kept them from being embarrassed by all this. And it looked like the case was going to be dragged out even longer. Since his arrest, there had been no way to communicate with his friends, secure funding, arrange for representation. A telegram he had tried to send to his father the day before had been returned for insufficient funds. He sighed and picked up his pen.

> BRENTSVILLE, Prince William County, Va., Aug 27, I am here incarcerated in jail, denied the free opportunity of advising with relatives or friends, or of engaging counsel to conduct my defense. I have never had so much as a preliminary examination before justice of the peace; have never been confronted with those witnesses on whose testimony alone my prosecution may hope in any contingency base my conviction; have never had an opportunity to converse with or to have examined a single witness in my behalf, and have under these circumstances been compelled to listen to

defamatory denunciations of the people and permitted to read newspaper articles written to embitter public feeling against me and to create in the judgment of the people my conviction of a crime, before I have been even arraigned therefore in any criminal forum of the country. I know how sensitive public opinion is and how easily it is operated upon to the prejudice of any one charged with a crime of this character, but surely it is bare justice to withhold popular out-cry against me until I have been convicted before a jury of my countrymen. Especially does this seem to me a right which I can confidently expect to have recognized by the press, since in no article that I have seen has my previous life for rectitude and integrity in such matters ever been assailed, and since I came to the community where arrest might reasonably have been expected and have never shrunk from any investigation of the case. I feel the deepest sorrow for all parties concerned in this most unfortunate affair, and no earthly ill will towards any who are engaged in an effort to rivet upon me a legal conviction and to place me in a felon's cell. But I am NOT GUILTY of the charge against me, and when the case is fully investigated and all the facts fully developed, I have no fears of a conviction by a jury. If I have violated any law let that law punish me through its recognized and sworn agencies. I am in the custody of the law and expect to be discharged as the law directs and don't ask a discharge in any other way.

At her home in Manassas, Fannie was still sequestered from those who would see her, complaining of ill health and refusing to see anyone besides the doctor and her attorney—and she only saw the latter when he insisted upon it.

Sinclair, the attorney, didn't need to see much of her, though, and when he visited, it was mostly to serve as another reassuring presence to the girl. Mostly he went about his own business, much of which involved talking to the press.

"I am thoroughly convinced that Miss Fewell has been villainously treated, and Clark will not be permitted to go unpunished," he told the *Alexandria Gazette*. But Sinclair opted not to press for an early trial, to allow Clark ample time to find counsel, and—perhaps—for Miss Fannie's nerves to settle down. Eventually, all sides got their ducks in rows and a trial was set for the following Monday, September 2.

William Fewell, as head of the family, was also making the rounds to newspaper offices. His daughter was the victim of a deep laid and hellish plot, he insisted to the *Gazette*. Yes, he had promised the authorities in Fredericksburg that he would not interfere with Jim while the trial was in progress, but if he had known the whole story then, there wouldn't be a trial at all; he would have blown Jim's brains out in the sight of judge and jury. To William's thinking, shooting was probably too good for any man who lured his daughter away from home by promising to marry her and then, upon growing tired of her, robbed and deserted her hundreds of miles away from home, so that she had to debase herself and beg her way back to Washington, leaving her very clothing behind to pay a $30 hotel bill in Missouri.

He had plenty of spleen to go around. He was astonished and infuriated that his trusted neighbor, Mrs. Hynson, would have assisted Jim in the abduction, even if she was Jim's relative. William had always viewed her as a friend, a lady in all ways, and worthy of her connections with the best people of the county.

Everyone in the county had an opinion, it seemed, and most were inclined against Jim. One person, in particular, was driven by William's comments— a person who was inclined to take matters to extremes. And that is how Lucien Fewell came to have two pistols in his pockets on August 31, walking up the same road to Brentsville that Jim had walked only four days earlier.

Witnesses sitting on the front porch of Kincheloe's store just across the street from the jail later said they saw Lucien "stealing cautiously towards the front door of the jail," but also said they wrote it off thinking it was the jailor's brother. Why a person with every reason to be on the property would be skulking about is unclear, and the witnesses never explained why this did not strike them as odd—a curious position to take, given the furor surrounding Jim's case, the well-publicized expectation of reprisals, and his own expressions of fear for his safety. One possible explanation is that Lucien's reputation was well established, and nobody wanted to tangle with him first thing in the morning. Another is that people knew what he was up to, and looked the other way, figuring that for once his belligerence was pointed in the right direction. That would also account for the fact that nobody was guarding the door to the jail despite the fact that public opinion was clearly set against the prisoner and violence had already been threatened. Sheriff John T. Goodwin later printed a card in the *Manassas Gazette* that stated the front door was left open at Jim's request—perhaps for fresh air— and that Goodwin was not 100 yards off at the time of the shooting. Whether Goodwin was covering his tracks or in earnest is lost to history.

The final point that remains unclear is why Jim had been relocated to a room on the ground floor. It was not unheard of for prisoners' families to pay off guards to leave doors unlocked or to doze off with a window open, but it seems unlikely the Clarks did so, and equally unlikely that the Fewells would have made such an arrangement for

Lucien's revenge plan—especially since Lucien didn't know which cell Jim was in. Perhaps the parade of visitors and gawkers was more easily accommodated by avoiding the stairwell. It is more likely, as the Washington, D.C., *National Daily Republican* reported on September 2, that the jailer was miffed by Jim's gibe about escaping by climbing up the chimney and moved him to a room with fewer holes in it.[23] In any event, Jim was in a ground-floor cell, the door of which was just steps away from the jail's front door. If Lucien had come in the front door, he would have seen Jim immediately and been at his cell door and firing within the span of three footsteps. Instead, he approached from the hall and Jim was alerted to a presence, if not danger, before actually seeing Lucien.

Jim did not go easily. He was lying on the bed when Lucien's face appeared at the iron grate of his door. Jim jumped up and ran to the corner on the right-hand side of the door. As he was running, Lucien fired and missed. Jim then ran to the other side of the door; Lucien shot and missed again, then put the pistol all the way through the grate in an attempt to acquire a better angle. Jim grabbed the pistol and tried to wrest it from Lucien. He failed, and Lucien then drew a second, smaller pistol and shot him in the chest. With his left arm hooked around the grate and a gun in each hand, Lucien was able to fire three times before anyone else came on the scene. Jim used every means at his disposal to defend himself; he used a table as a shield, and had thrown a pitcher, an inkstand, and a heavy glass salt cellar at Lucien's face; all were in

---

[23] Only the debtor's cells had fireplaces; jail cells for other criminals were much more secure and much less hospitable. Debtor's cells were more or less the equivalent of white-collar incarceration: Any person owed money could order a citizen's arrest, and the debtor either had to pay up on the spot or spend some period of time under lock and key. Because these situations were outside the court system, some measure of leniency was granted, including somewhat more comfortable quarters.

numberless fragments about the door.

Major William W. Thornton, who had been a captain in Jim's cavalry company during the war, was first to arrive on the scene, with deputy court clerk William E. Lipscomb. The two, who may have been among the witnesses on the porch of Kincheloe's store, came running at the sound of gunfire and arrived on the third shot. Thornton exhorted Lucien to stop.

"Major, let me alone," Lucien warned him. "I know what I am about." Thornton persisted. "Go away," Lucien snarled. "I don't want to hurt you."

Thornton then grabbed Lucien and attempted to drag him away, but with his arm hooked around the grate, Lucien was immovable. The men were unable to pry him loose before he had emptied both firearms into the cell. Upon concluding his job, Lucien walked out of the jail and escaped in the direction he had come. Distracted with the bleeding man in the cell, Thornton and Lipscomb let him go, and nobody else stopped him.

So, Lucien left the scene of the crime entirely unhindered—those in attendance were too concerned about Jim to stop him. He made first for a little belt of pines north of the jail where he reloaded his pistols. He then returned to Brentsville, passing immediately by the jail, and was walking back up the main street of town when he recognized his father's carriage heading toward him. There's no telling what ran through his head, but it wasn't his father at the reins. It was Harvey Varnes. Apparently, William Fewell had heard about Lucien's arrival in Bristow from the conductor of the morning train and, knowing his son but unable to leave his post, had sent Varnes to stop him. Varnes arrived ten minutes too late. The two men started for Manassas, but before they had gone 50 yards, the harness broke. They spent more than 15 minutes mending it, during which time several people passed them, but they were neither pursued nor accosted. Finally, they arrived in Manassas, where Lucien eventually gave himself up to John H. Butler, the justice of the peace.

Back at the jail, all was chaos. Jim, still in his cell surrounded by broken glass and furniture, was awake and moving around—and rational enough to ask that somebody stand outside and guard the window, in case Lucien came back to shoot him again.

Quick to arrive on the scene were Jim's brother-in-law, J. Milton Weedon, and Dr. Clement C. Barbour. They already planned to be in town for Jim's hearing, expecting Lucien to attack Jim in the street after the court proceedings. Instead, they arrived a half-hour after the shooting.

Jim knew he'd been shot in the chest. Upon examination, doctors found a navy ball had passed on the left side of the heart in close proximity to it and was lodged "in the back bone."

The Civil War, bloody as it was, had led to marvelous advancements in health care. Ambulance systems, immediacy of treatment, and sanitization of instruments were just some of the improvements that stemmed from care on the battlefield—not to mention a general rise in the population with medical experience; before the war, most new doctors were well-versed in book-learning but might never have administered treatment until encountering their first patient. However, treatment of wounds had only moved forward incrementally, and the wound Jim had suffered was not easily treated. Doctors also found a wound in his back where a second ball had penetrated a short distance into the flesh; this one was extracted.

Upon the completion of Jim's surgery, he was moved back upstairs to the debtor's cell. The iron bedstead and shuck mattress that had sufficed for him as a suspect were replaced with a wooden bedstead and a feather mattress. Meanwhile, a warrant was issued for Lucien's arrest, but Lucien had turned himself in to the Manassas magistrate before it was even drawn up. He hoped to obtain bail by a writ of habeas corpus, but was advised to go to jail instead and await the result of Jim's wounds. Thus, he returned to Brentsville late that afternoon and was locked in the room where he had shot Jim not eight hours earlier. Apparently a believer in locking the barn door after the horse has been shot and the shooter is asleep in a stall, Commonwealth's Attorney Sinclair called for a guard of eight men to be placed around the jail.

News traveled fast, and the *Manassas Gazette* (the masthead of which now boasted Varnes as "proprieter") pronounced judgment in favor of the shooter:

> Manassas, Va., Aug. 31 - Jas. F. Clark, the seducer of Miss Fannie Fewell, was shot, and probably killed, in the jail at Brentsville, this morning at about eight o'clock by her brother, Rhoda Fewell. Mr. Fewell came up on the night train from Lynchburg and got off at Bristoe Station, and walked over to Brentsville, and on going to the jail found the front door open. A black boy, the only person present, told him in which cell Clark was, and on going there, he found Clark lying on his bed. Seven shots were fired through the grating of the cell door, one of them taking effect in Clark's left breast, just below the heart. Mr. Fewell returned to Manassas and has surrendered himself into the hands of the authorities. It is thought Clark is dead by this time - eleven o'clock a.m.
>
> The brother of the wronged girl has the undoubted sympathies of the public with him, wondering why he did not kill her seducer before.
>
> Editor of Manassas Gazette

On the other hand, a correspondent for the *National Daily Republican* noted that "Clark is considered a dead shot, and if he should ever recover and regain his liberty he will probably make it warm for Mr. Fewell." As it turned out, Mr. Fewell did not have to worry.

Five doctors looked Jim over and agreed it was a dangerous wound and that "symptoms of a varied character may develop themselves at any time in the course of a few days." Elder Clark, who had visited his son two days earlier in preparation for the trial, traveled to Alexandria to acquire medicine and a doctor he trusted, Bedford Brown, before moving on to Brentsville, arriving Sunday morning. By Monday afternoon, Jim was declining rapidly.

He held on longer than expected, though. He rested, propped up on the feather bed because his wounds didn't allow him to lie flat. At first, there was little pain. Given the location of the bullet and the fact he appeared to do well initially, it would make sense that doctors would be reluctant to go poking around much for the bullet. When Dr. Brown finally admitted to Jim that the injuries were critical, the lawyer replied: "Yes, but I don't intend to give up until long after you do."

Lucien, still confined in the downstairs cell, was understandably anxious about Jim's fate and what it would mean for him. But when told death was imminent, he asked if "they would let the corpse stay up there all night?" Whether he asked this out of incredulity or superstition is unclear, but the answer was that they would—and Lucien, denied bail and in custody until his trial, remained below.

On Monday, Judge Aylet Nicol was busy in the courtroom. Among other cases to be heard, Lucien had applied for bail under a writ of habeas corpus. Nicol held the application for consideration for more than a week, ultimately rejecting it and setting a grand jury hearing for October. In the jail, Jim's pain from the chest wound apparently got much worse; he hadn't complained much about it before that day. He received assiduous medical attention—as well as the attention of many well-wishers. Numerous residents of Brentsville stopped by to offer comfort or advice. His brother-in-law, J. Milton Weedon, visited every day. His mother arrived a few minutes before he died. Notably absent from the recorded guest list were Jim's wife and children (though it is unclear if this is because they were absent or simply went unmentioned by the press). The list of visitors was made longer, however, by a parade of curious onlookers. Court was in session on Mondays, and an unusually large crowd was on hand, drawn by interest in the Clark-Fewell scandal. Though the guards that had been placed around the jail on Saturday were still in force, they did not try to stop any passersby whose curiosity or sympathy induced them to visit the dying man.

On Tuesday Jim started to spit blood, suffered a spasmodic hiccup and intense vomiting, and began wheezing with a "constant noise like that of a groan and cough." That afternoon, his mind began to wander. He lost consciousness around 4 p.m. and grew rapidly weaker until he breathed his last three hours later.

A coroner's jury was summoned and an inquest held. James R. Purcell, acting coroner, and the jury led by A.F. Woodyard, a farmer and justice of the peace, returned their verdict:

> The jurors sworn to inquire when and how and by what means the said James F. Clark came to his death, upon their oaths do say that the said J.F. Clark died on the 2nd day of September, 1872, about the hour of 7 o'clock p.m., from the effects of shots fired from pistols by and in the hands of one L.N. Fewell, on the morning of 31st day of August, 1872, he, the said James F. Clark, being then confined in a cell of the jail of the said county in the town of Brentsville.

Although massive advances had been made in the medical field as a result of the Civil War, it is still an understatement to refer to nineteenth-century surgical practices as "comparatively primitive" when placed against today's level of care. There were no X-rays, blood transfusions were not clearly understood and were believed to be dangerously risky, and obviously the concept of sterile conditions was a far cry from what we know today. For starters, the bullet probably would have been located with certainty, although if in a stable location, doctors still would have left it where it was rather than remove it. Jim would have had the benefit of reduced infection risk; he would have received a chest tube allowing the accumulating blood to drain and allow "normal" respiration to occur, albeit on a ventilator. Depending how much blood was collected out of the chest tube, he would have undergone surgery or simply been left alone until the bleeding clotted naturally and he could be weaned off the ventilator.

The shot that caused Jim's death was the one in his chest. The ball entered about an inch and a quarter to the left of the left nipple and inclined nearly horizontally to the right, passing directly over, if not wounding, the heart. Dr. Barbour and another doctor named Leary made a postmortem examination but were unable to discover the actual ball. They could only trace its course a short distance, though they were satisfied from the course it took that it lodged somewhere in the bowels. From the quantity of blood taken from Jim during the examination, they concluded that an internal hemorrhage began when he was shot and continued up to his death, but that he did not die of this; "death ensued from a lesion of the great sympathetic nerve."

With the benefit of modern medical knowledge, it can be guessed that a hemorrhage in the chest cavity actually was the likeliest cause of death, and a hemo-pneumo thorax being the most likely diagnosis. A lesion of the "great sympathetic nerve" would have explained the hiccupping, and so would blood in the lung. Alternately, it is possible the bullet did simply hit the esophagus, causing some irritation of the gastrointestinal tract by a slow bleed, causing the ensuing hiccup and vomiting. Since the bullet was never found, it is hard to reach any concrete conclusion. It is safe to say, however, that modern medicine would have allowed the "dead shot" Jim to "make it warm for Mr. Fewell."

Even as it was, things were plenty warm for Lucien, now facing a murder charge. The newspapers went wild with this development. The *Alexandria Gazette* reported,

> Clark is dead! And whether the enormity of his guilt was as great as it is now generally believed to have been is only known to the unfortunate survivor of the elopement in which he was implicated, for, so far as is known, he never breathed a word about the part the young lady took in that affair, except to say that he had not taken her away, and had not seduced her.

Jim was buried September 4 in Bellfair Mills, his childhood home, at his family plot in Chopawamsic. As his dying days had drawn a crowd, so did his funeral, including his family. "The parting with the corpse at the grave by the parents of the deceased, is described as being very affecting; causing nearly every one present to shed tears."

It is frustrating, though not surprising, that no notice was taken of Jim's widow. No diaries or letters are in the public archive, and in those days the newspapers were, for better or worse, more respectful of a woman's privacy. There is no way to know how she felt about her husband and the actions that led to his untimely end. We do know that although she was only 22 when he died, she never remarried, that she and her daughters lived with her brother, James, and his family for several years, and that later in life she lived with her elder daughter in New Jersey. She died there in 1896, and was buried with her brother and his family in Stafford, Virginia. It is a question for the ages whether she carried a torch for Jim Clark to the end of her days, or his actions simply put her off men altogether.

Chapter Six: Legal Eagles

*F*our days after the shooting, Lucien Fewell was still in jail, still brash and confident of acquittal, but also still waiting for the judge to decide on bail. Fannie, confined to her room, had no idea Jim Clark was dead. Her family had opted to keep it from her out of concern for her health— her doctor was afraid that in her already excited state, the news might kill her—but since she was still refusing to see anyone aside from her doctor and her lawyer, it was an easy secret to keep. The Fewells, of course, were not about to cheap out on their scion's defense. Regardless of how much trouble he'd gotten into over the years, and regardless of what individual family members might have felt about him and what he'd done, they joined forces and pulled together—which is how Eppa Hunton entered the picture.

Eppa Hunton II, attorney at law, knew Brentsville like the back of his hand. For years before the war, he had lived just up the street from the town square, and had been one of the first men in the town militia. For men such as Hunton, the war and its devastation were no longer a gaping wound by 1872, but the feelings had not yet subsided to a dull ache, either. The war was wrapped up in every aspect of one's existence; it was in the company one kept, the land one farmed, the laws and regulations one was subjected to. Such a pervasive influence was no longer the sole topic of conversation—it would be like obsessing about humidity or ragweed—but certain things brought such thoughts back to the front of one's mind. Jim Clark and Fannie had run away on the anniversary of First Manassas, and Jim had been shot one day after the anniversary of Second Manassas. It was a coincidence that inspired painful nostalgia.

Standing on the town square, for example, Hunton could see where his antebellum home had once stood. It had been demolished by Union soldiers while he was serving in the Eighth Virginia Infantry. It had been abandoned upon a Confederate retreat in 1862, and one of his slaves was living there when it was overrun. A soldier from Wisconsin

> found it occupied by a number of soldiers, who were taking it easy upon the handsome sofas chairs and lounges. In the parlor I observed a stalwart Pennsylvania Zouave beating away upon a piano while a dozen others were going it upon a regular 'break down.' In 'my lady's chamber' a squad of soldiers had taken up quarters, where they were cooking and washing. Her handsome mahogany bedstead was holding the elongated forms of four 'horrible Zouaves,' who declared to me that it was a d—d splendid sleeping machine. The Colonel's library had been completely stripped of all its books; private papers and letters scattered over the floor; writing desk and book-case partly mashed. It was sad to see this indiscriminate destruction of property and then reflect upon the causes which had produced it.

After referring to Hunton as one of the "blind and infatuated Virginia professionals [who] played an active part among the ranks of disunion in the contest with the union party which resulted so fatally to the peace and prosperity of the State," who was "'honored' with the position of Col. over a regiment of Virginia traitors" but who "followed the retreating forces of Beauregard, accompanied by his wife and two slaves," he went on to describe the slave inhabiting the Hunton home in what may or may not be a telling description of master-slave relations but is certainly a vivid example of a typical Northern perspective.

> In the kitchen I came across a sprightly negro woman who informed me that her master had left four of them behind with instructions to follow him as soon as he should send for them. Upon my pointing southward and asking her whether she intended going in that direction she gave me a knowing look and replied, "No, Master, We's gwine norf, whar de white folks don't whip de darkies." When asked what she could do to take care of herself, she promptly answered, "Why Master, if we colored folks can take care of da white people in dis country, we can take care of ourselves Norf." The shrewdness of this reply convinced me that these "ignorant darkies," now that they are at liberty to express their sentiments with out fear of the lash are "wide awake," and appreciate the difference between slavery and freedom.

Hunton did, indeed, number among the Virginia professionals; in fact, he was part of the cream of Prince William society. But he was not a shirker, as our Wisconsin wag would have it. Born in 1822, he was one of 11 children, nine of whom survived. His father died early on and left the family comparatively poor. Eppa was raised mostly by his mother, graduating from the New Baltimore Academy and then teaching school for a few years before studying law. He was admitted to the bar in 1843 and became commonwealth's attorney for Prince William County in 1847, re-elected to the position every term until 1861, when he joined the Confederate Army. A lifelong Democrat, he moved to Brentsville in 1849. He was involved in many land transactions related to the sale of Bristow lots after 1848 and actually sold land to Sinclair in 1850.

He was elected brigadier general of the county militia in 1857 and was among the "immediate secession" contingent voting in the state's 1861 convention. (The vote in favor of secession at the convention was 88-55. The popular vote was 128,884-32,134.)

Hunton was commissioned a colonel of the Eighth Virginia Infantry in 1861, participating in the Battle of First Manassas. Despite suffering from a debilitating fistula for the entirety of the war that kept him bedridden more than he would have preferred, he acquitted himself admirably, fighting in several major battles—including at Antietam and as part of Pickett's Charge at Gettysburg—in Lt. Gen. James Longstreet's division, Major General George Pickett's division, and the Department of Richmond. His action at Gettysburg earned him the rank of brigadier general, and he was present at the second battle of Cold Harbor and engaged General George Custer at Sailor's Creek on the way to Appomattox. Hunton was forced to surrender in that battle, miserably ill with diarrhea and continued agony from his fistula. Custer showed great generosity, sending a physician and a bottle of French brandy to the defeated officer.[24]

---

[24] Hunton's military medical history is difficult to read without cringing. After the battle of First Manassas, he suffered from an anal fistula (an abscess, or

Three days later, the Army of Northern Virginia surrendered, and Hunton, after a stint as a prisoner, returned home, settling in Warrenton. "From 1865-1872, I had all the business I could attend to. My income was a very fine one, and in 1867 I purchased a house from William H. Gaines and moved into it." He lived there with his wife, her sisters and mother, and his son, Eppa III, who attended school in Warrenton. Reconstruction rubbed Hunton the wrong way, as it did many gentlemen of the time, but it didn't affect him the way it did the Lucien Fewells:

> Notwithstanding the terrible condition of the country during this period of reconstruction, the business of the country went on. My practice was very large. I had a fine practice in Fauquier where I lived, in Prince William, where I lived before the war, and in Loudoun County, from which came six of the ten companies of my dear 8th Regiment. My practice in the three counties was very remunerative. I had purchased a residence in Warrenton, on Rappahannock Street, and paid for it. It was a very comfortable home. I had purchased eight or ten acres just outside of the town, for a pastureage for my horse and cow. I was doing very well indeed, but unfortunately, I went into politics.

---

infected cavity filled with pus, near the anus). After three months of intermittent sick leave, it still had not healed. He had surgery on it in November, but that, too, failed to heal properly, as did a series of cauterization treatments. He finally returned to his troops in March 1862, though still unfit for duty, and was on leave again in May and June. Ignoring his doctor, he rejoined his regiment for the Seven Days battles, falling frequently and once becoming separated from his command because he could not keep up. At the battle of Gettysburg, he was too sick to go into battle on foot and instead rode his horse. He was shot in the leg during the charge at Cemetery Heights and lost so much blood getting to a field hospital he could not return to the field.

On Friday, August 16, 1872, while Fannie had been making her way back to Washington from Missouri, Hunton had been nominated to run for a seat in the U.S. House of Representatives. The *Alexandria Gazette* gave him a glowing endorsement: "Those who may have had preferences for other gentlemen not only acquiesce in the result, but acquiesce cheerfully and will support the nomination heartily."

As a Democrat, Hunton was a virtual shoo-in, but he didn't have the job yet. Politics operated differently in those days—those elected to Congress in November 1872 were not sworn in until March of the following year, and did not actually begin legislating until December. In September of 1872, then, Hunton was still practicing law (and doing a little campaigning on the side). With his sterling reputation, the Fewells snapped him up for Lucien's defense. This was not Hunton's first encounter with the Fewells; he had been a trustee of Sarah Fewell's land when her first husband died intestate. No documents remain detailing Hunton's personal opinion of his new client, but the record shows he put in a solid effort preparing the defense.

Hunton was accustomed to joining legal forces with another war hero, William Henry Fitzhugh Payne, and he did so for Lucien's case. Payne was eight years Hunton's junior, born in 1830 in Fauquier County. He studied law at the University of Virginia, established his law practice in Warrenton, Virginia, in 1851 and served as commonwealth's attorney of Fauquier County. A year later, he married Mary Elizabeth Winston Payne, whose father, Col. W. Winter Payne, represented the Sumter district of Alabama in Congress from 1841 through 1848.

Payne enlisted as a private in early 1861 and participated in the occupation of Harpers Ferry in April. Later in the year, he became a captain in the Black Horse Cavalry, serving under J.E.B. Stuart. The type of unit and the name were a topic of later conversation with Major John Scott of Fauquier County, as Payne wrote later:

> The idea was that we were descendants of cavaliers. The company would be a cavalry troop. I called the Major's attention to the fact that the first standard borne by our tribe, the Saxons, when they landed at Than, was a banner with a white horse. It was agreed, therefore, that a horse, especially typical and representative of Virginia, should be adopted. We were all extreme pro-slavery men, but the Major in addition was in favor of opening the African slave trade and he suggested, therefore, that the horse should be black, and hence the troop was named the Black Horse Troop.

While such sentiments strike an appalling and sour note today (and rightly so), this is not a confession of guilt, nor a statement of defense on Payne's part. It was simply a part of who he was, the time and place in which he lived, and a view widely accepted by his peers. Payne was promoted to major of the Fourth Virginia Cavalry and commanded the regiment at the Battle of Williamsport during the Peninsula Campaign in 1862. He was severely wounded and captured by Union forces. After being exchanged, he returned to duty as the lieutenant colonel of the Second North Carolina Cavalry and fought in the Chancellorsville Campaign.

During the subsequent Gettysburg Campaign, he was captured at the Battle of Hanover in 1863 after being unhorsed and nearly drowning after being thrown headfirst into an open vat of tanning liquid (composed mostly of horse urine) used for making leather. Upon being released, he was promoted to brigadier general in November 1864 and led a brigade that year, participating in the battles of Opequon, Fisher's Hill, and Cedar Creek, then being badly wounded at the Battle of Five Forks. During the final operations around Richmond in early 1865, he commanded a cavalry brigade under Thomas T. Munford.

After the war, Payne remained an unrepentant Democrat and unreconstructed rebel. Like Hunton, his law practice thrived.

The third member of the defense team was Henry Wirtz Thomas, born in Leesburg on October 20, 1812. Like Hunton, Thomas had also started out as a school teacher, moving to Fairfax County in 1833 and becoming a major in the militia at the age of 26. He, too, served as commonwealth's attorney, and, in 1865, he was part of the committee that met with President Lincoln during re-establishment of civil government in Virginia. In 1866 he was appointed Judge of the Ninth Circuit, serving until 1869. "Judge T" often assisted Hunton and Payne on cases, and this would be no exception. In fact, Thomas conducted much of the courtroom questioning.

Still, Hunton was mindful of his role. The attention that could come with a high-profile murder case wouldn't hurt his political campaign (even if he was virtually guaranteed the seat), and having the Fewells and Merchants on his side wouldn't hurt, either. There was speculation that it would be impossible to get a jury, since by this time virtually everyone in a 20-mile radius had expressed opinions strong enough to disqualify them from involvement in the case. There seemed to be a geographic divide in these feelings. Most of the residents above Cedar Run felt Lucien's actions were justified; those who lived below the run expressed bitter feelings against him. It is a matter of speculation whether this was because most folks below the Run were more familiar with Lucien's fierce temper, or because Jim was more popular, or the concept of law and order was simply more ingrained.

Newspapers around the country also varied in their judgments. The *New York Tribune* flippantly declared, "We doubt this would be considered good form even among the Fijis." The *Fredericksburg News*, on the other hand, declared that "the unwritten law of Virginia is that death is the penalty of this crime. However guilty the woman may be, the man who assaults her purity or accomplishes her ruin, let him die the death." The *Washington Chronicle* chose to blame society, saying that Lucien "was goaded on to kill by a fear of public opinion. He killed him not for honor, but for selfishness; not to avenge his sister and punish a crime but to shield himself from the scorn of other men."

George Carr Round weighed in on September 11 with a long letter to the *Alexandria Daily State Journal*:

> The so-called Clark-Fewell sensation has developed into the Clark-Fewell tragedy. Your readers are acquainted with the main facts through the telegraph. One impression which has gone abroad I desire to correct. It is that public opinion about here justifies the act of Rhoda Fewell. I have heard the subject freely commented on by all classes of citizens, and I venture the opinion that not one out of ten of our citizens ever pretends to offer even an apology for the shooting of Clark while in the hands of the law. Even those who most severely denounced the actions of Clark and said that "Fewell ought to shoot him," stand aghast at the manner in which it was accomplished. How often are the public to be greeted with these ghastly tragedies? Probably until our wise(?) lawmakers at Richmond find a proper punishment for the crime of seduction, and a heavier penalty than twenty dollars for the crime of adultery.

Jim Clark's father was beside himself. Days after the funeral, he used the language of his pulpit and the public forum of his newspaper, the *Warren Sentinel*, to express his thoughts on the situation: "Never before have we so fully realized the full import of the words of King David when suffering under a similar affliction: 'my son Absalom, my son, my son Absalom! Would God I had died for thee, O Absalom, my son, my son?'" He also gave thanks for

> the kind and heart-felt sympathies of a great many of our citizens of the county, and many who were at Court from other counties, on the sad and mournful occasion, and we must especially name one noble spirit like the rose in the wilderness, a green spot in the desert, Mr. James Davies, an Englishman by birth, who kindly tendered to us his purse and his services in any way we might command them. He cheerfully volunteered to go to Alexandria for the coffin, &c. though he was threatened with chills. Such a gentleman will live while he lives, and after death will speak. May the good will of Him that dwelt in the bush be with him. And we take pleasure, also in making honorable mention of Major Thornton in tendering to us any money we might need, and other acts of courtesy and kindness, which we shall cherish in grateful reimburse.

Elder Clark's good will did not extend to Judge Sinclair. As the commonwealth's attorney, Sinclair was now in the dubious position of having to prosecute the murderer of a man he had been castigating only days earlier. It was a tricky position for any attorney, and while Sinclair had been in tricky positions before, this one was more personal than usual.

Sinclair was from an established family; his forbears had settled in the area before there even was a Brentsville. They purchased several town lots in 1823 and were active in the community. Sinclair himself had been born there in 1828; he was an active player in the Democratic State Convention in 1852 and around that time was elected to the House of Delegates—where, in 1855, he nominated Eppa Hunton as brigadier general for the fifth militia. Around this time he married Lucy Shackelford, the daughter of an upstanding local judge. Although the couple apparently had several children, none of them survived childhood. In 1857, Sinclair was appointed as a federal judge in the Utah Territory and went there to stabilize a situation in which President Buchanan feared a revolt by Mormons might occur. (It is unclear if Lucy joined him.)

~~~~~~~

The Mormon situation in Utah did not hold with the idea of American law and order, to say the least. Persecution in Missouri and Illinois—including the lynch-mob assassination of their leader, Joseph Smith, in 1844—had convinced Brigham Young and others that the national legal system was corrupt and they should maintain their own institutions of law and government. It was not resistance to the legal system itself so much as a fear that non-Mormons on the bench could (again) abuse their power and persecute the faithful. Thus, for Mormons, the granting of territorial status rather than statehood for Utah in the Compromise of 1850 was terrible news—it meant that three men who served separately as trial judges and jointly as the Territorial Supreme Court could review their own decisions on appeal in their own largely non-Mormon echo chamber, with no checks or balances. These judges had common-law jurisdiction courtesy of the U.S. Congress, and Mormons feared that the territorial legislature's laws would not hold sway—for example, the territory had no law prohibiting polygamy, but that might not matter to these judges. In an already hostile situation, things got off to a terrible start in 1851 with the first three judges—two non-Mormons, Perry Brocchus and Lemuel Brandenberry, and one Mormon, Zerubbabel Snow.

Within a month of their arrival, Brocchus and Brandenberry caused a fuss with a public lecture suggesting that the federal government could not redress wrongs committed by the gentiles in Illinois or Missouri. Young demanded an apology from Brocchus, who refused and, in a stunning display of inability to play nice, decided to take his marbles and go home—the marbles in this case being $24,000 in territorial funds, as well as the seal and records of Utah. The territorial legislature passed a resolution authorizing the U.S. Marshal to seize those items from territorial secretary Broughton D. Harris, who petitioned the Supreme Court for an injunction to prevent the seizure. Brocchus, still on the bench while the legislative aspects played out, heard the case with Brandenberry (Snow refused to attend)—and needless to say, the two judges granted the petition. Harris retained custody of the items, leaving the territory a week later.

Naturally, these events convinced the Mormons that everything they had suspected about a federal court was correct. In response, the territorial legislature took several steps, including essentially naming Snow the law of the land until President Millard Fillmore appointed new judges, allowing litigants to select their own judges, and allowing those with no legal training or experience to present their own cases.

Brocchus and Brandenberry, meanwhile, returned to Washington and stirred the pot by challenging Mormons to argue the legality of plural marriage from a national forum. A series of letters to the *New York Herald* in April 1852 did not admit polygamy's presence in the territory but outlined its legal and religious justifications. This set up a terrible situation for the next federal judges—Leonidas Shaver, in October 1852, followed by Chief Justice Lazarus Reed in June 1853—further exacerbated by Mormon control of all three branches of Utah government. During this period, Mormon litigants took their disputes to the ecclesiastical courts, the probate courts, or to Judge Snow.

In January 1854, the Utah legislature passed a measure—endorsed by Young but unheard of elsewhere in the United States—that said cases could be argued only before courts created by the governor and assembly. Mormons were outraged a year later when a new chief justice, John Fitch Kinney, declared that this measure violated the Organic Act that had established the territory. It was considered a blow below the belt, given that Kinney had enjoyed good relations with the Mormons as a lawyer in Lee County, Iowa, and later as an Iowa Supreme Court Justice. In response, Brigham Young argued that Kinney was off base and would have "to take that back." Arguments over the courts' powers continued to escalate, and Kinney, after suffering several setbacks, left the territory in April 1856.

The hostilities continued. That December, the only judge still on the federal bench, George P. Stiles, suffered the indignity of having his law books dumped into a privy and set on fire; he left the territory a few months later, so the federal bench was empty. The next year, President James Buchanan declared Utah in rebellion in June and sent an army to Utah, seeking to replace Young as governor. The Mormons rallied upon this news: Citizens prepared to defend themselves and the legislature passed a resolution seeking to maintain control of the courts. Young declared martial law.

Things remained tense throughout the fall. Young led a guerrilla attack on Army provision wagons. The Army remained encamped through the winter.

In March 1858, Young learned that the U.S. Senate had accepted the nomination of Alfred Cumming as governor and ordered his followers to prepare for a move to Provo and the destruction of Salt Lake City. Attempting to resolve the crisis, Buchanan issued a proclamation that pardoned the Mormons for treason, on the condition they accept federal authority. Young accepted Buchanan's terms and pardon, although he denied Utah had ever rebelled against the United States.

It was a lose-lose situation. Buchanan was criticized for miscommunication, for incurring the expense of sending troops to Utah on incorrect information, and for poor timing in dispatching those troops. The Mormons, on the other hand, faced more immediate and life-threatening problems: Crops had been ignored for most of the two-month planting season and livestock herds had been culled when the population had evacuated in anticipation of conflict. A year's worth of work improving their living conditions had essentially been lost. Plus, Utah was under nominal military occupation.

This, then, was the situation when Charles Sinclair arrived on the scene in June 1858, along with Cumming and fellow judges Delana R. Eccles and John Cradlebaugh. At that time, General Albert Sidney Johnston's army returned control of the executive and judicial branches to gentiles. In November, Sinclair opened court at Salt Lake City. His first move was an act of aggression, pushing for indictments of ex-Governor Young and other prominent Mormons for treason, intimidation of court, and polygamy. Sinclair asserted that Buchanan's pardon did not have full force and effect until a judge such as himself pronounced it valid. Even non-Mormon officials viewed this sort of saber-rattling as a step too far. The U.S. attorney in Utah, a non-Mormon, told the grand jury that Sinclair was out of bounds, and Governor Cumming also criticized the judges and refused to support their efforts. Sinclair responded harshly "and declared that he was now ready to do anything he could against both the church and people."

Sinclair's name was associated with another embarrassing courtroom gaffe—one tied to the first execution of a white man in Utah. Shoemaker (and non-Mormon) Thomas N. Ferguson asked his employer, Alexander Carpenter, for past wages and was refused. According to Ferguson, he went to a nearby saloon and had a "couple" of drinks. The next thing he remembered was sitting in jail charged with the murder of Carpenter, who had been shot on September 17, 1859. His trial was over quickly. He appeared before Sinclair and was found guilty, and—due to confusion with the calendar or something else—was sentenced to be hanged on a Sunday. Ferguson appealed to Cumming and the execution was rescheduled for Friday, October 28. On that day, Ferguson and his coffin were taken by wagon from the jail, across town, to about a quarter mile past the cemetery gate. As he mounted the scaffold, he was offered a chance for some last words. Some accounts claim he talked for as much as four to eight hours, but most accounts indicate he spoke less than an hour. The November 2, 1859, *Deseret News* printed his comments about Judge Sinclair:

> I was tried by the statutes of Utah Territory, which gives a man the privilege of being shot, beheaded or hanged; but was it given to me? No, it was not. All Judge Sinclair wanted was to sentence some one to be hanged, then he was willing to leave the Territory; and he had too much whiskey in his head to know the day he sentenced me to be executed on, and would not have known, if it had not been for the people of Utah laughing at him; it would have been Sunday. A nice Judge to send to any country.

While there are accounts of Sinclair being a drunk, it is difficult to corroborate the statements of journals with the facts. It is clear that Sinclair was frustrated and aggravated in his efforts—among other issues, Mormon jurors would not return verdicts against their own kind, and Young and the legislature withheld funds for court expenses. Ultimately, Sinclair departed Utah in 1859 with more of a whimper than a bang. By October he was in San Francisco, boarding a steamer for Panama en route back to

Washington, intending to testify before Congress about the state of the Utah judiciary. It appears he might have intended to return for a new session of court, but this did not happen. By March 1860 there were rumors of removal or resignation; he resigned April 2, as did Judge Cradlebaugh. A sympathetic report in the April 3 *Evening Star* reflected,

> The manner in which Judge Sinclair discharged the duties of his office, well known to all who have noted the progress of events in Utah, makes his resignation an event much to be regretted by all who favor the inflexible administration of law everywhere, upon which all hope of stemming the tide of popular demoralization under the Government of the United States rests.

No doubt, the Mormons were about as sorry to see Sinclair leave as he was to leave them. The reaction across the rest of the nation seemed to depend somewhat on geography. Western and Midwestern newspapers questioned the judges "whining because legal process is not summary enough in Utah to suit their views," while many in the East took a dim view of Mormonism and sided with Sinclair. (By January 1872, the *Alexandria Gazette* was proclaiming the end of Smith's vision altogether: "The News discusses Mormonism and sees the end of that monstrous delusion approaching.")

In any event, time marched on, and by October 1861, Sinclair was ready to join the War for Southern Independence and wrote to Virginia Gov. John Letcher, pleading for a job.

> In the general prostration of all professional pursuits, and hoping too to contribute something to our cause, in a position where I may be most efficient. I have concluded to apply for a staff

appointment in our army. I am told that there are places to be filled in the Commissary Department, & perhaps in the Quartermaster, Pay &c. Having been two years with an Army in Utah & somewhat observant of the details of its management, I think I can be serviceable in this way. With an assistant adjutant I had special occasion to know something; on account of our military complications in Utah. Independent of an earnest desire to be engaged in the public service at this crisis, I am wholly now unemployed and have been, some time having relinquished connection with the press. You will pardon me for adding that all of my property (not much anyhow) is tied up by the war & myself and family at expense.

There was something for everyone in the war; Sinclair's obituary credits him with working for the Confederate secret service—something virtually impossible to prove, and of which no records remain.

After the war, he edited the *Memphis Avalanche* for a brief period. Sinclair was still married, but apparently in name only. In divorce papers filed by Lucy in 1867, she affirms they had not lived together for five years and all children from the union had died. In 1869 or '70, Sinclair returned to his native county and again began practicing law: The *Manassas Gazette* in 1869 includes an advertisement for his legal services. On August 6, 1872, Judge Aylet Nicol appointed him to replace Jim Clark as commonwealth's attorney.

~~~~~~~

Thus, Sinclair found himself in an entirely unenviable position. Not only was he prosecuting the murder of a man he had recently vilified, he was also sitting in the seat of law only recently vacated by that murdered man. Despite his long associations with the area, it was easy to see the impropriety of a man playing both sides of the fence. Sinclair, no fool in a court of law or a court of public opinion, sought to assuage the anger expressed by Elder Clark (and, presumably, shared by others), publishing the following card in the *Alexandria Gazette* on September 21:

> No heart is penetrated with deeper grief than mine at the unfortunate position in which two respectable families have been placed. I had no idea of any attack from Fewell upon Clark, nor did I deem it necessary to call at that time for a guard around the jail. Public opinion was not aroused against Clark, in my judgment, though greatly excited, as to endanger his safety or the fairness of his trial while in prison, and I deemed him secure in prison. I wrote a brief and hasty order of arrest, such as in my judgment would have protected the officer in the capture and arrest of Fewell. I know of no concert in this case whatever; I have taken a rule against the sheriff of this county, the design of which is to bring out all the facts of this case. That rule will be put on trial. Until then let public judgment wait. This is no time for crimination or recrimination. With a saddened heart I write these lines, but I intend to do my duty fearless of the consequences.

Unsurprisingly, Sinclair's "just doing his job" argument did nothing to appease Elder Clark, especially considering how high tensions had been running in the community all along. So Elder Clark decided to pursue the best justice that money and influence could buy. The Fewells might have had popular opinion and local celebrity on their side, and Elder Clark might be stuck with Sinclair leading the prosecution, but he had an ace in the hole. He had a former governor.

Henry A. Wise was a charismatic speaker, well known and revered prior to the Civil War. He was also a longtime friend of Elder Clark, and readily agreed to take the case. Born in Drummondtown, Virginia, on December 3, 1806, Wise had studied law in Winchester and been admitted to the bar in 1828. He served in Congress from 1833 to 1844 and was the U.S. minister to Brazil from 1844 to 1847, where he stirred controversy for repeatedly criticizing the nation's participation in the international slave trade. The father of 14 children, he served a term as governor starting in 1856 during which he vacillated wildly on the issue of slavery. Torn between pleasing Northern allies and Southern constituents, he also seems to have struggled with the morality of the practice. He appears to have opposed secession more than slavery but concluded that a slave rebellion was a real and dangerous threat; thus, one of his last acts in office was to sign the death warrant of John Brown, after his October 16, 1859, raid on Harper's Ferry. When the war began, Wise served as a brigadier general in the Confederate Army of Northern Virginia and was with Robert E. Lee at Appomattox Court House, where he fought bravely but urged Lee to surrender. He took the loss very much to heart. "You may forgive us," he told Joshua Lawrence Chamberlain after the ceremony at Appomattox, "but we won't be forgiven. There is a rancor in our hearts, which you little dream of. We hate you, sir."

After the war, Wise resumed his practice of law in Richmond. He never sought a pardon for his Confederate service. He embraced emancipation for slaves, though not for the noble reasons one might hope: "I am now free of responsibility for their care and comfort, and I repeat I am content. They are naturally lazy and unsteady at work." But as time passed, he publicly deemphasized his role in Virginia's secession. He was getting on in years but remained a passionate and fiery orator and still drew crowds when he argued cases. He had recently published *Seven Decades of the Union*, a memoir of the public life of John Tyler that contained many of his own personal recollections.

Rounding out the prosecution was J.Y. Menifee. A 50-year-old widower, Menifee and his son had a law practice in Rappahannock. Menifee, a staunch Democrat, knew Wise from way back, and had been a senatorial elector in the 1850s, as well as commonwealth's attorney for Washington Court House. After the war, when a salt shortage threatened his county, he was named as agent to contract for and purchase 3,600 bushels of salt from the Salt Works in the State of Virginia, and to arrange for its transportation.

Meanwhile, Lucien's time behind bars was reportedly taking a toll on his health: He had come down with fever and ague—and ironically, though not surprisingly, was treated by the same Dr. Barbour who treated Jim Clark's gunshot wounds. (A bill for Barbour's services shows he charged $85 for his services for Jim—including the postmortem—and about $17 for Lucien's treatment.) Still, Lucien's spirits were lively and he showed little concern about the outcome of his trial, whenever and wherever it would be conducted. According to the *Fredericksburg Ledger*,

> Fewell expresses no fear of the result to himself. He is a young man of remarkably excitable disposition and determined character; some months since, he was found dying in an alley at Alexandria literally cut open, and for some time his life was despaired of but he now bears no marks of this injury.

So the waiting game continued. Lucien recovered from his fever, and soon enough, his arraignment date arrived.

Chapter Seven: Arraigned and Elected

Monday, October 7, 1872, finally arrived, bringing with it hordes of onlookers anxious to get a glimpse of the postbellum dream teams of Hunton-Payne and Sinclair-Wise. The *Alexandria Gazette* marveled at the crowd: "Prince William never probably witnessed a larger attendance on her courts than that which was gathered here to-day to listen to the arguments which the able and brilliant counsel on both sides are well qualified and prepared to deliver in this case, to the result of which so many look forward with an intensity of interest equal, if not stronger, than that displayed in the Mary Harris, or the more recent Black-McKaig cases."[25]

---

[25] In 1865, Mary Harris, the 19-year-old daughter of Irish immigrants, traveled from Iowa to Washington, D.C., where she shot her longtime suitor, 33-year-old Adoniram Judson Burroughs, after reading of his marriage to socialite Amelia Boggs. It was the second court case of temporary insanity heard in the United

And the October 8 *New York Herald* set the scene by describing the defendant as

> naturally of a reckless, dare-devil disposition, but his recklessness of getting into scrapes is fully equaled by his ingenuity in getting out of them. Naturally of an agreeable and friendly disposition, people readily forgive in "Rhoda" what they would have considered criminal in others. Rhoda seemed to have no idea of law, and he would be at one time the terror of the community, and at another, its spoiled petted child. It was the exploits of "Rhoda" and one or two other similar characters that caused the Reconstruction Committee in December 1869 to summon George C. Round, a lawyer of Manassas, to testify before them in regard thereto. It is supposed the State of Virginia would have been admitted before the holidays had it not been for "Rhoda."

Inside the courthouse, Judge Aylett Nicol gaveled in

States (the first was in 1859, when Dan Sickles was acquitted on that defense after killing his wife's lover, Francis Barton Key, son of national anthem composer Francis Scott Key), and Harris was found innocent on what amounted to a PMS defense: "insane from moral causes, aggravated by disease of the body."

William McKaig owned a prosperous iron operation in Cumberland, Maryland. A childhood friend of Myra Black, he courted her publicly, ultimately seducing her and then using the threat of exposure to keep her under his control, apparently impregnating her in 1870. When Myra's father found out, he shot McKaig in the arm. He was awaiting indictment when Myra's brother, Harry, returned home for a visit, learned the whole story, and shot McKaig three times in view of at least 20 witnesses, reportedly saying, "That's what you get for ruining my sister and for trying to send my father to the penitentiary, and I have got another shot for any damned scoundrel who says I've done what was wrong." The jury apparently had no such scoundrels, and Black was acquitted at trial in 1871, to deafening cheers of well-wishers.

early. Born March 11, 1822, Nicol had spent some time in Washington, Virginia, but by 1850, he served as a Deputy Clerk for the Prince William County Court. Now in his late 40s, he lived in Brentsville with four daughters and two sons. A fifth Nicol daughter was married to Dr. Barbour, who had ministered to Jim Clark in his last hours and tended to Lucien's fever the month afterward. Still considered relatively young for a judgeship, Nicol nonetheless "possessed the confidence of the entire community over which he presides," according to the October 8 *Alexandria Gazette*. He was also no stranger to Lucien Fewell, having represented George Jones in 1868 after Lucien had kicked the man in the face for being a "damned Yankee." He had also served with Jim Clark on the Union Church board of trustees, a group that had met several times in 1871, when George M. Goodwin sold a piece of property to the trustees for a church to be used by various denominations. It was a small town, and such associations were hardly unusual, but it is a little surprising that Hunton did not express more concern regarding the judge's personal experiences with the parties in question.

The grand jury was called, sworn in, and sent into seclusion, and events began in earnest.[26] Sinclair kicked things off by raising the issue of whether the sheriff should be removed from his office for neglect of duty in allowing Jim to be killed in the first place. Sinclair's main stated objective here was to determine culpability (whether the sheriff's or the jailer's) in allowing the jail door to be left open. His unspoken intention was to illustrate that Rhoda acted independently, and that there was no collusion on the part of those paid to protect Jim. Hunton opposed this motion, saying it would affect the defense's case. Nicol ruled for a continuance until after Lucien's trial was concluded.

---

[26] Arraignment events from here on are drawn from the October 8 and 9 *Alexandria Gazette*.

The court recessed, and Hunton took advantage of the lull to get in a little politicking. The green outside the courthouse was now packed with picnickers awaiting afternoon action, and Hunton addressed the friendly and enthusiastic crowd, assuring them of the importance of voting for Greeley—and, no doubt, himself—and exhorting them to get to the polls on November 5.

Once assorted other matters were attended to, the grand jury brought in two true bills for murder. The first was against Lucien Fewell for killing James Clark:

Prince William County, to wit:

In the County Court of said county the jurors of the Commonwealth of Virginia, in and for the body of the county of Prince William, and now attending the said court, upon their oath present that Lucien N. Fewell, of the said county, on the 31st day of August, 1872, with force and arms in the county aforesaid, in and upon the body of one James F. Clark, in the peace of said Commonwealth then and there being, feloniously, willfully, and with malice aforethought, did make an assault; and that the said Lucien N. Fewell, with certain pistols then and there charged with gunpowder and certain leaden bullets, which he, the said Fewell, in his hands then and there had held, then and there feloniously, willfully, and of his malice aforethought did discharge and shoot off against and upon the body of the said James F. Clark, and that the said Lucien N. Fewell, with the leaden bullets aforesaid, then and there, by the force of the gunpowder aforesaid, shot off as aforesaid, then and there feloniously, willfully, and with malice aforethought, did strike, penetrate, and wound him, the said James F. Clark, in and upon the left side of the breast, and in and upon the back of him, the said James F. Clark, then and there, with the leaden bullets aforesaid, so as aforesaid, discharged and shot out the pistols aforesaid, by the said Lucien F. Fewell, in and upon the left side of the breast and in and upon the back of him, the said James F. Clark, giving to him, the said James F. Clark, then and there, with the leaden bullets of aforesaid so as aforesaid, discharged and shot out of the pistols aforesaid by the said Lucien N. Fewell, in and upon the left side of the breast and in and upon the back of him, the said James F. Clark, two mortal wounds, of the depth of ___inches and breadth of __ inches, of which said mortal wounds he, the said James F. Clark, from the said 31st day of August in the year aforesaid to the 2d day of September, in the year aforesaid, in the county aforesaid, did languish, and languishing did live, on which said 2d day of September, 1872, the said James F. Clark, in the county aforesaid, of the said mortal wounds died. And so the jurors aforesaid, upon their oath aforesaid, do say that the said Lucien N. Fewell, him the said James F. Clark, in the manner and form aforesaid, feloniously, willfully, and of his malice aforethought, did kill and murder against the peace and dignity of the Commonwealth of Virginia. — Charles E. Sinclair, Attorney for the Commonwealth, Prince William County. A true bill: Allen Howison, Foreman of the Jury.

With the indictment read into the record, the case of *Commonwealth v. Fewell* was finally called—and immediately stalled. Payne moved for a month's continuance, stating that one of his witnesses was sick and would be unable to attend before the next term of the court. For reasons that are unclear, Wise, for the prosecution, was not in the room at that moment and a delay was sought by the Commonwealth, leading to another half-hour recess.

Wise was there when court resumed, ready and willing to put on a show, to the delight of the assembled onlookers. Payne restated the cause for continuing the case. This led to some discussion, and some frustration, since Payne preferred not to disclose the name and character of the missing witness, saying only that a detective was currently engaged in tracking down the party.

Wise rose then, and the crowd that had turned out to see a legal spectacle was not disappointed. Though somewhat feebler than in his fiery early years, his wit and lungs were as strong as ever. The rules that applied to the defense, Wise proclaimed, also applied to the Commonwealth. "If Fewell's life is to be tried, another has been taken, gone past recovery, and a living issue is to be tried," he argued earnestly. "I want to defend the justice of this Commonwealth and the dead, the dead as well as the fallen, the fallen as well as the dead." It was reasonable for the defense to seek extra time to procure witnesses, he acknowledged—but then he whirled on that argument and insisted that the judge could not grant a continuance if this was simply a delaying tactic designed to provide time for the strong feelings that the killing had created to subside.

Payne replied that Wise had nothing to fear: One important witness was sick and another lived in the District of Columbia, and the case would be materially affected by these witnesses.

Wise's sparkling rhetoric may have won over the crowd, but Judge Nicol was swayed by Payne. He sustained the motion for postponement, the trial was set for the following month, and Rhoda was consigned to jail until November.

It may seem strange now that Fannie's behavior in the proceedings was completely immaterial to the case. Hunton didn't know if Fannie was truly an innocent, misled by a cad; a flighty child who misconstrued friendly flirting on Jim's part; or a gold-digging homewrecker out to get herself a man. More important, he didn't care. What actually took place with Fannie didn't matter; what mattered was Lucien's beliefs about what took place.

It must also be noted that the concept of law and order in 1872 Virginia did not quite match modern perceptions of due process. It is likely that for many people, just the word "honor" conjures up movie images of overheated Southern gentlemen rising angrily in the midst of a ball or dinner and demanding "satisfaction." There are few, if any, such images involving Northerners. These images are not entirely grounded in fantasy. Partly rooted in the cultural difference of the early settlers and partly based on their economies, there was a significant cultural schism between North and South. Further, in the North, crowded, urban environments led to an even greater shifting away from earlier ideals of honor toward a quiet, personal quality that was more often labeled "integrity." This makes sense; if you live in a city of immigrants and cannot name the last five generations of your neighbors' "people," you are far less likely to go sticking your nose in their business and more likely to praise the qualities of restraint and piety. Not so in the South. The code of honor there required a man to have a reputation for honesty, martial courage, self-sufficiency and mastery over one's family, and a willingness to use violence to defend any perceived slight to his own person or threat to his family.

Dueling was part and parcel of the honor code. Although the North can claim ownership of the nation's most famous duel—that between Aaron Burr and Alexander Hamilton in 1804—it is true that the practice of dueling persisted far longer in the South than it did in the North. The Anti-Dueling Act had passed in 1810, but such confrontations still happened frequently with limited prosecutions or convictions. Bladensburg, where Fannie and Jim had caught the train to Baltimore, was one of the more famous dueling grounds of the region.

Thus, the issue of Lucien's innocence or guilt did not necessarily stem directly from the fact that he killed Jim. For many, it had more to do with the method. In that time, a duel or similar confrontation would have been an acceptable outcome for what Jim had ostensibly done to Fannie—but it is one thing to challenge a man to a fair fight, or call him out on a public street; it is quite another to shoot him, unarmed, trapped in a jail cell.

Therefore, the trial was not going to focus on Lucien's actions as much as it would focus on his motivations. Unlike his previous drunken brawling, the actions in this case were, after a fashion, defensible in court, and that was how Hunton planned to map out his defense.

For the rest of the month, the lawyers went to work researching their case. Payne paid a visit to Fredericksburg to gather information. One witness—Hartman, who had handled Fannie's trunk and gotten her on the train that fateful night—vanished altogether, apparently fearing arrest. Hunton continued his legal work, but his mind was really on the election. The campaign was on.

~~~~~~~

For what has gone down in history as a relative non-event, the election of 1872 nonetheless had its fair share of nastiness and media backbiting. *Harper's Weekly* cartoonist Thomas Nast, infamous for not pulling his punches, had a field day with Greeley, skewering him for his stance on reconciliation: Greeley shaking hands with a Confederate who has just shot a Union soldier; Greeley on a pirate ship beckoning the "Ship of State" to come closer while Confederate pirates hidden below wait to spring out and attack. The Democrats sank to the same level, portraying Grant as a drunken idiot who voted for Buchanan in 1856.

But cartoons don't win campaigns; money and organization do. And on those grounds, Republicans again carried the day. Those running the campaign did their homework, targeted the critical states of North Carolina, Maine, and Ohio, and hired 300 people to parse every word Greeley had ever published for ammunition against him. Meanwhile, the loose coalition of liberals could not or would not work together and coalesce. Greeley himself stepped in to fill the gap—possibly one of the worst things he could have done.

In the nineteenth century, presidential candidates were considered above such demeaning tasks as explaining themselves in person or going out and hobnobbing with the general rabble. They had people to do that for them, while they were expected to maintain a dignified silence and think deep thoughts that would be put into action upon arrival in the White House. Grant was lucky in this regard—he could hide behind tradition with full recognition of his shortcomings as a public speaker and lack of powerful presence.

Greeley started out strong in this regard as well. He resigned from the *Tribune* and stayed at his farm. And while everything had looked rosy in mid-July—a toss-up, at least—things were going the other direction by mid-September. With the campaign losing steam, Greeley (though hardly a young man any longer) took his own advice and went west. In the space of ten days, he gave more than 200 speeches. While his output might be admirable, the results were not; he reintroduced the idea of peaceful secession, criticized Union soldiers for holding a convention and stirring up partisan feelings, and basically declared war on black voters everywhere, going so far as to say his opposition to slavery "might have been a mistake."

Greeley's running mate, Gratz Brown, did nothing to mitigate such disasters; in fact, he threw gasoline on the fire. At the Yale commencement in July, Brown delivered a drunken tirade in which he compared the university unfavorably with those in the West, and congratulated Greeley on having "the largest head in America." A popular joke at the time revolved around a Brown gaffe from his 1870 campaign for governor, when he had gotten so drunk he buttered a slice of watermelon.

On October 8, the day after Lucien's arraignment, Pennsylvania and Indiana held state and congressional elections. Republicans carried Pennsylvania and most of Indiana, although Democrats squeaked out a gubernatorial win there. It was a harbinger of November.

But in late October, Greeley largely dropped out of sight, although his political machine kept up the campaign. Mary Greeley, who had suffered from tuberculosis for much of her life, had been especially sickly since her return in June from a trip to Europe and had taken a turn for the worse, so he stayed home to care for her. She died October 30, a week before the election. For all that their marriage had been an unhappy one, Greeley was devastated. "I am not dead but I wish I were," he wrote to a friend. "My house is desolate, my future dark, my heart a stone."

~~~~~~~

Lucien may have followed the political races in the newspapers, given there wasn't much else to do in jail. He would have watched the trees on the ridge turn from a blanket of green to a wash of orange and gold. The *Alexandria Gazette* reported that subpoenas had been sent during the month to Harold Snowden, James W. Carr, and M.D. Ball. And so, he waited—but not patiently.

The October 24 *Alexandria Gazette* included an item stating that Lucien had attempted to escape, apparently getting so far as undoing two of the locks on the iron grating door of his cell before being caught by one of the guards on duty. "Fewell asserted that he did not do it, but at the same time told the jailer that the locks were worthless, and that he could get out at any moment if he so desired."

This led to another minor media flurry: Lucien may

have recognized the error of his bragging ways, or he may have been unjustly accused. Either way, the next day he had written a card for the *Manassas Gazette*, reprinted October 29 in the pro-Republican Richmond *Daily State Journal*:

> The Alexandria Gazette of yesterday has a letter written from Brentsville, October 23, in which it is said I attempted to escape from the jail at that place on Sunday last. I most emphatically and unequivocally deny the charge and instead of making any such attempt I have shown conclusively to several persons who have visited me since that time, and in the presence of the jailor, that I could have gotten out at any time I chose to do so. I do not wish to escape, but expect to be discharged by a jury of my countrymen and not only discharged but justified in what I have done, and believe that said letter was written solely with a purpose to prejudice my case.

Given that Jim had similarly sniffy views of the jail's lack of fortification (not to mention the fact that a lack of security contributed to his death and the current inmate's incarceration), it seems possible Lucien was telling the truth. But that gave rise to a different set of complaints, as voiced by the *Daily State Journal*:

> 1: If Fewell could escape at any time from the jail as he states, what is to be thought of the administration of justice in Prince William County? It seizes a man accused of crime who has voluntarily returned to be arrested, confines him in a narrow cell and leaves the jail open so that he can be conveniently shot through the grated door of his cell!! It allows him to be brutally murdered

in broad daylight. Then, when it has arrested and indicted the murderer, it goes through the farce of confinement in a jail from which "he can escape any time"!!

2: Fewell does not try to escape because he is confident of being not only discharged, but justified for what he has done. The previous history of this case would seem to give ground for such a confidence on his part. The way has been smoothed for him to commit a cold-blooded and brutal murder, and, as he says, the doors were left open for his escape, the trial is to be a mere farce! A jury sworn to execute the law are to perjure themselves by setting it aside and justifying the crime they have sworn to punish! The character of the dead man is to be forever blackened with no chance for defence, and an assassin is to be let loose on society.

There is no way to say how this article affected readers. Presumably it had much the same effect as such articles do today: energizing those in agreement and engendering sneers among those opposed. It is also safe to assume that—again, as is the case today—the next day's news overtook any strong opinions one way or the other. In the case of the *State Journal,* that news included several columns about State Fair contests and, of course, the presidential election. (Naturally, the Republican paper endorsed Grant.)

As it turned out, the election interfered with Lucien's trial. The October 17 issue of the *Daily Phoenix* in Columbia, S.C., reprinted an article from the *Manassas Gazette* explaining the logistical problem: "In consequence of the Presidential election which comes off on Tuesday, the trial of L. N. Fewell was set for Wednesday of the November County Court instead of Monday as was first understood. This will give witnesses and others who have to attend the trial an opportunity to vote on Tuesday before coming to court." So Lucien got to spend two more days in jail, while the rest of the population decided the fate of the nation.

~~~~~~~

In the week before Election Day, campaign fever seemed to taper off, rather than ramp up. The state and congressional elections had been clear indicators of which way the wind was blowing; all the Republicans needed to do was make sure people showed up at the polls.

But there was one last bit of excitement before the polls opened. Victoria Woodhull, the New York suffragette, had pretty much fallen off the radar after her nomination in June, plagued by her fringe position, the fact that her core constituency had no legal right to vote, and (not least of all) lack of funding. Woodhull and her sister, Tennie Claflin, had managed to alienate communists and capitalists alike, and they were struggling just to find living quarters. Woodhull's running mate, Frederick Douglass, had never responded to the party's nomination—and was stumping for Grant, not her. Now, in an act of desperation, the sisters published a story they had been sitting on for a year.

Henry Ward Beecher, a renowned preacher and brother of abolitionist author Harriet Beecher Stowe, supported women's suffrage, but disdained Woodhull's propositions of equality and female empowerment. This led to a simmering resentment between the two. The sisters had learned, through a series of friend-of-a-friend exchanges, that Beecher had been indulging in extramarital dalliances with Elizabeth Tilton, a married member of his church. After pouring the story out to a meeting of the American Association of Spiritualists, Woodhull published it in her newspaper when the Boston press said the story was too obscene to print—correctly, as it turned out. Beecher didn't take it lying down. Two members of his church ordered copies of the paper, specifying mail delivery. The moment they were received, warrants were issued for violation of the law prohibiting the sending of obscene material through the mail.

Thus it was that the first female presidential candidate was incarcerated on obscenity charges, and could not even try to cast a vote for herself.

On November 5, the bars all closed, and the polls opened. There was some civil disobedience: Susan B. Anthony tried to cast her ballot and was arrested and fined $100. But for the most part, balloting was quiet and went as expected. Grant carried all but six states in the presidential election. (Georgia, Kentucky, Maryland, Missouri, Tennessee, and Texas swung for Greeley.) Virginia, in its first election since being readmitted to the Union, cast its 11 electoral votes for Ulysses S. Grant (who got 50.47 percent of the popular vote to Greeley's 49.49 percent), and Democrats were neck-and-neck with Republicans in congressional and local contests. Hunton defeated Edward Daniels, a Republican carpetbagger from the North, by a vote of 11,782 to 9,178. His term would begin in March the following year, and he would take his seat in Washington more than a year later, in December.

With the election thus concluded, it was time to get on with the trial.

Chapter Eight: Opening Arguments

Newspapers in the 1870s were, in some respects, recognizable precursors of the modern fish-wrapper. They were generally local in nature but included bits on world affairs. They were advertising-driven. One intriguing similarity between those papers and the media of today (including online media) that might not seem immediately obvious is what might be called the "cut-and-paste" effect. Local papers were, in fact, hyperlocal, and often just broadsheets of four to eight pages produced by one or two people. Thus, a large amount of copy was reprinted from one paper to another, often verbatim, sometimes credited, sometimes not.

But papers of the past also had many distinct differences from what you see in today's *New York Times*. They were not split into sections; fashion items abutted police reports and shared pages with train schedules and crop predictions. Many Southern papers did not splash the biggest news across the front page, which was reserved largely for long-running advertisements (in the case of the

Gazette, a front-page ad for liver treatment was notable for often featuring the only illustration in the entire newspaper) and, usually, one item of a higher aesthetic level—a poem or short story, perhaps, something high in tone and generally with some kind of moral.

Most notable, however, was the issue of editorial bias. There was no pretense of impartiality in the nineteenth century; an editor's opinion was right out there in the open for all to see. The industry was generally relied upon to provide information, certainly, but it was by no means expected to deliver this asset in a neutral fashion. Editors had carte blanche to tell readers not only the who-what-when-where of an issue, but also why the editor considered it important and exactly how readers ought to feel about it.

Editors also had the flexibility to devote a majority of an issue's space to major news while ignoring other events. Thus, Lucien's murder trial garnered gallons of ink. The story gained national attention, described in newspapers from New York to Missouri. A German-language newspaper in Baltimore, *Der Deutsche Correspondent*, followed the trial with as breathless an interest as any of its English-language counterparts.

~~~~~~~

Wednesday, November 6, dawned gray and misty. Rain, so desperately sought in June, pelted the autumn leaves and turned the roads to mud. The Fewell case would not be called until late morning, and Sinclair sent Wise a telegram in Richmond asking him to come. Wise replied that he could not arrive before Friday and asked if the case could be continued. Sinclair sent a follow-up telegram urging haste: "To be tried; come immediately. Bring the letters.—

CHARLES E. SINCLAIR."[27]

The weather hadn't done much to hold the crowd down, though it was smaller than the gathering at the October session when the case had been called but postponed. Another possible reason for fewer attendees was something the papers at the time referred to as the "horse disease," an outbreak of equine flu that was later recognized as the Great Epizootic (animal epidemic) of 1872, one of the most destructive epidemics in history.

In the 1870s, horse and mule power was what the gasoline engine is to modern transportation and commerce. The census of 1870 counted approximately 8 million equines for 40 million humans. The flu virus started in Ontario, Canada, in early October and swept south to Cuba and west to Arizona within 90 days. Reports of the disease in Baltimore began around October 24 and in Portsmouth, Virginia, on November 1. Official estimates put the number of afflicted horses at between 80 percent and 99 percent, and once infected, horses stayed sick for about two weeks with a debilitating fever and inflammation of the respiratory mucous membrane. Worse yet, having the disease did not confer immunity from a second attack. The day Lucien was to appear in court, the November 6 *Alexandria Gazette* described the extent of the effect:

> So many horses are now sick with it that business has been considerably interfered with and the streets present an almost Sunday appearance from the absence of vehicles. Some of the bakers and milk men carried their cans and baskets around this morning on their own shoulders, and some of the butchers ... have engaged laborers to draw

---

[27] Except where otherwise noted, all coverage of the trial in this chapter comes from the *Alexandria Gazette*.

their wagons to market tomorrow morning. The wagons of Cameron Mills were drawn this morning by oxen. All the horses in both the livery stables and nearly all private horses in the city are sick, and the disease has attacked mules on the canal, but only four fatal cases have as yet been reported.

The effect of this was comparable to modern Americans waking up one day and one in every five of them finding their gas tanks filled with sugar. Horses were too sick to pull wagons full of cargo—including coal, which meant trains couldn't run. Farmers couldn't get produce to town. In the West, the U.S. Cavalry and Apaches fought on foot, both sides' mounts too sick to carry riders. A later report suggested a mortality rate of about 2 percent, although it ranged up to 10 percent in some areas.

~~~~~~~

But court was in session, and regardless of transportation and weather obstacles, the relevant parties (excepting Wise) all arrived on time. (None of the Clark family chose to attend.) Jury selection began at 11 a.m., and although Hunton half-expected Sinclair and Menifee to request a continuance, they said they were ready; Hunton, Thomas, and Payne followed suit from their side of the room. People craned for a look when jailer John S. Goodwin brought in Lucien and seated him behind his counsel. The November 7 *Alexandria Gazette* described him as

> a genteel looking man, about twenty-seven years old, about five feet ten inches high, weighing from one hundred and thirty to one hundred and forty pounds, with brown hair and eyes, good forehead, high cheek bones, straight and prominent nose,

and being blanched by sickness and confinement in jail, and being dressed nicely, presented a trim, jaunty, and rather prepossessing appearance. He was perfectly self-possessed, and smoked his white clay pipe with an air of nonchalance, evidently induced by his belief that he had done what was right, and that he would be sustained in by those of his countrymen who might be selected to try him.

Judge Nicol called upon the defendant to rise. William E. Lipscomb, the assistant clerk of the court, read the indictment as it had been handed down the month before. "Not guilty," Lucien replied airily.

With that, the process began in earnest. As the rain drummed on the high roof of the courthouse, the list of prospective jurors summoned for the trial was read, and the men interviewed accordingly. The first four stated that their minds were made up as to the verdict they would give and were consequently set aside. The defense then struck four more men, and the jury was composed of those who were left.[28] Most who made the final cut also admitted to having opinions as to Lucien's guilt or innocence, but affirmed that their decision of a verdict would be formed from the evidence elicited during the trial. Whether they were sincere believers in the judicial system or simply better liars than the others is a matter of conjecture. Either way, the jury was sworn in and Nicol called a one-hour recess.

When court resumed, it was still raining, and Wise was still absent. At this point, Sinclair and Menifee did move that the case be continued until next morning, when they hoped the former governor would be in attendance, citing

---

[28] The jury foreman was Allen Howison. Other jurors were John Sewell, W.H. Poland, G.S. Pickett, D.A. Pickett, W.F. Skillman, J.P. Smith, J.N. Otterback, C.E. Tyler, R.A. Foley, M.W. Nalles, J.M. Shirley, and E.J.T. Clark.

the fact that Wise had in his possession papers containing matters of importance connected with the case, and that knowledge of all the preliminary proceedings of the trial would be of importance. Hunton and Payne immediately objected and Nicol overruled the motion. It was a good sign, Hunton noted smugly: A delay had been readily made for the defense to locate missing witnesses, but the prosecution would not get one day of grace.

But Sinclair appeared unfazed. He went ahead with his opening statement, the first point of which addressed the somewhat unorthodox involvement of the absent Wise. Sinclair's nose may have been out of joint behind closed doors, but he was going to put on the best public face he could about Elder Clark's insistence on an augmented prosecution team. "The cry of blood money might be raised with reference to the employment of assistant counsel for the prosecution," Sinclair said, but it was unsubstantiated. "If ever a prosecuting attorney felt the need of assistance, it is now, and in the case before the court I feel that need in every fiber of my body, and in every effort of my mind." Further, he added, the employment of such assistant counsel was by no means unusual.

That out of the way, Sinclair moved on to the case itself. "Clark, when shot down in his cell in the jail, had been convicted of no crime that would stamp his brow with shame," Sinclair reminded the jury.

> He was confined in jail for examination, and until he was examined and found guilty, he was entitled to the protection of the law. Lucien Fewell does not think he committed any crime, and surrendered himself to the officers of the law under that supposition, not seeming to understand that when the shield of the State is thrown around a man as it was around Clark in prison, that man's

person is sacred, and an offense against him is an offense against the Commonwealth.

Sinclair urged the jury to remember the anguish of the dead man's wife, the misery of his children, and the sorrow of his father, so debilitated that although he was in Brentsville, he was unable to come into the courthouse. Even if James Clark were guilty of the accusation, Sinclair argued, his crime was not sufficient for the terrible expiation it had met. "All men are weak, and the sin of the dead man might be that of the living. If it could be proved that Clark had seduced his victim and set on fire the temple of innocence, and laughed at the conflagration, there might be palliation for his murder," Sinclair said, "but even in that case there would be none for shooting him down like a dog when in the hands of the law." He concluded by urging the jury to judge between the friends of the dead and the living, and to give a verdict that they would have no cause to regret in later years.

Then it was Payne's turn. "Lucien Fewell would have been branded with everlasting disgrace had he not have acted as he did in doing what he could to wipe out the shame that had been inflicted upon his family," he insisted. The local papers had urged Lucien to avenge his sister's honor, but as soon as he did, they flipped their position and demanded he be punished. As to Elder Clark, "though he might hesitate to come into court, he had no hesitancy in using his own purse and that of his friends, and in invoking the aid of a powerful secret organization to supply funds with which to secure the ablest counsel in the State to assist in the prosecution." This reference to a "powerful, secret organization" is quite sensational, but it's hard to guess what Payne might have been trying to imply. Wise was a Freemason, but there's no record that Elder Clark was. Payne could have meant the Klan, but it seems unlikely, given not only the group's diminished capacity by this period, but also Wise's careful cultivation of his postwar reputation as a Republican-leaning civil rights advocate.

Thus, Payne continued, Lucien had not only to meet the demands of the State, but the revenge of Jim's friends as well. "The prisoner has now been confined in jail a long time; his health is suffering, and the verdict to be rendered must be no compromise; he is either guilty or must be set free." He went on to point out that "Judge Sinclair said that if Clark had set the human heart on fire and brought disgrace on a worthy family, there might be palliation for the crime. Disgrace has been brought to a worthy family, and the heart set on fire ... nothing short of those conditions would have induced [Lucien] to commit that deed."

Payne went on a bit of a stem-winder, continuing his argument until after dark, listing similar cases where the accused took the law into their own hands and were acquitted (to much applause from the spectators), and assuring the jurors that "from the time of the patriarchs down to the present such crimes as adultery and seduction were considered as beyond the pale of law and subject to the punishment of the sufferers."

He also gave an excruciatingly detailed account of the acquaintance between James Clark, "the Claude Melnotte of Manassas,"[29] and Fannie Fewell until the former's death, how Jim abducted Fannie, "defiled her ... basely deserted her ... robbed her of the little money she had and then left

---

[29] In *The Lady of Lyons*, a five-act melodrama written in 1838 by Edward Bulwer-Lytton, Claude Melnotte is the son of a gardener for Pauline Deschapelles, with whom he is in love. When Pauline jilts the Marquis Beauséant, the Marquis persuades Melnotte to disguise himself as a foreign prince and trick Pauline into marrying him. When Melnotte takes Pauline to his widowed mother's home after the marriage, she discovers the ruse and gets the marriage annulled. Melnotte enlists in the army to assuage his remorse. Pauline's father is then threatened with bankruptcy, and Beauséant is willing to pay the debt if Pauline will marry him. Melnotte becomes a war hero, and Pauline realizes that she is truly in love with Melnotte after all.

her again with the hope that she, in her distress, might be forced to join that unfortunate class whose only object while they live is to conceal themselves from their friends."

At the conclusion of this speech, court adjourned until the following morning, Lucien returned to his cell, and sheriff's deputies William E. Goodwin and Charles E. Butler, charged with keeping the jury members together and preventing them from communicating with anyone else, escorted them across the street to accommodations at Reid's Hotel.

It should be recalled that nineteenth-century newspapers were structured differently from modern ones, and that "page one news" is a fairly recent (if already obsolete) turn of phrase. By Thursday, however, election reports had receded somewhat, and the trial was high-profile enough that Wednesday's proceedings merited two columns on page 2.

In Brentsville, the second day of the trial saw fewer in attendance, at least in part due to flooding at Broad Run, but the crowd that gathered still packed the courtroom.[30] Among the onlookers, any issue of guilt in the case had taken a back seat to wagering whether the jury would bother to leave the box before declaring Lucien innocent. Inside the courthouse, the trial resumed at 10 a.m. Wise's chair was still empty, though Sinclair had sent another telegram to Richmond detailing the previous day's events and urging the governor to hurry up. It was to be a long day full of testimony, but the main event was not expected until that afternoon, when Fannie would take the stand.

The prosecution moved through its witnesses briskly and efficiently. The court first heard from Thornton and Lipscomb, who testified as the first responders on the

---

[30] Brentsville's location as the county seat of Prince William had been criticized for this very reason, as it was located near several water courses, including Broad, Cedar, and Slaty Runs. This was, in fact, one argument for the removal of the court to Manassas when the issue was resurrected 20 years later.

scene after Lucien opened fire into Jim's cell. Thornton recounted how he had seen Lucien fire two shots, and how Lucien had insisted to him, "Major, let me alone; I know what I am about." Lipscomb elaborated with details about the struggle between Lucien and Thornton. Next to testify was Oscar Powell, the boy who had been on the jail's second floor and told Lucien what cell Jim occupied.

Drs. Barbour and Leary, the physicians who performed the post-mortem examination of Jim, testified briefly about their findings, basically stating that Jim did, indeed, die of gunshot wounds. They were followed by a man named Thomas K. Davis, who stated that he had been at Bristoe station that fateful morning and that Lucien had said he was going to Brentsville to "shoot that damned scoundrel" for seducing Fannie.[31] Davis said Lucien seemed "perfectly frantic and bent upon the purpose he had come for ... he spoke of nothing but his intention to kill Clark."

At this point, Jim's dying declaration was read into the court record. With that, the prosecution rested. It was 12:20 p.m. Wise still had not made it to the courthouse.

Now it was time for the defense to roll into action. The first witness for that side was *Alexandria Gazette* reporter Harold Snowden, called for his recollections of Jim's "confession," given during the interview a few days before his death. Hunton's purpose was twofold: first, to indicate that everything Jim said had made it into the article; and second, to introduce the article into evidence as the item that incited Lucien to action. Sinclair objected, stating the article was not part of the res gestae, which refers to the start-to-end period of the felony. After a period of debate on both sides, Nicol allowed it to be admitted and Payne

---

[31] The November 8 *Evening Star* report says Lucien was seeking a horse to ride to Brentsville and that he was "sent to a colored man, from whom he procured one." No other record of a horse remains, however, and if Lucien had been riding rather than walking, he would have arrived in Brentsville much earlier than the time of the murder.

read the entire thing.

This would have been a full day in itself, but all had been prelude to the arrival of Fannie.

There is no record of when Fannie found out that Jim was dead, or how she reacted—only that she did not know in September, but probably did by the time Lucien was arraigned in October. In any event, she had composed herself for this appearance. Accompanied by her stepmother, Virginia B. "Maggie" Mankin Fewell, as well as Benjamin Merchant, Fannie had come to Brentsville via Bristoe Station because of the flooding. The *Alexandria Gazette* described her as a "bright and pretty-looking, light haired, blue-eyed, and rosy-cheeked girl, about sixteen years old, and rather small for her age ... [who] wore a dark dress with white stripes, a red sack, and a straw hat with a blue veil." She moved with grace and poise as she approached the stand, and did not look at her brother. On the stand, she gave her evidence not as a statement, but as a series of replies to numerous questions, most of which were put forward by the defense's Thomas.

> Mr. Clark had promised before I left Virginia to marry me when I reached Washington. When we arrived in Bladensburg I asked him why he did not do so; he said it was too early in the morning. I asked him again when we reached Baltimore to marry me; he said it was impossible—that he was a married man, and it would be bigamy, a penitentiary offense, to marry while he had a wife living. After supper; Clark went down into the office of the hotel; about ten o'clock he returned to my room and found me in tears. He told me that I might as well become resigned to my fate; that if I had made a sacrifice in leaving home with him, he also had made sacrifices for me. I told him if he did not intend to marry me I would return to my home. He said that our fates were

linked irrevocably, that I had taken a step which I could not recall, that my family would not receive me and the world would not believe me faultless. He also said that if I left him then he would leave me and I would have no protector.

Thomas steered Fannie through her trip west, and asked about her return home.

I saw a notice in a Cincinnati paper that a man by the name of Clark had deserted his wife, and that she was without money or friends in that city; a few days afterwards a publication appeared in the same journal congratulating Mr. and Mrs. Clark upon having met by accident on the train, as they were each going east in search of the other. This paragraph was uttered false; I did not see Clark from the time I left Mexico until I arrived in Washington ... I reached Washington about 10 p. m. [Sunday night] and had heard Mr. Clark speak of a friend who was clerk at Boyle's Hotel; I knew no one in Washington; called a policeman and asked him to conduct me to Boyle's Hotel; inquired if John R. Lee was registered there; he replied "yes," and went to the room which he thought Clark occupied; he returned and said he was not in his room, and had probably left the city; I asked to be shown to a room. In a short time the clerk knocked at my door and said he had mistaken another for Mr. Clark's room, and that he had just entered the hotel. I requested that he should be brought to me. When he entered my room he seemed astonished and exclaimed, 'My God, how did you manage to get here?' Mr. Clark spent this night with me; when I awoke I examined my pocket book, and found $26 of the $30 which I had when I arrived in Washington gone; I thought I had been robbed and told him of it, and he said he had taken the money. He was angry that the publication had appeared in the Cincinnati Commercial setting forth that Mrs. Clark had been abandoned by her husband and was in destitute condition; he said this might be seen by my family and lead them to search more diligently for me. He announced his intention to go to Fredericksburg and collect some money that was due him there; he asked me to lend some more of what I had left; he took five dollars; I then had a two dollar note and some small change remaining.

Fannie's grasp of arithmetic leaves something to be desired. It is unclear how she came to have more than $30 in her possession upon arriving in Washington when she had to leave her clothing in Missouri to pay her hotel bill and required a charitable handout for a train ticket from Cincinnati to Washington. It is possible she received some cash with her train ticket, but even then, she claims Jim took $26, leaving her with $4, but then she gives him $5 more and has $2 to spare. Thomas did not pursue this issue, however, and asked her to describe the last she saw of Jim.

He left me the same morning (Monday) for Fredericksburg, telling me that I must still pass as Mrs. J. R. Lee. I stayed [at the hotel] until Saturday night, never during that time having left the hotel but on one occasion, and then in company with Mr. Clark. I was brought away by Mr. Merchant, my brother in law.

A brief cross-examination took place, probably conducted by Sinclair, during which Fannie averred that she "did not accept Mr. Clark's advances until I supposed he was divorced from his wife ... I inquired, and was told that they did not live happily together. After they had been gone some time I received a note from Mr. Clark asking me to meet him at Mrs. Hynson's, in which he said that he was separated from his wife, and wanted to see more of me now."

Georgianna Weedon Hynson's role in the whole matter was thus called into question. Jim's niece and the wife of Charles L. Hynson, who owned a Manassas general store, she held a respectable position in town and had been friendly with the Fewells for years. When asked about the propriety of her actions, Fannie waxed a tad indignant. "I did not feel that it was morally wrong for Mr. Clark to pay his addresses to me; under the circumstances, it did not occur to me that I should not go to Washington and be married when I had every assurance that he was an unmarried man and was also told he was divorced by Mrs. Hynson, who said she had letters in her possession to confirm this statement."

The prosecution then gingerly prodded what happened between Fannie and Jim when it was clear they would not be married. "I knew that I was deceived and ought not to remain with him longer than the night we spent in Baltimore," she replied. "But where could I go? We passed the night in Baltimore together as man and wife; this was after he told me he could not marry me."

Calm and collected, she spoke distinctly. Those in attendance were completely still; her words were audible in every part of the courtroom. At this point, the prosecution asked for a continuance; Fannie's letters to Jim, considered key evidence, were with Wise, who was now expected to be in court the next morning. Hunton and Payne resisted the motion for adjournment, alleging that they would allow the letters, when ready to be presented, to go to the jury, after they were proven to be those written by Fannie, and Nicol agreed to this.

The rest of the day was anticlimactic. The defense

proposed to introduce Thomas M. Sullivan, a policeman from Washington, but the court declined to receive his evidence. J. L. Sinclair and Col. M. D. Ball followed up on Snowden's testimony and also shared their recollections of Jim's comments in the days before his death. At the conclusion of Ball's evidence, the court adjourned, to resume at 10:30 the next morning. Fannie and her family stayed at a friend's house. Jury members spent their second night across the street at Reid's.

~~~~~~~

Better late than never, Wise finally arrived in Brentsville on Friday. The ex-governor's presence would have created a stir even in the most mundane of circumstances, and these were anything but. First, he had to account for his absence of the past two days, and second, he was carrying evidence that would further whet the public's appetite for salacious details.

The absence was easily explained. His seeming dereliction of duty stemmed from the fact he had never received Sinclair's second telegram telling him there would be no continuance. When Sinclair's telegram of November 7 arrived informing him of the progress of the trial, he started from Richmond immediately.

Next, the prosecution made a motion to introduce Fannie as witness for the defense, to be further cross-examined by the prosecution. Nicol rejected this, however. After reviewing the agreement of the previous day, he concluded that she could be introduced only as the witness for the Commonwealth. This was yet another blow to Sinclair and his group: It meant they couldn't cross-examine Fannie, nor impeach her, and were limited in the sort of questions they could ask her. It would require some careful footwork when she returned to the stand.

Wise now revealed his fascinating cargo: the letters Fannie had written to Jim while they both lived at

Manassas, along with the one she wrote him while sequestered at Boyle's hotel on August 22, after their fateful trip west. Hunton and Payne agreed that Fannie, with her delicate health and mental state, shouldn't be on the stand any more than necessary, so they acknowledged the letters' authenticity. The courtroom was nonplused by the ardent nature of the letters, even in consideration of a 16-year-old girl's emotions running wild. The fourth letter introduced into evidence, for example, was quite flirtatious:

> I long for the sound of the freight whistle, and still I dream for fear my darling will not come, but will hope for the best. And just to think he is going to leave so soon again — going off on the 12 o'clock train to B. Now you could not defer your trip to-day, but I know you can to-night. We are all going after raspberries tomorrow, about two miles down the road, and I want you to go and may be we will have to have a little talk. Now do this pet, for your little girl.

Once this was completed, letters from Jim to Fannie were also introduced into evidence, including the one Merchant produced in August referring to Fannie as "a little flirt." The other two were both sent to Fannie while she was in Missouri:

> My Darling little Girl: I telegraphed this morning as soon as I reached here and got my breakfast and although it is now after three o'clock, I have not heard a word from them (parties Clark hoped to get money from). I truly and greatly hope to hear to-day, so as to have you come up tonight, and I could meet you and go on to Cincinnati but have been disappointed. If you knew how I have felt, darling, since I left you, you would never

doubt or distrust me, I never felt as lonely and miserable in my life. If I don't hear by eight o'clock tonight I am going to Cincinnati to night; will get there by 8 o'clock in the morning, and if I do not hear from them to-morrow, I will go on to Washington and send you money back from there. Oh, how I do hate this arrangement and I am really afraid you will have to come to Cincinnati by yourself, anyhow, If you do, you can take the next night train at Mexico, and get to Cincinnati at 6 next night, and I will meet you then, if possible. Don't get mad with me darling, or discouraged because of the delay, for as God is my judge, it is no fault of mine. Take good care of yourself darling, and just as soon as I can hear I will telegraph you.

Yours devotedly.

The second, addressed to Mrs. Fannie S. Clark at Ringo House, was addressed like the first:

My Darling little girl: In addition to what I wrote this evening I think it best to write again. It is now 5 o'clock, and still no answer. If I do not hear by half past eight I shall go to Cincinnati to night, and if in no other way will borrow enough to bring you to that place, and send it to you, so that you can leave to-morrow night. Oh darling, if I only had you with me tonight. You do not know how much I missed your dear little hand on my own in the train. When you get on the train, get the conductor to see that your baggage is properly attended to, if you want to change cars here. I will send you a money order, and you can collect it yourself. I want you to take the letters and photograph out of the trunk and put them in your pocket. You know the photograph I mean, the picture of somebody when she was small (referring to Jim's wife). I believe though, it is an ambrotype and is in the bottom of the trunk. It should be so that I cannot meet you at the depot at Cincinnati, you must go to the Galt House and register as Mrs. J. M. Moore, N. C., and I will find you. It may be that I cannot get off from Taylor Thornton but I do not apprehend any difficulty. I will send you a telegraph money order for enough to get you a ticket to Washington and to pay your expenses to Cincinnati, and after you get there I will meet you. Bring all letters that may come for me. I hope to be with you in a day or two, darling, and until then I hope you will try to be happy. You can tell Mr. Ringo that I could not return as expected, and will send him whatever I may not have paid him. If you leave to-morrow night you will get to Cincinnati Thursday night at 9. Good-bye till we meet. Ever and devotedly yours. Destroy these letters, or take mighty good care of them.

After extended discussion of the letters, the prosecution began its rebuttal by calling William Wright, conductor of the freight train on which Fannie left Manassas. He verified that the train left the station at 12:39 a. m. but that William Fewell stopped the train and went through the caboose.

When about a mile and a half from the place, I observed an old gentleman who appeared to be very restless. Soon after I saw a lady; I walked up to her and asked her if she wasn't Miss. Fewell. She said yes and told me she was going to Washington to marry a man by the name of Lee. I remonstrated gently with her, told her that I was much older than she, and advised her to return to her father, but she said she had fully made up her mind to go. We arrived at Alexandria at 3:30. There was a hack to which I escorted her. I saw a man on the pavement; they saluted each other, he helped her into the hack and got in with her; the old man got in also.

At 1 p.m., Gov. Wise asked the court to adjourn until Saturday morning, as two of the witnesses for the Commonwealth were not present and could not arrive before that. After considerable discussion, Nicol decided to adjourn.

These events were recounted in Saturday's *Gazette* juxtaposed with another item: "A young woman, in Baltimore, on Wednesday committed suicide by taking laudanum. She said she had been betrayed by and ruined by a young man who had promised to marry her."

Fannie, on the other hand, very much alive, was back in the witness's chair on Saturday morning, after Wise solicitously asked about her health and whether she was able to come into court. Upon taking her seat, she was asked to explain the letters that had been read before the court in her absence the day before, in chronological order. "In the sentence 'It will be a day or two before I can decide at what time I can leave,' I meant leave for Washington to be married. 'But don't think I have given it out for I would not for the world,' means that I thought a great deal of Mr. Clark, and was anxious to marry him." Wise pushed Fannie on this matter, asking whether she really preferred Jim to the world, and she replied in the affirmative.

When asked about the timing of the undated letters, Fannie was hazy. But she was emphatic about her collaborator. "I left these notes at the house of Mrs. Hynson, she sent the first five. She dictated them all, and examined them after I wrote them, although she did not dictate the sentence in which the words 'respectful or disrespectful' are mentioned." Fannie went on to say she did not know exactly when Jim's wife left Manassas but that she had gone before Fannie wrote any letters. When pressed about the letter referring to Lizzie and attending church, Fannie replied that she had asked him to remain until Sunday because "I wanted to go to church, and Mrs. Hynson told me to put it in; 'I want you to go down to church, Lizzie and I are going.' Lizzie is intended for Mrs. Hynson; Mr. Clark and I called her Lizzie; he addressed his letters to me 'in care of Lizzie Twyman,' a name he gave Mrs. Hynson. She sent for me to her house to write my letters to him. She was my aide, abettor, and counselor."

It is unclear whether Fannie was actually telling the truth, merely believed she was telling the truth, or was intentionally throwing Mrs. Hynson under the bus in an effort to magnify the extent to which she was misled about Jim's availability and build the case for her own innocence. Regardless, Thomas objected that this line of questioning was not rebutting testimony. Nicol overruled him, and Wise continued, asking Fannie about lines in her second letter:

> I am not mad with you and I have never heard that you said anything respectful or disrespectful about me, except what Walter M. told me: The person I alluded to was Walter Merchant. He was a friend of mine and my family; I had learned that Mr. Clark had made some remarks about me in his store; I asked Walter what Mr. Clark had said and he replied that Mr. Clark had not said anything particularly about me.

In this same letter, "I alluded to a fishing party, but did not go on that occasion; I had gone fishing before that; Mr. Clark met me on the creek; I did not seek his company."

Finally, Fannie defended her request to have letters destroyed:

> "My reason for saying that was because Mr. Clark had asked if any of my family suspected us; they did not like him and I asked him to destroy my letters because he had requested me on the other hand to destroy his lest they should fall into the hands of my family. I never heard that any person suspected me of any thing else; if they did, they certainly had no right to do so; I never took but one buggy ride with Mr. Clark, and that was to church."

Wise then moved on to the third letter, written faintly in pencil on a small piece of paper. After asking several questions trying to pin down when the letter was written, he asked about the line, "Don't think my seeming negligence is an indication that my feelings toward you have changed, but you become dearer to me every day, and I agree with you in the arrangements you have made for me to leave with you, and hope it will not be long before we can be together, to be separated no more." Fannie replied that she was referring to her impending marriage, and further, "Mrs. Hynson dictated that letter."

"Why was it written on such a small piece of paper?" Wise asked.

"It was all that was convenient," was the simple reply.

Fannie also said that Mrs. Hynson dictated every word of the fifth letter. "Mr. Clark and myself were never alone at Mrs. Hynson's; she or her husband were always present." She did attest to writing the letter at Boyle's herself. She also testified that the two letters Jim sent her in Missouri arrived after her departure for Cincinnati. They were apparently forwarded to Manassas, taken into the possession of her family and kept from her sight. With this, Fannie's testimony was concluded and she was relieved of all further court attendance.

Following Fannie to the stand was Jim's brother-in-law, G.M. Weedon. The line of questioning directed at him appears to have been an effort to pin down the timeline for Fannie's and Jim's exploits. But Weedon said he was not sure when Jim decamped his wife and children from Manassas. ""I do not know exactly when Clark traveled from Manassas to Prince George's County; I only know that he stayed one night on the way at my house. He brought his wife and his two children with him. I think it was between the 16th and 20th of June that Clark came. When he left my house with his family, he travelled to his home in Prince George's County." One point he was certain on was the family had only had three bags with them, and no furniture. This is peculiar for someone looking to pull up stakes and relocate, especially since nobody had any recollection of the family selling off any furniture. (Further, there are no ads in the *Alexandria Gazette*, although it is possible that ads were only placed in the local Manassas paper.)

With this, the prosecution closed its case at 3 p.m., although there was discussion of allowing Mrs. Hynson on the stand when court resumed Monday, assuming she was able to attend.

Chapter Nine: The Verdict

Sunday was a day of rest: Newspapers did not publish and court was out of session. When Monday's *Alexandria Gazette* hit the streets, however, the trial was not the biggest news of the day. Over the weekend, the town of Boston suffered a devastating fire that still ranks as one of the most costly fire-related property losses in American history. It began in a commercial warehouse on Summer Street and took 12 hours to fight. Before it was over, it had killed at least 30 people, destroyed 776 buildings and 65 acres of Boston's downtown, and caused $73.5 million in damage. As with the more infamous and more devastating Chicago fire of the year before, much of the damage was ascribed to dry wooden structures, failure to follow building regulations, and insufficient water systems. Also to blame were the flammable wooden Mansard roofs common on most buildings, which allowed the fire to travel far above ground and even across streets to other buildings.

One problem Boston firefighters faced that Chicago had not was a lack of horsepower, literally. The Epizootic had rendered the city nearly horseless for a week before the fire broke out, and that night only five of the city's steamers were drawn by horses; the rest were pulled by gangs of men. As far as timing went, it ultimately presented only a small delay, but every delay is a problem when a wooden city is burning.

News of the fire reached Brentsville on Monday and was the topic of much discussion as court resumed. Mrs. Hynson was in attendance, but she had been detained and apparently arrived too late to be examined, although she wished to give her testimony. It's an indication of the scandal surrounding the case that when she was not allowed to testify (thus getting her version of events circulated in the public), she filed an affidavit with George C. Round, who served as notary public, detailing what she would have said on the stand, which apparently was mostly an effort to clear herself of any involvement in the affair (and perhaps, to some extent, an effort to clear her dead relative's reputation). The *Alexandria Gazette* published a synopsis:

> She has known both of the parties to the elopement all of her life, and while she does not know when they became acquainted is inclined to believe that the introduction did not take place at her house; she remembers, however, having seen them both at her house at a dancing party given in the latter part of the winter of 1871-72. The Fewell family ... had always been very intimate with her, and Fannie had always been a constant visitor at her house and she had always looked upon her in the light of a very near relation, but she does not think the number or frequency of her (Fannie's) visits increased after Mr. Clark came to the village and often became a guest at her

husband's house; she recollects that Mr. Clark and Miss Fewell were members of a fishing party, of which she was one, that had gone to Millford Mills during the month of May, and that they conversed on that occasion. ... She had never encouraged any intimacy between them, and she never told Miss Fannie that she knew Clark to be separated from his wife, and had papers in her possession to confirm that assertion; no money had ever passed through her hands, either directly or indirectly, from Clark to Miss Fewell, and she did not know of Miss Fewell's having a sum of any amount in her possession until she was informed of that fact by another, to whom it was entrusted one day when Miss Fannie took a drive with a young man; that (Hynson) had never corresponded with Mr. Clark under her own name or a fictitious one, and was not known to him by the nom de plume of Lizzie Twyneman; that she had never inquired at the post office for letters for Lizzie Twyneman, and had never seen any so addressed on but one occasion, and under these circumstances:

"Miss Fewell was at our house one morning, and asked me to let my servant girl, Bertie Robinson, go to the post office for her; Fannie told her to ask for her mail and for Lizzie Twyneman's. On her return, she brought one letter for Lizzie Twyneman and one for Fannie; I saw the former letter, and noticed it was postmarked Alexandria; I asked her who Lizzie Twyneman was; she replied, 'the girl at Noonnie's.' (Noonnie was a pet name she had given Mrs. Merchant.) I did not know the name of the servant at Mrs. Merchant's at that time, nor do I know it now; she then put the two letters in her pocket and walked out of the house."

The affidavit continues: "I had never heard Fannie speak in affectionate terms of Mr. Clark; on the contrary, she told me several times, both before and after she became acquainted with Mr. Clark, that she intended to elope with a young man who was then living in Fredericksburg. I not only never dictated any of these letters, but to my knowledge none of them were written at my house. Mr. Clark did not leave his clothes with me; he took his meals at my house after his wife left, and remained during the night once or twice; was invited to stay much oftener but generally declined and would leave about 9 or 10 p.m. on the plea of having some visiting to do, and go to his own home; (Hynson) often visited Mrs. Clark and thought her husband was devoted to her; never knew of any arrangement between Mr. Clark and Fannie to meet at my house; have always had a great deal of company, and they sometimes met there though without any knowledge on my part of concert between them, have once or twice heard Mr. Clark speak in light terms of Miss Fewell, and she always acted when with me, as if his presence was not particularly agreeable to her."

The glaring contrast between Hynson's version of events and Fannie's is fascinating. Perhaps if Hynson had been subject to cross-examination, it would be clear who was closer to telling the truth. And there is no clear indication why the attorneys spurned her testimony. Obviously, it did the defense no favors, since it makes Fannie look less like a gullible child led along by trusted adults and friends, diminishing her brother's motive. Perhaps the prosecution felt that Hynson's comments would only confuse the issue—or, worse, increase the jury's impression of Jim's culpability in the affair.

In any event, Hynson did not get her day in court, and

the case proceeded without delving into this tangent. Instead, the counsel for both sides expressed readiness to present closing arguments. Hunton and Payne, however, objected to the involvement of Wise (and his infamous oratorical skills) as he was private counsel, not an attorney for the Commonwealth. Nicol deliberated over this but decided the prosecution had the right to employ assistant counsel in closing arguments and assign them their place in the argument. With that, court adjourned until 10 a.m. Tuesday.

On the morning of Tuesday, November 12, Nicol read to the jury the instructions prepared mostly by the counsel, with such corrections as he deemed necessary. It is an indication of how sensational this case was that the *Alexandria Gazette*, after printing an abridged version of the instructions, printed the instructions in full (nearly 2,000 words) on page 1 of the following day's paper.[32]

The prosecution's eight instructions were clear, and boiled down to essentially one concept. If the jury believed that "sufficient time for cooling" had occurred between the time of the offense and the time of the killing, or that Lucien showed "thought, caution and design" in procuring weapons best suited for the purpose of killing Jim, then Jim had been killed in revenge "willfully, deliberately, maliciously, premeditatedly, and with malice aforethought," and Lucien should be found guilty of murder in the first degree.

The instructions by the defense were similarly repetitive, with their 11 instructions revolving around two central themes. First, if Lucien was "so deranged that he was deprived of his memory and understanding so as to be unaware of the nature, character and consequences of the act he committed, or to be unable to discriminate between right and wrong in reference to that particular act" at the

---

[32] The full text of the *Gazette*'s reprint can be found in the appendix.

time of Jim's killing, he should be acquitted. Second, if the jury felt that Lucien was justified in killing Jim, "then the place or manner of his executing his purpose is immaterial and should not be regarded by the jury as affecting in any manner their verdict." For good measure, the defense's final instruction reminded the jury that if they had any reasonable doubt about any aspect of the case, Lucien was entitled to its benefit and should be acquitted.

Once both sets of instructions had been read to the jury, court adjourned. Wednesday, then, would be the day of judgment.

On Wednesday morning, Nicol presented additional instructions to the jury, touching on the plea of insanity:

> The insanity contemplated by the series of instructions granted the defense in this case may proceed from one of the two distinct species of disease of the mind—either of which, if a person was laboring under at the time of committing the act, might render him irresponsible therefore, however criminal such an act might be in a person free from disease. The first is when the disease so affects the mental or reasoning faculties of the brain that the person subject to it is unable to determine the nature and quality of the act he is doing—or, if he does know it, he does not know that it is wrong. The other is when the disease so affects the moral faculties that the person subject to it is liable at any time to break out into such paroxysms of violence that it is impossible for him not to give way to them, and this though the person at the time is fully conscious of the nature and quality of the act he is doing and that it is wrong. The difficulty in such cases is to determine whether the act proceeded from passion or malice on the one side, or from a diseased mind upon the other. It is for the jury to say if they believe the

prisoner committed the homicide with which he is charged, from all the facts in evidence before them, whether he was at the time of committing such act, laboring under either of the aforesaid diseases of the mind, and so affected thereby as to render him irresponsible for such act.

This definition of insanity must have caused some eye-rolling among Lucien's neighbors and acquaintances, who were all too familiar with "paroxysms of violence" occurring "at any time" despite Lucien being "fully conscious of the nature and quality of the act he is doing and that it is wrong." Whether it had been within his power to resist acting on impulse was irrelevant: He hadn't resisted—had almost never resisted—and who on a jury would assume they could outdo a man's own assessment of his self-control?

This bit of theater out of the way, closing arguments commenced. Menifee went first, for the prosecution. No details were printed, but the *Gazette* deemed the argument "an able one, and in which the law and the testimony was discussed at length."

At this point, Hunton, Payne, and Thomas made a last-ditch effort to keep Wise from speaking, submitting a proposal to give the case to the jury without further argument. Nicol presented this option to the prosecution, which predictably declined to accept, and led Wise to quip to Thomas, who was next to speak, that he could not be caught, as Wise knew Thomas "intus it in cute"—inside and out.

Thomas used his time before the jury to stress the importance of the issues at stake: not just the future of the prisoner, but the emotional repercussions for two families, and the well-being of society itself. "Every man's house is his castle," he reminded the jury, and when Jim (or any man) sought to defy protection of said castle and its inmates, he must be prepared to face the consequences.

Thomas based the grounds of the defense, as Payne had, on the two pleas of justification and insanity. Regarding the insanity angle, he called attention to the instructions submitted by the defense relevant to insanity, and read from "Ray on Diseases of the Mind" to show that there can be a moral derangement, unaccompanied by any symptoms of physical disease.[33] To substantiate his position on justification, he rehashed the case evidence and cited legal precedents showing that the "higher law" of public opinion had always extenuated actions such as those Lucien committed. He made specific mention of two notable precedents: the Richardson-McFarland case and the Grant-Pollard case.

~~~~~~~

While the cases Thomas cited as precedent drew heavily on the concept of honor, his inclusion of the Pollard-Grant verdict may have been a tad below the belt, given Wise's involvement with the defense in that case. On November 24, 1868, Henry Rives Pollard, publisher and editor of the Richmond, Virginia, *Southern Opinion*, was shot outside the door of his office. James Grant, scion of one of the wealthiest families in town, had threatened Pollard for publishing an article attacking the virtue of Grant's sister, Mary, by purporting she had eloped with a man named Horace Ford. The veracity of this report was immaterial; once the story was out, a family's reputation was ruined. And Grant's sister was hardly being singled out: The *Opinion* was little more than a scandal sheet, and Pollard routinely carried three guns on his person in self-

---

[33] Isaac Ray was the leading forensic psychiatrist of the 1800s. In 1838, he published *A Treatise on the Medical Jurisprudence of Insanity*, the foremost writing on that topic for many years. He was among the first to recommend passage of laws to secure the rights of the mentally ill and define civil and criminal relationships of the insane.

defense against indignant—and, perhaps, injured—parties. Shortly after the shooting, James Grant was found in a building across the street from Pollard's office, holed up in a third-floor room with four guns, including a double-barreled shotgun—one barrel loaded with buckshot, the other barrel recently fired. The family hired a stellar team of defense lawyers, including Wise's son and law partner, John S. Wise. The senior Wise visited the crime scene on the day of the killing to take measurement, and later testified that incriminating marks on the windowsill were circumstantial, not made by muzzle flash, and would have resulted in bullets missing Pollard by 18 feet, thus attempting to raise the possibility that Pollard had been shot from some other room of the unlocked and thoroughly searched building. The inclusion of the Wise family in this case was particularly disturbing for Pollard's family: Wise was a frequent target of the late Pollard's writing, and in fact Pollard had been involved in a brawl in Maryland earlier that year with two Wise cousins where gunshots were exchanged. Ultimately, Grant was found not guilty.

Almost exactly one year later, on November 25, 1869, Daniel McFarland walked into the *New York Tribune* office and fatally shot Tribune editor Albert Richardson, who had planned to marry McFarland's actress ex-wife, Abby Sage McFarland. The trial focused less on the facts of the murder and more on the behavior of Abby McFarland, alternately portrayed as an adulteress who drove her husband to murderous insanity and a hapless victim fleeing a drunken, abusive husband. Interestingly, the prosecution's ability was questioned in that case, as well: Doubting the district attorney's abilities, Abby's supporters brought in former judge and congressman Noah Davis to assist. McFarland, not to be outmatched, hired John Graham as his attorney, who had been associate council in the Sickles case and would use the same temporary insanity plea that got Sickles acquitted. The trial was a high-profile affair, with Abby's relatives and friends, including Horace Greeley, testifying to the miserable state of the McFarland marriage. The defense spotlighted Abby's adultery with Albert Richardson and argued that an intercepted letter from Albert to Abby, coupled with Daniel McFarland's family history of mental instability, allegedly triggered the insanity in McFarland that led to the shooting. After five weeks in court, the jury deliberated nearly two hours before finding Daniel McFarland not guilty.

~~~~~~~

With these precedents well established, Thomas sat down and Hunton closed the defense's arguments. He began by stating that the refusal of the prosecution to send the case to jury without closing arguments indicated their lack of confidence. He also took a swipe at Sinclair, saying he had expected to square off against the Commonwealth, but the Commonwealth had taken a back seat to private counsel, and this anomaly was not merely grounds but virtually a requirement for acquittal.

Hunton specifically discussed Thomas K. Davis's comment that Lucien had given the seduction of his sister as a reason for killing Jim. From there, he went on to give a dramatic depiction of Jim luring Fannie to her downfall. He thrashed the prosecution for casting aspersions on Fannie's reputation for chastity—then went on to say that even if they were correct, justification was still a cause for acquittal because Lucien would have had to know of his sister's former bad character when he killed Jim.

Finally, Hunton said it was evident that Jim considered jail a safe haven, and that being informed of this was the provocation for Lucien to act. The circumstances attending Miss Fewell's abduction were clear justification for action: When a man's wife or daughter was seduced, the laws of Virginia conferred upon the injured party the privilege of taking the life of the seducer. But then he addressed the defense of insanity, also citing the McFarland-Richardson case. All told, Hunton talked for nearly two hours.

It is interesting that the defense tried to play both sides of the fence: Lucien had every right to kill Jim—but he was clearly insane when he committed this perfectly justifiable act. It is not, however, surprising: Even in modern courtrooms, attorneys will offer seemingly conflicting arguments when it serves their purpose and a case can be viewed in more than one way.

When Hunton was done, the crowd must have grown a little restless, as the best had been saved for last: Wise closed the argument for the prosecution. He blamed the changing times and loose morality for the tragedy that had occurred, harping on free love "and the other isms of the day, not sparing Greeleyism," which he deemed "immeasurably the worst of all." Contrary to the position of the defense, he insisted that no matter how worked up Lucien was, there was no excuse for murder—and besides, no evidence had been presented indicating Lucien's state of mind when he pulled the triggers. And that was that. Despite the vitriol of the defense, Wise's speech clocked in at a fraction of Hunton's.

The jury took even less time than Wise. Members did leave the jury box, as it turned out. They retired to consider a verdict at 1:30—and returned at 1:35. Foreman John S. Ewell presented the unsurprising verdict: "We of the jury, find the prisoner not guilty as charged in the indictment." Whether the jury reached this verdict because they determined Lucien had been justified in his actions or if they thought him temporarily insane was not revealed; as the *Fremont (Ohio) Weekly Journal* put it, "the jury did not take the pains to draw nice distinctions, and brought in a simple verdict of not guilty."

It didn't matter. Applause shook the courtroom, with much cheering and stomping. Lucien was excused, and was mobbed by rowdy friends congratulating him as he left the prisoner's box. The crowd spilled out of the courthouse and along the green, crossing the street to Reid's Hotel for a raucous celebration. The large hotel (which was also where the jury had been sequestered) was overrun by revelers for several hours, through dinnertime.

Joseph Reid's place was a welcoming spot on a large and spacious property. Reid and his wife had been in the hospitality business for several years, owning by turns a bar room, a bowling saloon, a boarding house, and now the hotel. By virtue of its location across the street from the courthouse—and a well-stocked bar—the hotel was a prime spot frequented by all manner of guests; "here the nestors of law and politics talked it over ... here stories and jokes were told galore."

When the celebration had wound down, Lucien was driven to Manassas, accompanied by a reporter for the *Baltimore Sun*, who snagged an interview that was astonishingly candid, ridiculously brash, or both. Lucien, typically cocky, bragged that he had made all his moves in broad daylight, had clearly communicated his intention to at least one friend along the way, and had dallied along the way back to Manassas with nobody pursuing him for arrest. He shrugged off the horror of incarceration; the jail was so insecure, he said, that many nights he would take off his shoes, remove the door to his cell and wander the building at his leisure. (The fact that he'd spent enough time there in the past to know every corner blindfolded does not appear to have come up.)

The law having been served and the scandal thus more or less concluded, Brentsville was finally able to get back to its normal, quiet, sleepy self.

Epilogue: From Presidents to Pistol Johnnie

*W*ith the salacious details out of the way, the majority of newspapers devoted a maximum of three lines to the verdict: "The trial of Lucien Fewell for the murder of James F. Clark has been concluded, and the prisoner acquitted." But it was inevitable that the verdict would stir a few passions on either side of the fence. The *Daily State Journal* reported that the "Northern press are quite unanimous in condemning the acquittal of Fewell," and proceeded to devote a column to reprints of outraged rhetoric. The November 20 *Baltimore Sun* said that

> If Fewell had waited till Clark had been released from jail and then proceeded to "execute" him, the story would have been the old one of summary vengeance openly and fearlessly taken ... We solemnly protest against this assumption by private individuals of the right to take life, either in cases of adultery or seduction, deliberately after the fact.

The November 21 *New York Times* took Southerners to task more directly:

> For such a murder as Fewell brazenly confesses that he committed, there is no extenuation in its provocation. The assassin, his jury, and his adulators ought to be anxious now only for oblivion, they can be remembered only with contempt so long as courage in personal action and decency in the administration of the law are respected among men.

Southern papers retaliated. The November 30 *Memphis Public Ledger* acidly noted that

> The New York World of last Sunday has an editorial which must have been written when the editor was not in. It goes into the detail of the famous Fewell-Clark case ... and grows faintly humorous over the murder of Clark ... it is known in the sanctum of all rural papers that the Virginia jury did not "praise the murderess" or say anything about the lady in question; that she ... never was on trial for anything ... the World's critic of Southern habits and society seems to have a vivid and correct comprehension of the whole affair. ... We admire enterprise, and shall look to the world now for the very latest news, even down to the death of General Jackson.

But after the predictable outrage from various corners, the nation's fascination with Brentsville quickly faded. There were other headlines to write, other sensational stories to embellish and embroider in a bid to increase sales.

~~~~~~~

Not least of these was Greeley's death on November 29. His political defeat on the heels of his wife's death proved too much: The editor more or less went out of his head two weeks after the election. The November 30 *New York Sun* reported that the "disease first developed itself violently two weeks ago tonight at a meeting of the trustees of the Tribune ... then came the consultation and the unanimous verdict of the doctors that acute mania had set in ... Nervous excitement, disappointed hopes, and loss of sleep doubtless produced the fatal disorder, while a terrible mental strain proving too great for the exhausted physical system, doubtless hastened the result." Greeley died at Choate House's sanitarium (now Marks Hall) in Pleasantville, New York.

His death came before the Electoral College met. He would have received 66 electoral votes; instead, those votes were scattered among the other candidates. However, three of Georgia's electoral votes were left blank in honor of him. (Other sources report Greeley receiving three electoral votes posthumously, with those votes being disallowed by Congress.)

~~~~~~~

Victoria Woodhull and Tennie Claflin spent the month of November in jail before somehow raising $16,000 bail, but a cycle of arrests and hearings and releases persisted, while actual trials for their alleged crimes were delayed. Acquitted on a technicality, the sisters had some small taste of validation in 1875 when Elizabeth Tilton's husband, Theodore, sued Beecher for "alienation of affection." The trial in 1875 resulted in a hung jury.

In June 1876, the *Weekly* folded. Depressed and depleted, the sisters sailed for Europe in July 1877 and settled in England where Victoria Woodhull continued lecturing to make a living. Tennie Claflin married Francis Cook, Viscount of Montserrat, Portugal, in 1885; soon after, Queen Victoria created a Cook Baronetcy, meaning Tennie became Lady Cook. Tennie also lectured on women's rights and suffrage, rallying for a women's home-front militia in England during World War I. She died in 1923.

Victoria Woodhull also found love, marrying wealthy banker John Biddulph Martin in 1883, and under the name Victoria Woodhull Martin established *The Humanitarian* magazine in 1892, running it for nine years with the help of her daughter, Zula. After her husband died in 1901, she gave up publishing and retired to the English countryside. She died in 1927.

~~~~~~~

Grant's second term was as beleaguered as his first. The nation plunged into the financial Panic of 1873; financial entities that owned railroad stocks and bonds were ruined, and the New York Stock Exchange suspended trading for ten days in October. Grant approved an injection of cash into the system, but that didn't prevent a five-year industrial depression in which 89 out of 364 railroads went bankrupt. Congress, in its perennial desire to shape the economy, debated an inflationary policy to stimulate the economy and passed what became known as the Inflation Bill on April 14, 1874. Supported by farmers and laborers for its intention to add $64 million in greenbacks to circulation, the bill was opposed by Eastern bankers because it would have weakened the dollar. Grant wound up vetoing the bill, kicking off a Republican commitment to a strong, gold-backed dollar. But Grant's troubles weren't just financial: He faced charges of misconduct in nearly all federal departments, especially in the Treasury and Interior departments. Having apparently learned nothing from his first term in office, he continued to defend corrupt associates in the face of accusations and congressional investigations.

Opting not to run for a third term in 1876, Grant and his family departed on a two-year world tour, dining with Queen Victoria and meeting with the emperor of Japan. This tour did much to restore his reputation and popularity, and in 1880 his name again was bandied about for a third run at the presidency. That year's Republican convention in Chicago marked the first such gathering in which delegates attended from every state in the Union. But the scene was somewhat reminiscent of that at the 1872 Liberal Republican convention: The first ballot had Grant at 304, James G. Blaine at 284, John Sherman at 93, and the rest scattered to minor candidates, meaning none had the 370 votes needed for nomination. Subsequent ballots resulted in a continued standoff between Grant and Blaine. After 36 ballots, several delegates peeled off from Blaine and others to back a compromise candidate: Representative James A. Garfield of Ohio, who accepted the nomination and ultimately won the election to become the nation's 20th president.

The world tour and campaign over, Grant was now home, jobless, and broke. He went in on a project to build a railroad from Oaxaca to Mexico City, but the plan failed and the railroad went bankrupt. At the same time, his son was involved with some shady dealings on Wall Street that put his firm on the verge of collapse. Grant approached businessman William Henry Vanderbilt, who gave Grant a personal loan of $150,000. Grant invested the money in the firm, but it was not enough to save the firm from failure. Grant, now destitute, sold off Civil War mementos and all other assets to repay what he could of the debt.

Desperate for funds, Grant wrote several articles on his Civil War campaigns, which were well received by critics. Editor Robert Underwood Johnson suggested that Grant write his memoirs, as other war heroes had done. Around the same time, Grant learned that he was suffering from throat cancer. He took up the book project, making a last-ditch effort to provide for his family after his death. Mark Twain offered to buy the works, proposing a 75-percent royalty. Grant plugged away on the book, even through cancer treatments, and finished it shortly before he died. The book did well, and Grant accomplished his goal: The proceeds took care of his family after his death.

Grant's memoir is an interesting read. There is a fair amount of personal detail, with straightforward portrayals of battles against both the South and internal army foes. Grant portrays himself as honest and honorable, but it is difficult to read the book and not think of the troubles that go unmentioned and the postwar troubles that led him to be writing the book in the first place.

Grant died July 23, 1885, at the age of 63. After private services, Grant's body traveled by special train to West Point and New York City. Thousands of veterans marched with Grant's casket to Riverside Park, where he was laid to rest, first in a temporary tomb, and finally in a sarcophagus in a circular atrium at the General Grant National Memorial ("Grant's Tomb"), the largest mausoleum in North America. Grant's pallbearers were representative of the reunifying nation: Union Generals William Tecumseh Sherman and Philip Sheridan were joined by Confederates Simon Bolivar Buckner and Joseph Johnston.

~~~~~~~

Out of the limelight, life in Prince William County went on. Manassas was incorporated in 1873, declared a town by the General Assembly. Among those serving on the first town council were Varnes, Hynson, Round, and William Fewell.

An 1878 business license lists the senior Fewell as branching into commerce: "successor to L.B. Butler; Will continue the mercantile business at the old stand, corner of Centre & East Street, Country produce of all kinds." He served as mayor from 1882-1884. Twenty years after the referendum that spelled James Clark's downfall, Manassas would finally wrest the title of county seat from Brentsville, thanks largely to its railroad access and extensive land donations by Geroge Carr Round and others. Brentsville has been built on a hill to avoid flooding, but railroad planners tried to avoid the added effort of such construction. Unable to get a spur built, Brentsville essentially disappeared from the map, allowing it to maintain its rural nature. Upon ceasing incarceration operations, the jail building was used for several purposes, including a dormitory for a girls' school in the late 1890s, a private home in 1910, and an office space in 1975. As a result of historical interest and local efforts, many town sites, including the courthouse and the jail, were added to the National Register of Historic Places in 1990.

It is, perhaps, to be expected that a place with so much tragic history would fuel the imagination, and Brentsville has attracted its share of supernatural and paranormal adventure seekers. The courthouse complex was featured on a 2009 episode of the SyFy network's show *Ghost Hunters*; apparently, the team heard some knocking and got some electromagnetic field readings inside the jail, which had no electricity at the time.

Site officials have shared other reports of knocking sounds and apparitions in the jail, as well as the sound of voices and figures drifting past the courthouse windows. Some say it is the ghost of Agnes, the slave who killed her master and staved off execution for a few weeks by claiming pregnancy. Some believe it is Jim, seeking Lucien.[34]

~~~~~~~

---

[34] The author feels obliged to report that neither she nor anyone in her family experienced anything remotely spooky in frequent visits to the site. That said, we are scoffers and unlikely to be attractive to ghosts.

James F. Clark's body certainly did not rest in eternal peace. He and Elder Clark (who died in November 1882 after a short bout of paralysis, possibly from a stroke) were buried with much of the rest of the family at Chopawamsic, off what is now MCB-1 on Quantico Marine Base. In the 1940s, the government acquired much of the land around there through eminent domain, and two years later paid to relocate more than 1,500 bodies out of intended bombing range areas. Two new cemeteries were created, both maintained by the Marine Corps: Carver Cemetery was established for the relocated bodies of blacks, near the intersection of Garrisonville and Brent Town roads; and Cedar Run Cemetery was established for whites. The Clark family plot is now there. Elder Clark's headstone has a CSA marker beside it for his service to the Confederacy and is marked SS. V.D.M (scilicet verbi divini minister, or Minister of the Divine Word) in recognition of his lifelong religious service. At some point, Jim Clark's headstone was broken and a repair was attempted—but it was a sloppy job, with dribbles of glue running along the bottom. The stone reads:

IN MEMORIAM
JAMES F. CLARK
Died Sept 2. 1872
From a wound received by the hands of an
assassin
Aged 28 years
Though young in the legal profession, yet he
attained a respectable position at the bar
Generous, noble, spirited and a true friend. Loved
in life and mourned in death by all who knew him.
Requiescat en pace

Jim's older daughter, Laura, married a man named Jesse Stone, had seven children, and died in New Jersey in 1952.

His younger daughter, Bertha, remained unwed and died in Virginia around 1944.

~~~~~~~

Judge Aylett Nicol continued on the bench until his death. Caught up in a property dispute in 1876, he faced charges of misconduct and bribery. As it turned out, the "Boss Tweed of Prince William County" was cleared by the House of Delegates and found eligible for reappointment. Nicol died on March 10, 1878, and was buried in Brentsville. His son, Charles E. Nicol, followed in his footsteps, serving as judge of the Sixteenth Circuit of Virginia.

~~~~~~~

Charles Sinclair, after stepping into Jim's spot as commonwealth's attorney, followed further in his footsteps a couple years later, assuming editorship of the *Manassas Gazette* in June 1874. He was elected to the state Senate in 1875 and served two terms. He died of apoplexy in March 1887.

~~~~~~~

By the mid-1870s, Henry Wise had become estranged from the state's Conservative Party leaders. But after carefully cultivating a Republican reputation, he eventually soured on Grant, if not the party: "General Grant had an opportunity, after being freed from Stevens, Stanton, Seward, and Greeley, to have inaugurated a patriotic policy which would have poured balm into the wounds of war and have restored halcyon days of peace to the South. I had a hope at one time he would allow the good genius of the country to be his genius and if he had he would have left his office and left this world for a better, happy and blessed. But he has proved himself to be but a military martinet—has obeyed the orders of the hydra monster Congress and has 'broken owners.' I give up all hope in him." Still, his sons John Sergeant Wise and Richard Alsop Wise both later affiliated with the Republican Party and served in Congress. Wise returned to Washington for the last time in 1876 to argue a disputed-election case before a committee of the House of Representatives. He died later that year, on September 12, after a lingering illness, at age 70.

~~~~~~~

Eppa Hunton continued the string of illustrious successes he had already demonstrated himself capable of. His congressional term began in March 1873 and he took his seat in the House in December that year. Most notable in his congressional career was his service on the Electoral Commission in the disputed Hayes-Tilden election of 1876. Democrat Samuel J. Tilden had won the popular vote by almost a quarter of a million votes, but he did not have a clear Electoral College majority over Republican Rutherford B. Hayes. Tilden received 184 electoral votes; Hayes 165. The remaining 20 (four from Florida, eight from Louisiana, seven from South Carolina, and one from Oregon) were in dispute. Since a total of 185 votes constituted an Electoral College majority, Tilden needed only one of the disputed votes, while Hayes needed all 20. With a Republican Senate and Democratic House, it was unlikely Congress would be able to resolve the dispute with a vote, and there was a real danger of the nation flaring into war again. Hunton, needless to say, was in Tilden's camp, and sought to get Tilden seated by legal and peaceful means. But his recognition that more war would be bad for Virginia outweighed his partisanship, and he ultimately backed the Compromise of 1877, which awarded all 20 electoral votes to Hayes, in return for which the Republicans agreed to withdraw federal troops from the South, ending Reconstruction and essentially giving the South back to Democrats (and, not coincidentally, dismantling virtually all of the work done to enfranchise black voters).

Hunton served in the House until 1881, then stepped down, declaring himself finished with politics. He went on to form a lucrative law partnership in Washington, but in 1892, he was appointed to the U.S. Senate to fill a vacancy left by the death of John S. Barbour (who had succeeded Hunton in the House). Hunton won the ensuing special election and remained in the Senate through 1895, when the term expired, then returned to Warrenton to again resume his law practice. He died in Richmond in 1908.

Hunton's son, Eppa Hunton III, wound up marrying two of William Fitzhugh Payne's daughters. He married Erva, the eldest, in 1884, but she was frail and died in 1897. The younger Hunton then married Erva's sister, Virginia, in 1901: Their children were the only ones who could boast having two Confederate general officers for grandfathers. The same year as his second marriage, Eppa Hunton III also co-founded the notable Richmond law firm Hunton and Williams, beginning a legal dynasty in Virginia that is carried on today by Eppa Hunton VI.

~~~~~~~

William Fitzhugh Payne, like his former partner, was also bitten by the politics bug and served in the Virginia legislature from 1879-1880, then served as general counsel for Southern Railway. He died at home in Washington, D.C., on March 29, 1904. The March 30 *Richmond Times Dispatch* headlined a front-page obituary, "A Noble Virginian Crosses the River," in which it referred to Payne as "perhaps the most celebrated general officer of the Confederate army living in Virginia, with the exception of Gen. Fitzhugh Lee."

~~~~~~~

Henry Wirtz Thomas continued on the bench and, like his compatriots, dabbled in politics, serving in the state senate from 1871-1875 and as lieutenant governor from 1875-1878. He died in 1890.

~~~~~~~

Benjamin Dyer Merchant remained a town leader and continued to run his store in Manassas until 1905. He served as commissioner of the revenue and participated in several civic groups. His wife, Betty, died in 1900. In 1902, the United Daughters of the Confederacy presented him with the Southern Cross of Honor, in recognition of his service. He lived out his days attending annual Confederate reunions, and died in 1913 at his son's Baltimore home at the age of 74. His family continued on the path of commercial success, founding Merchant Tire and Auto in 1934, which expanded along the East Coast in ensuing decades until its parent company was bought in 2000. The Merchants are still one of the most distinguished families in Manassas, known for their support of the arts community.

~~~~~~~

In its article describing Lucien's attempt to escape from jail, the *Daily State Journal* of October 29, 1872, had closed with this: "We wish no ill to Rhoda Fewell. We hope he may live to repent of his terrible crimes, become a good man, and undo some of the great wrong he has done."

The *State Journal*'s hopes were in vain, as it turned out. While spending a few months in jail and being tried for murder might be a sign to some men to play things safe, Lucien only stayed on the straight and narrow for about a year. In December 1873, he was back before the grand jury facing an accusation of attacking a man named John Varns and another accusation that he "feloniously and maliciously did cut with intent" Charles Hynson—whether for the Hynson family's role in the Clark case or some other offense is unclear. After some time in jail, he was released on $1,000 bail. The outcome of this case is unknown.

But in July 1876, Lucien was in jail again. This time, Charles Brawner accused his stepfather, saying Lucien "did unlawfully assault, beat, and ill-treat one Sarah E. Fewell." This was not viewed lightly by the court officials at Manassas, who found him guilty and sentenced him to a year in jail and a $50 fine. However, Aylett Nicol issued a writ of habeas corpus, and in a document dated July 12, Lucien filed a counter complaint that he had been examined by an imposter:

> To the Hon. A. Nicol, Judge of the County Court of Prince William County. Your petitioner, Lucien N. Fewell represents that on the 9th day of July 1876, he was arrested in the Town of Manassas, Prince William County, Virginia on complaint of one C.E. Brawner, that your petitioner did unlawfully assault and beat one, Sarah E. Fewell, and further your petitioner represents that the said complaint of the said C. E. Brawner was made before one D. W. Whiting, pretending to be a justice of the peace of Prince William County, but in fact merely a private citizen having vacated his position of Justice to which he was elected on the (blank) day of (blank) 187(blank), by resignation on the (blank) day of (blank) 187(blank), a considerable time previous to hearing the said complaint of the said C. E. Brawner. Your petitioner further represents that the said D. W. Whiting, pretending to be a justice as aforesaid, in

obedience to the prayer of the said complaint of said C. E. Brawner issued on the 9th day of July 1876, a warrant for the arrest of your petitioner, which was executed on the same day, and in force and of the command of said warrant he was returned before the said Whiting, pretending to be a justice as aforesaid, on the said 9th day July 1876 and forthwith tried, found guilty and sentenced to 12 months imprisonment in the County jail of Prince William County and to pay a fine of $50 by the said Whiting, pretending to be a justice as aforesaid. Your petitioner, further represents that the said Whiting in pretence of his said judgment of fine and imprisonment issued a (not legible) on the 9th day of July 1876, directed to the sergeant of the corporation of Manassas, and the jailor of Prince William County whereby the said Sergeant was commanded to convey the body of your petitioner to the said jailor and into his hands safely deliver the same, and the said jailor was commanded the same to receive, and to safely keep confined for the term of twelve months, and there after unless and until he shall have paid the sum of 450 to the Commonwealth of Virginia, in accordance with the said judgment of the said Whiting, pretending to be a justice as aforesaid. As your petitioner is advised the entire proceedings by which he was arrested, tried, imprisoned, and fined is unauthorized by and contrary to law, and that he is detained without lawful authority, he therefore prays the Commonwealth most gracious writ of habeas corpus may be awarded to him, directed to the jailor of Prince William County requiring him to bring before you the body of your petitioner, with the cause of his detention, so that the same may be inquired into, and all such relief afforded unto your petitioner. L. N. Fewell

Nicol found in favor of Lucien. He was ordered discharged.

In August, Lucien was on the other side of the law, accusing John McCulloh Smith of breaking into his house and making off with

> one over coat of the value of ($45.00) forty-five dollars, and one pair of pants of the value of ($8.00) eight dollars and three boots of the value of $2.50 each and four pair of drawers of the value of $1.50 per pair and four shirts of the value of $1.00 each and 4 pocket-handkerchiefs of the value of 20 cents each and eight pairs of socks of the value of 30 cents per pair and one hat of the value of $4.00 and one traveling valise of the value of $8.50 and one other valise of the value of $3.50 and one pair of carpet slippers of the value of seventy cents.

After this, Lucien appears to have stayed out of trouble for some time. It's not until May 1877 that he's in the court records again—this time for defrauding a man named Joseph Yohner regarding the purchase of a $100 horse. Lucien must have been in some straits by now, for he apparently lied about owning property in Manassas that would serve as collateral for the purchase.

Lucien knocked around Virginia for a bit longer, but sometime before 1880 he lit out for the territories. In 1880, Sarah was living with her son Charles and his family, with no mention of Lucien—who, according to a family document, was in Colorado that year, with an October wedding to a Tennessee-native widow named Mary Maple Rouse who had two children from a previous marriage. Two years later, the family had landed in New Mexico, where they had two more children, Willie Spitberg Fewell, born May 5, 1882, and William Fewell, born May 30, 1885.

The 1885 New Mexico territorial census lists Lucien as a stage driver.

For a time, Lucien seemed a better fit in New Mexico than Virginia. While his drinking and brawling did not abate, what was viewed as barbaric and dangerous behavior in Manassas was apparently par for the course out West. Adopting the colorful moniker of Pistol Johnny, Lucien was involved in a series of exploits uproariously reported by several newspapers. In 1881, less than a month after the death of Billy the Kid, the following appeared in the August 11 issue of the St. Clairsville, Ohio, *Belmont Chronicle*:

> William "the Kid," who died in his stocking feet in New Mexico a short time since, has a worthy successor in a party styled "Pistol Johnny," "held up" at a New Mexican town the other day, and didn't rob anybody, either, a local paper remarking that he is too much of a gentleman to do that. All he did was to go around with thirty of his followers and make the publicans "set 'em up for the boys." Pistol Johnny is a nice man.

In 1883, he apparently was not so nice: The April 6 *San Francisco Chronicle* says that "John Fewell, known in Santa Fe as Pistol John, was cut across the throat with a razor in the hands of Lou Taylor, who was arrested and jailed. Pistol John may live if he is treated right by the doctors." Pistol John healed up just fine, as it turned out.

The emphasis was on "new" in New Mexico at that time. A missionary from Pennsylvania wrote an account of her experiences in Ranchos de Taos in 1884, teaching school to Spanish-speaking children in a Mexican plaza and living among a "peculiar people." Alice Hyson recounts an 85-mile stage ride from Santa Fe to Taos with Pistol Johnny, as well as the Presbyterian minister and his wife. Hyson notes, be it wryly or with relief, that "Pistol

Johnnie had no occasion to use firearms on that trip."

But by 1886, Lucien was facing another murder rap, this time for killing Edward Norman Bachelor on August 18 in Espanola after weeks of enmity. It began, as so many of Lucien's exploits did, in a saloon. Bachelor was drinking when Lucien came in and sat down. The two argued about a financial transaction that had occurred in the Espanola court, where Lucien had gone against Bachelor. Words in the saloon escalated into a fist fight out in the street, where Lucien threw Bachelor to the ground and "gave him a severe whipping." When he finally let Bachelor get up, Bachelor attacked again and Lucien ran off, Bachelor chasing him with a plank of wood.

For weeks after that, the two snarled and exchanged threats whenever running across each other, until things came to a head on August 18. Bachelor was again in the saloon, playing cards with several other persons, including the saloon's proprietor. Lucien came in to settle up an account, but as the proprietor laid his change on the bar, Bachelor came up and told Lucien, "We will settle that thing now," and hit him in the head, though witnesses differed as to whether it was with a clenched fist or open hand. Lucien staggered toward the door with Bachelor in pursuit, when Lucien fired his gun twice in rapid succession. Both shots hit Bachelor, who died shortly thereafter. When Bachelor's body was moved, a large revolver was found on his person, which in 1886 New Mexico could mean something or nothing in terms of his intentions.

As he had done in Brentsville, Lucien fled the scene of the slaying, this time hiding behind a boarding house. The housekeeper soon found him, and told him to go to his room and stay there until the authorities arrested him—which he did.

The court case dragged on for some time. The Rio Arriba court found Lucien guilty of third-degree murder and sentenced him to ten years in the penitentiary. A motion for a new trial was overruled, and the case was then appealed on several technicalities. In 1888, Lucien was granted a new trial based on a technical error in sentencing instructions. Frank Bond, a prominent New Mexico entrepreneur, said the story ended this way:

> The three Bachelor Brothers were ex-buffalo hunters out of Dodge City. ... Two of them finally secured a tie contract and moved to Tres Piedras. The youngest brother remained at Espanola and secured a job as a caretaker of the engines in the roundhouse at Espanola for the [Denver and Rio Grande Western Railroad]. They had a friend who visited them from Santa Fe occasionally with the good sounding sobriquet of Pistol Johnny. He was a dangerous man drunk or sober, particularly so when drinking, very treacherous. He got in an altercation one night with Bachelor and killed him. The Bachelors spent a lot of money they could ill afford in prosecuting him, and he finally went free. I recall while attending the trial at Tierra Amarilla, one of the Bachelors' tie men came to him and told him that he was wasting his money in prosecuting John, that he had three good boys with good horses and good guns, and if he would just say the word, they would be glad to accommodate their good friend Bachelor by shooting down Johnny on his way from Tierra Amarilla to Santa Fe. "But," I said, "you would have to kill Frank Chavez, the sheriff," as he was a brave man, and would put up a fight. He grinned and said that another one would not matter in the least.

Either way, Lucien was back on the street and boozing it up in the 1890s. There is a mention in the January 10, 1891, issue of the *Albuquerque Weekly Citizen* that "Johnny

Fewell has opened a billiard Hall at Lamy." An account eight months later in the August 29 *Albuquerque Weekly Citizen* describes him getting into a "friendly scuffle" with someone named George Eickleberger at Eakin's saloon. As was usually the case, the other party got the worst of it; Eickleberger was "thrown to the floor, breaking both bones in the right leg above the ankle." The paper termed it an "unfortunate scuffle, and Pistol Johnny very much regrets the accident." But Lucien was on the receiving end in 1893: The April 21 Santa Fe *New Mexican* reported that Lucien and

> Geo. Doty became involved in an altercation over the job of driving one of Patterson & Co's night hacks, night before last, and Doty made his revolver serve as a club. He was arrested on the charge of assault with intent to kill, and today Squire Garcia placed him under $300 bonds for appearance before the district court and $200 bonds to keep the peace.

By 1894, Lucien had struck out on his own—whether he couldn't get along with employers or was moving up in the world is unclear. Based on the *New Mexican*, it was the former; a March 2 note from his old boss read as follows:

> I desire to inform the public that Mr. L. N. Fewell, better known as "Pistol John," is no longer in my employ. He has purchased one bus and one hack from Val. Schick, but has nothing to do with my barn whatever. Thos. A. Herlow.

A notice in the same paper on May 7 reports that Lucien "will hereafter leave the Claire hotel daily for Cochitt with his stage, leaving Santa Fe at 8 o'clock, arriving at destination at 3 o'clock p.m. Leaving Allerton 8 o'clock, arriving in Santa Fe at 4 p.m. on same day. Hacks and buses to and from the depot."

This left plenty of time for entertainment, however. By that year, he reportedly found an even more dangerous way to pass the time than bar fights, when another resident introduced a dancing bear attraction to the town. According to a February 18 story datelined Santa Fe in the New York *Sun*:

> Tripelett's pet cinnamon bear Mary is not in good humor these days. This is the time of year that she prefers to devote to sleep, and she doesn't like to be aroused and yanked about for the amusement of frivolous persons. If she could have her own way she would lie curled up in a dark corner most of the time and come out only on warm days to eat a few lumps of sugar and drink a bottle of sweet soda, just as if she were at home in some canyon of the Rocky Mountains. Not that she would get sugar and bottled soda water at home, but her diet would be equally light, and her midwinters naps would not be disturbed by Tripelett and Pistol Johnny and their inconsiderate folks.

> Because he persists in disturbing Mary at inopportune times, Tripelett wears surgeons bandages on his face and hands and swears when anybody slaps him on the left shoulder. Pistol Johnny is still intact, but he treats Mary with marked respect. One evening, when he was full of courage and rye, Pistol Johnny attempted to show the crowd how friendly he was with Mary by shaking hands with her.

> Mary resented the familiarity and seizing Johnny around the waist, she dexterously laid him upon his back, and then turned around and deliberately

sat on him. Then she "jounced" up and down like a child trying a spring-cushion chair, until Johnny's intermittent and explosive yells brought Tripelett to the rescue with a club.[35]

It is intriguing to consider how the papers would have responded to such shenanigans had they occurred in Manhattan, or even Washington D.C.

The last lengthy article on Lucien's exploits is a May 12, 1899, account in the Santa Fe *New Mexican:*

AN EMBUDO MAN
He Amused Himself, but Is in Jail for His Fun
LN Fewell, alias Pistol Johnny, was arrested last evening in a Santa Fe saloon by Sheriff H.C. Kinsell. Fewell whose residence is at Embudo, where his wife keeps a restaurant, took a double-barreled shot gun in the other evening and chased his family out of the house to the depot, it is alleged. He then went to the depot in order to chase his family back to the house, but this time several other people interfered. Railway Agent Wusson took the gun and pounded it over Fewell's back, then locked him up in the depot. A deputy sheriff was summoned and proceeded to take Fewell to jail but the prisoner managed to escape and made his way to Santa Fe. He is now lodged in the Santa Fe jail.

Lucien dropped out of the public eye after that. In

---

[35] A longer and even more fantastical version of this tale, wherein Johnny does a fandango with the bear, appears in a magazine article by Allen Kelly. In that telling, the bear's name is Juanita, her owner is a Mexican man named Juan who is injured and must temporarily house Juanita with a butcher named Trimble, and Pistol Johnny is described as, "in spite of his war-like, self-chosen pseudonym, notoriously the most harmless person in the ancient pueblo."

1900, he was working as a carpenter in Raton, New Mexico. His son, William, was now 15 and apparently attending school away from home. True to form, the last news article mentioning Lucien in the Albuquerque *Daily Sun* has him pleading guilty to assault with intent to murder in October 1900. The district attorney recommended a two-year sentence in the penitentiary, suspended pending good behavior. Extensive searching turned up no death records for the man, but by 1910, Lucien's widow was living in San Francisco with her daughter.[36] Family legend has it that he died when he was trampled trying to stop a runaway horse team dragging a wagon with a woman and child inside. There is no record to corroborate this, nor does the story particularly conform to anything previously exhibited in Lucien's character, but it is the sort of redemptive ending one might hope for such a man.

~~~~~~~

It does not appear that Lucien ever returned to Virginia after leaving. There is no mention of him in local newspapers, except for his illegal exploits out west. So it is possible that Fannie never saw him again after 1880—but she had moved on by then in her own life. Like the fictional Mabel Lee, she appears to have put her past behind her and moved on to a successful marriage. For all her distress at the time of the trial, she was married two years later to a farmer named James Edgar Trimmer (in Washington, D.C., no less, where Jim had promised to wed her before). Aside from a few years spent in Ohio, they remained in the Virginia-Washington area most of their lives and had four children. It appears to have been a

---

[36] There is one more newspaper mention of Pistol John: In the summer of 1972, a century after the Clark-Fewell murder trial, the El Paso *Herald Post* reported that Pistol John failed to place in races at New Mexico's Ruidoso Downs.

happy marriage, though Fannie was apparently always frail and James Trimmer, like James Clark, would meet a tragic end.

James Trimmer appears to have suffered from nervous exhaustion, and was committed to the Government Hospital for the Insane, where he died November 7, 1909. The story was circulated around Manassas that he died of pneumonia, but news accounts indicate more was afoot. Trimmer reportedly had broken ribs and a dislocated eye, as well as a healing burn mark on his arm, to the dismay of family members who insisted he was not a violent man and demanded an investigation. But nothing came of it: A coroner's jury declared his death was the result of pneumonia and broken ribs incurred when Trimmer fell over his cot in an attempt to rip the grate off his window and escape the hospital.

Fannie died five years later, on August 31, 1914, at her daughter's house in Harrisonburg, Virginia. An invalid, she apparently lived with her daughter for two or three years before that, dying two months after a hip fracture. She was buried in Manassas; Merchant and Nicol descendants were among her pallbearers. Far from her past being buried with her, she had apparently buried it long before: Her obituary makes no mention of her youthful adventure, nor of her avenging brother.

Appendix

On Wednesday, November 13, the Alexandria Gazette ran the full transcript of the instructions to the jury in Lucien Fewell's murder trial. It is reprinted here.

Instructions by the Prosecution:

First if the jury believe from the evidence that the accused from any cause of grudge or from any provocation no matter what so that there was a sufficient time for cooling after the cause of grudge or provocation was given or after knowledge or information of such cause or provocation was had by the accused killed the deceased in revenge willfully, deliberately, maliciously, premeditatedly, and with malice aforethought, then the killing was murder in the first degree and the jury should so find by their verdict.

Second, if the jury believe from the evidence that the deceased, Jas. F. Clark, did not induce Fannie Fewell to leave her home by any acts of his own or of others assisting him with intent to defile her and that he did defile her and that the accused was informed thereof and believed the same to true and that for a considerable time thereafter sufficient for cooling time in revenge for said wrong done to his sister by the deceased, did willfully, deliberately, maliciously, premeditatedly and with malice aforethought kill the said Clark, then it was murder in the first degree and the jury ought so to find in their verdict.

Third, if the jury believe from the evidence that James F. Clark, the deceased, did commit adultery with Fannie Fewell, the sister of the accused, and caused her to commit fornication and by having carnal knowledge of her with her consent and the accused after being informed of his sister's shame did not kill him in the first transport of passion but had time for cooling and showed "thought, caution and design" in procuring weapons best suited to the use of them he intended and in the mode of killing the deceased, and did kill him willfully, deliberately, maliciously, premeditatedly, and with malice aforethought, then the wrong done to his sister by the deceased was no justification and no extenuation or mitigation of the homicide and the killing was murder in the first degree and the jury ought so to find by their verdict.

Fourth, if the jury believe from the evidence that the accused knew the deceased, Jas. F. Clark, had been committed to the jail of Prince William County for safekeeping to answer the charge of fraudulently abducting with intent to defile Fannie Fewell and that thereafter he left the neighborhood of the deceased and went on a journey to the county of Albemarle or elsewhere and had sufficient time for the blood to cool and for reason to resume its way before killing the deceased, and that he returned and went to the cell of the deceased prepared with deadly weapons for the purpose of killing and what he did without other circumstances or causes of provocation or justification, then those aforesaid willfully, deliberately, maliciously, premeditatedly, and with malice aforethought killed the deceased and then it was murder in the first degree and the and the jury should so find in their verdict.

Fifth, if the jury believe from the evidence that the accused when he saw or was informed of an article in the Alexandria Gazette now put in evidence by him in this trial was at a considerable distance from the jail of Prince William County and that it took considerable time sufficient for the blood to cool and for reason to resume her sway before he could reach said jail from the place where he then was and said the matter contained in said article caused him to form a purpose and a plan to kill James F. Clark, and to prepare himself with deadly weapons selected to suit to carry out and execute his purpose at the place where they were to be used and that he did go to said jail and to the cell where the deceased was confined and after declaring his purpose to kill said Clark and did shoot and kill him, willfully, deliberately, maliciously, premeditatedly, and with malice aforethought, the provocation contained in the matter of said article is no justification and no extenuation or mitigation of the homicide and the killing was murder in the first degree and the and the jury should so find in their verdict.

Seventh,[37] if the jury believe from the evidence that the accused contrived and planned, willfully, deliberately, maliciously, premeditatedly, as aforesaid, whilst said Clark was a prisoner in jail in the safekeeping of the law, then no provocation can justify or palliate the homicide and the killing was murder in the first degree, &c.

Eighth, if the jury believe from the evidence that the death wound of James F. Clark by the prisoner whilst he (the prisoner) was smarting under a provocation so recent and so strong that the prisoner may be considered as not being at the moment the master of his own understanding and the prisoner was in no great danger of losing his life or sustaining great bodily harm, the offense was manslaughter but if the jury believe from the evidence that after the provocation there was sufficient time for the blood to cool and for reason to resume its seat before the mortal wound was given, and that the accused displayed thought, contrivance and design in the mode of preparing himself with weapons or in any other way, such exercise of contrivance and design is in evidence, rather of the possession of reason and judgement than of violence and ungovernable passion and unless rebutted by sufficient evidence to the contrary, the killing was murder in the first degree &c.

---

[37] It is unclear if the newspaper inadvertently omitted the sixth item or the items were misnumbered.

Instructions by the Defense

First, If at the time the prisoner committed the act charged upon him from an association of the deceased with his real or fancied troubles, arising from the abduction, debauching, or abandonment of his sister after she had been debauched, his mind became so deranged that he was deprived of his memory and understanding so as to be unaware of the nature, character and consequences of the act he committed, or to be unable to discriminate between right and wrong in reference to that particular act, at the very time of its commission, he is entitled to acquittal.

Second, If at the time the prisoner committed the act charged upon him he was by reason of the causes aforesaid thrown into a state of excitement and frenzy, in which he was divested of his reason and judgment, and was from mental disease incapable of governing himself in reference to the deceased, he is not responsible for the act.

Third, if by reason of the causes as aforesaid the prisoner's mind was so controlled and operated upon that he could not resist, or that he could not control the impulse which prompted the act complained of, he is not responsible, provided such impulse was not of anger or revenge, or other kindred evil passions.

Fourth, If the prisoner was deprived of his reason before and at the time the act was committed, and on account of the conduct of the deceased in the abduction or seduction of his sister, the jury have the right from their own knowledge of human nature and the tendencies of the human mind, to judge whether the act complained of was not the result of an ungovernable frenzy, sufficient to unsettle his faculties, and by an insane impulse deprived the mind of its controlling and directing power, thereby rendering him legally irresponsible for what he did.

Fifth, If the jury believe that by reason of the abduction or seduction of his sister, the letter which deceased wrote to her, the card of the prisoner issued by him whilst in custody, and all the circumstances attending upon the abduction or seduction as came to his knowledge, and the declaration of the deceased that there was no law to punish him, the prisoner committed the act, then the jury have the right to judge whether the moral or mental faculties of the prisoner were not so diseased by reason thereof, as to deprive his mind of its controlling powers, and to render him irresponsible therefore.

Sixth, If the jury shall believe that the act complained of was the offspring or product of mental disease in the prisoner, then and in that case neither delusion or knowledge of right or wrong, nor design or cunning in planning or executing the killing, will render the prisoner responsible for the act, and that he is entitled to an acquittal.

Seventh, if the jury believe from the evidence that when the prisoner committed the act for which he has been indicted, he was either by physical disease or some moral cause not voluntarily induced by himself or both operating on his mental faculties unable to control his will and actions with reason and judgment in reference to the act or acts committed, then in judgment of the law, he was insane and could not be guilty of the offense charged in the indictment.

Eighth, or if the jury shall believe at the time of committing the said act or acts as aforesaid, the prisoner was moved thereto by an impulse controlling his will and his judgment too powerful for him to resist and the said impulse arose from causes physical or moral or from both combined not ordinarily produced by himself, he is entitled to a verdict of not guilty and the court further instructs the jury that all symptoms and tests of disease of the mental or moral faculties are purely matters of fact to be determined by the jury.

Ninth, if the jury believe from the evidence that the prisoner is not responsible for the act or acts committed by him aforesaid because of the diseased or insane condition of the mind as aforesaid at the time of committing the same or from any other sufficient cause arising out of the evidence then the prisoner is entitled to a verdict of not guilty though the said act or acts were committed upon the person of the deceased while in jail under process of law.

Tenth, if the jury believe from the evidence that the prisoner slew the deceased in the jail in the county that from the fact and evidence in this case he was justifiable or irresponsible for the homicide that then the place or manner of his executing his purpose is immaterial and should not be regarded by the jury as affecting in any manner their verdict.

Eleventh, if the jury shall entertain any reasonable

doubt of any fact essential to the conviction of the prisoner then he is entitled to the benefit of said doubt and as a consequence thereof to a verdict of acquittal provided if the jury shall believe from the evidence that the prisoner committed the homicide with which he is charged to render him irresponsible therefore because of insanity at the time of committing the deed such insanity must be proved to the satisfaction of the jury.

Acknowledgments

*T*his was a difficult book to research. No family diaries or letters were available, so nearly all the narrative is taken from newspaper reporting of court proceedings. Especially distressing is that a 1905 fire destroyed the offices and archives of the *Manassas Gazette*, which would have provided a much richer tapestry. (A couple issues remain, as well as reprints in other papers, but the rest is up in smoke.)

It is also annoying, as a modern American, that women's views are so dismally represented in these reports, which curtailed the amount of information I was able to find on Lucien Fewell's mother, Elizabeth, and on James Clark's wife, Mary. (It is also annoying that women reportedly fainted so much in moments of stress and chaos—and that it was taken for granted.)

The book as it did come into being could not have happened without the help of a whole village. First, I am indebted to Ron Turner and Morgan Breeden, who blazed the trail on this story. I am not sure I ever would have

241

started this project if they had not paved the way.

At the other end of the process, this book would not exist without the endless support and patience of David A. Ross and Kelly Huddleston at Open Books, whose professionalism and dedication are second to none. I know it's not easy to work with a Type A diva like me, and I'm so grateful for how you both took me, my scattered brain, and all my nitpicking in stride.

Jane Sthreshley and Mary Jane Zelnick generously shared family photos and anecdotes with warmest regards, and Ben Merchant's enthusiasm for his family history was a terrific shot in the arm when I needed it.

Rodney Ross at the National Archives and Mary Katherine Dellinger at the Manassas Museum also provided crucial documents, and their patience and amazing research abilities are second to none. The medical speculations of Dr. Kim Toone and her buddies were likewise invaluable, and Commonwealth's Attorney Paul Ebert generously took time to explain some of the finer points of courtroom procedure and protocol.

I am also indebted to the staff at Brentsville Courthouse—particularly Mike Riley, for first sharing this story with me, and Bill Backus, for jail tours and wide-ranging discussions of Brentsville—and the staff at the Bull Run Regional Library's RELIC Room, who never tired of answering questions and figuring out which material would best serve my needs.

My dear friends Heather Shannon and Allison Kerns provided insightful reviews, and their strong editorial skills made the manuscript much more compelling—while their generous doses of snark made me much less neurotic.

But I am most grateful to my parents, John and Nancy, and to my family—especially my husband, John, whose love, patience, and encouragement were a greater boon than he could possibly imagine, and my son, Thomas, who not only put me in position to learn about this story, but also put up with more bad moods, despondency, and absenteeism than any kid should have to. I owe this book and so much more to you both.

References

Prologue: A Matter of Honor

The heft of two pistols . . . Alexandria Gazette, August 31, 1872.

In 1872, Virginians were starting to take the railroad for granted again . . . David Maurer, "Torrential Rains are Measured by the Flood of 1870," *Daily Progress*, Dec. 1, 1991.

Then the war ended, and the Orange & Alexandria had merged with the Manassas line . . . Charles Siegel, *The Orange & Alexandria Railroad, 2002–2012*, April 20, 2012.

Chapter One: Religion, Railroads, and Rebellion

The Clarks were longtime Virginians . . . Marshall Wingfield, *A History of Caroline County, Virginia,* Baltimore, Md., Genealogical Publishing Co., 2005, p. 177.

In his younger years, he worked as a millwright . . . R.H. Pittman, *Biographical History of Primitive or Old-School Baptist Ministers of the United States; Including a Brief Treatise on the Subject of Deacons, Their Duties, Etc., With Some Personal Mention of These Offices,* Anderson, Ind.: Herald Printing Co., 1909, p. 64.

The bridge was not free . . . *Political Arena,* December 30, 1828.

"I wish them to specify the number in family . . ." Political Arena, June 24, 1828.

Coalter was not entirely unreasonable . . . *Political Arena,* December 10, 1828.

Elder Clark was a diligent scholar . . . Pittman, 1909, p. 64.

As with most people in most historical periods, the anti-missionists were not motivated by a few overwhelming social or economic factors . . . James R. Mathis, *The Making of the Primitive Baptists: A Cultural and Intellectual History of the Antimission Movement, 1800–1840,* New York: Routledge, 2004, p. 5.

Baptists had to contend not only with other Christian denominations . . . Mathis, 2004, p. 7.

Held at Occoquan Church that year, six participating Virginia churches— Occoquan, White Oak, Frying Pan, Mount Pleasant, Fredericksburg, and Bethlehem—bonded . . . Garnett Ryland, *The Baptists of Virginia, 1699– 1926,* Richmond, Va.: Virginia Baptist Board of Missions and Education, 1955, p. 251.

This, then, made up the world into which James Clark was born . . . U.S. Census, 1850.

This is distinct from, but patterned on, the older American Baptist Foreign Mission Society . . . David Charles Laubach, *American Baptist Home Mission Roots, 1824–2010,* Valley Forge, Pa.: American Baptist Home Mission Societies, 2010, p. 4.

The year Jim was born, Southern Baptists challenged this ruling . . . Mary Burnham Putnam, *The Baptists and Slavery: 1840–1845,* Ann Arbor, Mich.: George Wahr, 1913, pp. 46, 77.

In 1853, he commenced publication of Zion's Advocate . . . Pittman, 1909, p. 65.

*Some time in the early 1850s, Elder Clark took a tack of his own . . .*W.M.
Smoot, *Reminiscences of the Baptists of Virginia*, Occoquan, Va.:
printed at Office of Sectarian, 1902, pp. 40–41.

"It is clear that the same identical individual. . ." John Clark, "The
Regeneration of the Soul," in *Exposure of Heresies Propagated by Some
Old School Baptists*, undated.

*For several years, Southeast faithful referred to themselves as "Beebe Baptists" or
"Clark Baptists . . .*Hoyt D.F. Sparks, *Primitive Baptist History*, Hoyt
Sparks, 2014.

*This rift never really got mended . . .*Personal correspondence with Primitive
Baptist Elder Robert Webb, March 29, 2015.

Today, Primitive Baptists are a small but zealous group . . . "Primitive
Baptists," *About Religion* website, undated.

*In 1860, he gained further distinction . . .*John Clark, "Discourse of Elder
John Clark, upon the Subject of 'The Relation of Master and
Servant,'" *The Primitive Baptist*, August 25, 1860.

And Noah began to be an husbandman . . . Gn 9:20–27.

*After receiving "an ordinary education" . . .*Bristol News*, Sept. 10, 1872; U.S.
Census, 1860.

His older brother, Thomas . . . "Cedar Run Cemetery" *Stafford County
Cemeteries and Churches* website, undated.

*Some 3,668 miles of track were laid in less than 20 years . . .*Jane Scully, "The
Life and Times of the Manassas Gap Railroad," *Fairfax County,
Virginia* web page, undated.

*The line, completed in three years . . .*Scully, undated.

*The legislature approved the plan in March 1853 . . .*Scully, undated.

*By 1856, the Manassas Gap Railroad had promoted William . . .*Benjamin
Homans, *The United States Railroad Directory for 1856*, New York: B.
Homans, 1856, p. 70.

*Buying up the land and preparing it for track was expensive . . .*Scully, undated.

Sanford had been executor of his father's estate . . .U.S. Census, 1810; Thurman family website, undated; Prince William County, *Will Book L.* p. 90–91.

Lucien and Hayden were no longer the babies of the family . . .U.S. Census, 1860.

After the Battle of Manassas . . . "Clark, James F., Co. A," Fourth Virginia Cavalry, muster roll, 1861–1865.

His father appears to have signed up as well . . .Homer Musselman, "Civil War Veterans," *Stafford County Military Information,* website, Feb. 7, 2001.

The Prince William Cavalry, as it was called, had come into existence in Brentsville . . .Kenneth L. Stiles, *4th Virginia Cavalry,* The Virginia Regimental Histories Series, 2nd ed., Lynchburg, Va. . . .H.E. Howard, 1985, p. 1.

It officially formed September 4 and assembled September 19 at Sangster's Crossroads . . .Stiles, 1985, p. 7.

"Fresh beef but with little salt" . . .Stiles, 1985, p. 8.

Merchant earned a promotion to 2nd Lieutenant . . .John T. Toler, "From Captor to Prisoner: Lt. Ben Merchant, CSA, Was One of the 'Immortal 600,'" *Warrenton Lifestyle Magazine,* February 2013, p. 28.

They were mustered into Company H . . . "Fewell, L.N., Co. H," 17th Virginia Infantry, muster rolls, 1862; "Fewell, W.H., Co. H," 17th Virginia Infantry, muster rolls, 1862.

Officially, the first Federal prisoner listed in the Civil War was Pvt. Manuel C. Caustin . . .Carlton Fletcher, "Manuel C. Causten, Prisoner of War," *Glover Park History* website, undated.

Lucien got sick . . . "Fewell, L.N., Co. H," 1862.

The Seven Days battles began . . .Stephen W. Sears, *To The Gates of Richmond: The Peninsula Campaign,* New York: Houghton Mifflin Harcourt, 2001, pp. 277–279.

Lee ordered his Army of Northern Virginia to converge . . .Sears, 2001, pp. 277–279.

Huger missed the battle entirely . . .Sears, 2001, pp. 283–292.

Justice and Vengeance

The assaults by the divisions of A.P. Hill and Longstreet . . .Sears, 2001, p. 294.

"We were ordered to charge a battery on the opposite hill . . .George Wise, *History of the Seventeenth Virginia Infantry, C.S.A,* Baltimore: Kelly, Piet & Co., 1870. p. 76.

In their first combat experience . . .Wise, 1870, p. 80.

The Confederate brigades met stiff resistance . . .Sears, 2001, pp. 295–299.

Edgar Warfield, a private serving with the Fewells . . .Edgar Warfield, *Manassas to Appomattox: The Civil War Memoirs of Pvt. Edgar Warfield, 17th Virginia Infantry,* McLean, Va.: EPM Publications Inc., 1996 (reprint) pp. 77–78

"I had been assigned to look after the slightly wounded . . ." Warfield, 1996, pp. 79–80.

Hayden Fewell was dead . . . "Fewell, W.H., Co. H," 1862.

The battle was tactically inconclusive . . .Sears, 2001, p. 307.

"Could the other commands have cooperated in this action, the result would have proved most disastrous to the enemy . . ." quoted in Sears, 2001, p. 307.

Eppa Hunton, a colonel of the 8th Virginia Infantry . . .Eppa Hunton, *Autobiography of Eppa Hunton,* Richmond Va.: William Byrd Press, 1933.p. 72.

Hayden Fewell was gone . . .Confederate States Auditor for the War Department, register of claims of deceased officers and soldiers from Virginia which were filed for settlement, January 19, 1863.

A tally sheet of his effects . . .Confederate Controllers Office, descriptive list and account of pay and clothing, November 9, 1862.

Elder Clark's church was playing a key role . . . Virginia Civil War Trails marker, Stafford, Va.

Lucien began 1863 away from his regiment . . . "Fewell, L.N., Co. H," 1863.

As the war progressed . . .Warfield, 1996, p. 144.

"Nothing for ourselves or horses since April 29 . . ." Quoted in Stiles, 1985, p. 27.

In October of that year . . . Toler, 2013, p. 28.

James Clark appears to have served with the 4th Virginia Cavalry without interruption . . . "Clark, James F., Co. A," 1864.

It is possible he was shot in the lungs . . . *Fredericksburg Ledger*, Sept. 3, 1872.

When the campaign in northern Virginia began in May 1864 . . . Warfield, 1996, p. 147.

On October 14 of that year . . . Jan Townsend, *The Civil War in Prince William County*, Prince William County, Va.: Prince William County Historical Commission, 2011, p. 36.

In March 1864, Mosby's Rangers attempted to interrupt the Union supply line at Bristoe Station: Townsend, 2011, p. 37.

Warfield "took advantage of the opportunity to mark afresh the grave of my brother . . ." Warfield, 1996, p. 147.

"the explosion was heard distinctly . . ." Warfield, 1996, p. 152.

So began business as usual on July 30 . . . Lee A. Wallace Jr., *Seventeenth Virginia Infantry (The Virginia Regimental Histories Series)*, 1st ed., Lynchburg, Va.: H.E. Howard, 1990, p. 66.

Following the Battle of New Orleans in 1862 . . . Terry L. Jones, "The Beast in the Big Easy," *New York Times*, May 18, 2012.

Fewell was imprisoned . . . Wallace, 1990, p. 66; "Fewell, L.N., Co. H," 1864.

He had been captured . . . Headquarters Department of Virginia, Parole of Honor for James F. Clark, April 28, 1865.

Merchant, however, had the most harrowing experience . . . Toler, 2013, pp. 30–34.

Chapter Two: The Lightning-Rod Man and the Lawyer

A month after Lee's surrender . . . Library of Virginia, *Reconstruction*, web page, undated.

More than 40,000 of her residents had died . . . Ronald L. Heinemann, John G. Kolp, Anthony S Parent, Jr., William G. Shade, *Old Dominion, New Commonwealth: A History of Virginia, 1607–2007*, Charlottesville, Va.: University of Virginia Press, 2007, p. 245.

John T. Trowbridge, a Northerner who visited Virginia at that time described the area . . . Quoted in Virginius Dabney, *Virginia: The New Dominion, A History from 1607 to the Present*, New York: Doubleday and Company, 1971, p. 353.

He urged magnanimity to the rebels . . . Henry Luther Stoddard, *Horace Greeley: Printer, Editor, Crusader,* G. P. Putnam's Sons, 1946, pp. 231–234.

Later newspaper accounts described his courtroom style . . . *New York Herald,* Oct. 8, 1872.

But on May 27, 1867 . . . Ronald Ray Turner, *Prince William County, Virginia, Marriages: 1854–1938*, Manassas, Va., 2002b, p. 21; U.S. Census, 1870.

State voter registration reflected huge demographic changes . . . Heinemann et al., 2007, pp. 247–252.

"idiots and lunatics . . ." 1868 Virginia Constitution, quoted in Julian A.C. Chandler, *The History of Suffrage in Virginia,* Baltimore, Md.: Johns Hopkins Press, 1901, p. 333.

Benjamin Merchant was part of that large group . . . John T. Toler, "From Captor to Prisoner: Lt. Ben Merchant, CSA, Was One of the 'Immortal 600,'" *Warrenton Lifestyle Magazine*, February 2013, p. 34; Turner, 2002b, p. 21.

Slaves made up 28 percent of the population . . . National Park Service, "Civil War," *Prince William Forest,* web page, undated-a.

"protection of the white race . . ." Richmond Daily Enquirer & Examiner, March 26, 1868.

Even Virginia historian Virginius Dabney . . . Dabney, 1971, pp. 365–369.

. . . the KKK's presence in the state . . . John T. Kneebone, "Ku Klux Klan in Virginia, " *Encyclopedia Virginia,* Virginia Foundation for the Humanities, April 21, 2015.

Those born after 1820 were largely responsible for altering and expanding feminine power . . . Jane Turner Censer, *The Reconstruction of White Southern Womanhood, 1865–1895,* Baton Rouge, La.: Louisiana State University Press, 2003, p. 6.

Nearly all widows under 25 remarried . . . Robert Kenzer, "The Uncertainty of Life: A Profile of Virginia's *Civil War Widows*," in Joan E. Cashin, *The War Was You and Me: Civilians in the American Civil War.* Princeton, N.J.: Princeton University Press, 2002, p. 126, Table 2.

Like his brother, he was 5-foot-8, but he had auburn hair and hazel eyes . . . "Fewell, L.N., Co. H," oath of allegiance to the United States, June 19, 1865.

Her late husband, William, had been a prosperous farmer . . . U.S. Census, 1860; "William Brawner," findagrave.com, January 16, 2007.

The gay season is fast approaching . . . "Charles Edwin Brawner, Fan of Manassas Winters," *Brawner Bulletin,* family newsletter, Summer 1997, p. 3.

Sarah Brawner, as befitted a woman of her age and station, was also busy organizing the Ladies Memorial Association of Manassas . . . Confederated Southern Memorial Association, *History of the Confederated Memorial Associations of the South,* New Orleans, La.: Graham Press, 1904, p. 282.

On July 1, 1868, the pupils of Clover Hill School . . . Confederated Southern Memorial Association, 1904, p. 282.

The ladies of Manassas were further assisted by William Sanford Fewell . . . Jeffrey M. Poulin, "A Brief History of the Manassas and

Confederate Cemeteries," in *Manassas City Cemetery*, Manassas Va.: Prince William County Genealogical Society, 1990, unnumbered page.

Although the Manassas Ladies did receive a letter of thanks from General Robert E. Lee . . . Caroline L. Janney, *Burying the Dead but Not the Past: Ladies' Memorial Associations and the Lost Cause (Civil War America)*, University of North Carolina Press, 2008, pp. 1–3.

In June 1867, however, an altercation with resident Israel Jones left Lucien accountable . . . Ronald Ray Turner, *Prince William County Virginia Clerk's Loose Papers, Volume IV, Selected Transcripts 1811-1899*, 2004b, p. 241.

In February, he was again before a magistrate . . . Turner, 2004b, pp. 239–240.

Tragedy struck the Fewells the following month . . . *Manassas City Cemetery*, Manassas Va.: Prince William County Genealogical Society, 1990, p. 10.

Records indicate Lucien appeared in court in May, July, August, and September . . . Turner, 2004b, passim.

Plenty of veterans went on to violence-free lives, but plenty of others didn't . . . Censer, 2003, p. 36.

In July 1869, he placed ads in the New York papers seeking owners of a sword . . . J. Fred Pierson, *Ramapo to Chancellorsville and Beyond*, Richmond, Va.: A. Scott, 2002.

In May 1869, Lucien drew the ire of new Commonwealth's Attorney George C. Round . . . Ronald Ray Turner, *Prince William County Virginia: Clerk's Loose Papers, Vol. III: Selected Transcripts 1804–1899, Indictments, Juries, and Trials*, Prince William County, 2004a, p. 96; George Carr Round, Commonwealth's Attorney for Prince William County, Virginia, letter to the House Reconstruction Committee, September 13, 1869.

"Soon after I settled at Manassas, I found that a young man . . ." George Carr Round, remarks made before the House Reconstruction Committee, December 18, 1869.

On January 3, 1870 . . . Turner, 2004b, p. 101.

Charles, now 19, was an express agent . . . U.S. Census, 1870.

An express agent's job was to ship packages . . . *Railroad Job Descriptions*, website, May 28, 2000.

In December of that year, Elijah B. Georgia hauled Lucien . . . Ronald Ray Turner, *L.N. Fewell*, web page, undated-c.

Beauregard made light of the incident . . . General P.T. Beauregard, "The First Battle of Bull Run," reprinted on *Shotgun's Home of the Civil War* website, February 16, 2002.

McLean, who was too old to fight in the war, made a nice living during the war . . . Frank P. Cauble, *Biography of Wilmer McLean, May 3, 1814-June 5, 1882*, Lynchburg, Virginia: H.E. Howard, 1987, pp. 61–62

A document from 1871 indicates Lucien represented himself in getting Sarah's dower . . . Ronald Ray Turner, *Prince William County Virginia: Clerk's Loose Papers, Volume IX, Selected Transcripts*, Prince William County, 2006c, p. 119; Chancery Records Index, Library of Virginia, Lucien Fewell & Wife vs. James R. Brawner et al., 1871.

But he was back to mixing it up and in jail in February 1872 . . . Turner, 2004a, p. 107.

The Brentsville jail was built some time between 1820 and 1822 . . . Interviews with site staff; Prince William County, *Brentsville Courthouse Historic Centre*, undated-a.

"Next to the substitution of sawdust packages for counterfeit money . . ." Plain *Directions for the Construction and Erection of Lightning-Rods*, New York: Handicraft Publication Company, 1871, p. 27.

. . . *most companies preferred door-to-door salesmen* . . . Arwen Mohun, "Lightning Rods and the Commodification of Risk in Nineteenth Century America," in *Playing With Fire: Histories of the Lightning Rod*, Peter Heering, Oliver Hochadel, and David J. Rhees, eds., Philadelphia, Pa.: American Philosophical Society for its *Transactions* series, Vol. 99, 2009, p. 174.

"But in spite of my treatment . . ." Herman Melville, "The Lightning Rod Man," originally in *Putnam's Monthly Magazine*, August 1854.

In 1860, there were 20 establishments in the country . . .Alfred Judson Henry, *Recent Practice in the Erection of Lightning Conductors,* Washington D.C.: Weather Bureau, 1906, p. 9.

Most systems cost between $65 and $200 . . .Mohun, 2009, p. 175.

"These pamphlets are a formulaic compendium . . ." Mohun, 2009, p. 175.

By 1870, patriarch William and all his daughters, including young Fannie, were living with the Merchants: U.S. Census, 1870.

When William remarried in July 1871 . . .District of Columbia, Select Marriages, 1830-1921, Ancestry.com., undated.

Jousting in Virginia . . .Peter C. Stewart, *Early Professional Baseball in Hampton Roads: A History, 1884-1928,* North Carolina: McFarland, 2010, p. 4; Lon Savage, "Local Spas Cured Ailments Galore," *A Guide to Historic Salem,* Vol. 4, No. 2, 1998.

Born in 1838 in rural Homer, Ohio, Victoria California Canning . . .Myra MacPherson, *The Scarlet Sisters: Sex, Suffrage, and Scandal in the Gilded Age,* New York: Twelve, 2014, passim.

Mary Greeley . . .Barbara Goldsmith, *Other Powers: The Age of Suffrage, Spiritualism, and the Scandalous Victoria Woodhull,* New York: Alfred A. Knopf, 1998, pp. 55, 58.

She hired a Fox sister . . .Barbara Weisberg, *Talking to the Dead,* New York: Harper Collins, 2009, p. 116.

Confederate first lady Varina Davis took in a show by Margaretta Fox . . .Varina Davis, *Jefferson Davis: Ex-President of the Confederate States of America, A Memoir by his Wife,* Vol. 1, p. 548; Feather Schwartz Foster, "The Sons of Jefferson Davis," *Presidential History Blog,* May 1, 2014.

The hard-scrabble Claflin family sought to cash in . . .MacPherson, 2014, passim.

Mabel Lee . . .Christian Reid (Frances Christine Fisher), *Mabel Lee,* Appleton, 1870.

Jim dabbled in newspapers . . . "VNP Acquires Pages and Pages of Page County Newspaper", *Fit to Print* blog, Virginia Newspaper Project at the Library of Virginia, October 23, 2012.

He had "deep blue eyes, light hair, and fair skin; a frank countenance, pleasant address, and agreeable manners" . . .*Bristol News*, Sept. 10, 1872.

On October 24, 1868, he married Mary Elizabeth Lee . . .*Fredericksburg Ledger*, October 27, 1868; *"runaway marriage"* . . .*New York Herald*, October 8, 1872.

William Lee was a farmer in Stafford County . . .U.S. Census, 1860; "Ancestors and Family History of Kevin James Devine and Etoye D. Johnson," Ancestry.com, undated.

On July 5, 1869, the day after Elder Clark's birthday . . . "Laura Lee Clark," werelate.org, October 25, 2011.

It is unclear how long the young family stayed in Washington City . . .U.S. Census, 1870.

Jim was well known and respected enough to be elected Commonwealth's attorney . . .Congressional Serial Set, *The Miscellaneous Documents of the House of Representatives for the First Session of the Forty-Second Congress*, Washington, D.C.: U.S. Government Printing Office, 1871.

Chapter Three: Two Towns and Party Politics

To look at it now, it is hard to believe Brentsville was ever a bustling center of anything . . .Prince William County, undated-a.

The town was established on 50 acres in 1820 . . .Ronald Ray Turner, *The Removal of the Courthouse from Brentsville to Manassas: Fraud or Sour Grapes*, Prince William County, undated-e.

The jail was notoriously problematic . . . Ronald Ray Turner, *Brentsville Jail Escape*, undated-a.

One of the less pleasant aspects of Brentsville's history . . . Prince William County, *The Underground Railroad Connection to Prince William County at Brentsville*, undated-c.

In 1833, a free black from Ohio named William Hyden . . . Bill Backus, "William Hyden," *Brentsville Neighbors*, March 2014.

In 1850, a slave named Agnes was hanged on the gallows . . . Ronald Ray Turner, *Commonwealth vs. Agnes*, undated-b.

Described as a white male laborer, Burgess was convicted of the murder of Charles Gollyhorn . . . *The Telescope*, August 13, 1825. Reprinted in Vols. 1–2, New York: William Burnett & Company, 1824, p. 44.

Jesse Fouks was a former slave . . . Andrew C. Banks, "A Shocking Death!" *Brentsville Neighbors*, April 2014, pp. 5–6.

As the nation girded for war . . . *Brentsville Courthouse and Jail, Prince William County*, waymarking.com, undated.

Confederate partisan units operated in Brentsville throughout the war . . . Prince William County, undated-a.

Despite the ravages of war, Brentsville limped on as the county seat during peace time . . . Prince William County, "Brentsville Historic Complex," YouTube, uploaded Jan. 10, 2011.

The first school for white children was formed in 1871 . . . Eugene M. Scheel, *Crossroads and Corners: A Tour of the Villages, Towns, and Post Offices of Prince William County, Virginia, Past and Present*, Prince William County, Va.: Historic Prince William Inc., 1996, p. 16.

A place of indeterminate origin . . . Kathleen Mulvaney and The Manassas Museum Association, *Manassas: A Place of Passages*, Charleston, S.C.: Acadia Publishing, 1999, p. 9.

The Manassas Gap ran the gamut of railroad involvement in the war . . . John Browne, "Manassas Gap Railroad," *The Story of Ravensworth*, undated.

. . . for the people's use once more . . . Dennis Droppa, "Piedmont Railroaders," *Norfolk Southern Railway* web page, 2002.

William Sanford Fewell laid out the first section of the future town of Manassas . . . "Who Remembers?" *Manassas Journal*, Nov. 7, 1935; U.S. National Register of Historic Places, National Park Service, National Register of Historic Places, Manassas Historic District registration, May 10, 1988.

A tract dated 1869 indicates the area was home to a school, churches, and two hotels . . . Mulvaney, 1999, p. 10.

He relocated his family there in early January . . . *Alexandria Gazette,* January 15, 1872.

He was warmly supported in convention by the county . . . *New York Herald,* October 8, 1872.

Betty had another daughter . . . U.S. Census, 1880.

It began with the struggle over the county seat . . . Turner, undated-e.

On March 12, 1872, the General Assembly issued a bill . . . *Acts and Joint Resolutions Passed by the General Assembly of the State of Virginia at its Session of 1871–72,* Richmond, Va.: R.F. Walker, Superintendent of Public Printing, 1872, pp. 219-221.

Greeley's candidacy did not begin with the Democrats . . . William Gillette, "Election of 1872," in Arthur Schlesinger, Jr., ed., *History of American Presidential Elections, 1789–2001,* Vol. IV, 1971, pp. 1305–1306.

A number of likely candidates had already dropped out . . . Gillette, 1971, pp. 1307–1309.

On the first ballot . . . Gillette, 1971, p. 1311.

"If there is one quality . . ." *Harper's Weekly,* May 18, 1872, reprinted in Arthur Schlesinger, Jr., ed., *History of American Presidential Elections, 1789–2001,* Vol. IV, 1971, p. 1356.

"This is the most preposterous. . ." George Templeton Strong, diary, quoted in Gillette, 1971, p. 1316.

Woodhull before the House Judiciary Committee . . . Myra, MacPherson, *The Scarlet Sisters: Sex, Suffrage, and Scandal in the Gilded Age,* New York: Twelve, 2014, pp. 64–65.

Woodhull nomination . . . MacPherson, 2014, pp. 163–173.

Courthouse vote . . . Turner, undated-d.

Republican convention . . . Gillette, 1971, p. 1320.

Democratic convention . . . Gillete, 1971, p. 1318.

Clark's departure . . . New York Herald, October 8, 1872.

Chapter Four: Manassas to Missouri— and Back

Elite women were still figuring out how to deal . . . Censer, 2003, p. 77.

Georgianna Weedon Hynson, his niece and an old friend of Fannie's family . . . "Fewell Trial Update," *The Bell Ringer*, June 2006.

"I did not feel that it was morally wrong. . ." Alexandria Gazette, Nov. 8, 1872.

The Rennert House . . . S. Arnold, "Business and Finance: Robert Rennert," *German Marylanders*, undated.

In 1885, the building was demolished . . . William Dunn, Master in Chancery of the Circuit Court for Baltimore City, "Clarence M. Mitchell, Jr. Courthouse," *Explore Baltimore Heritage*, undated.

The Dolley Varden . . . Natalie Ferguson, "A Brief History of the Dolly Varden Dress Craze," *A Frolic Through Time: Experiments in Period Dressmaking and, of Course, the Occasional Side Trip*, Saturday, August 23, 2008.

The Hotel Rennert . . . See Frances F. Beirne, *The Amiable Baltimoreans,* Baltimore, Md.: JHU Press, 1984; Jacques Kelly, "A Once-Grand Summer Resort," *Baltimore Sun,* July 9, 2010.

The Ringo House was a famous and fancy hotel . . . Joan Gilbert, "The Ringo and Tom Bass," *Saddle and Bridle*, undated.

Boyle's Hotel . . . William H. Boyd, *Boyd's Directory of the District of Columbia,* Washington, D.C., 1877.

Chapter Five: The Lawyer, on the Wrong Side of the Law

Edrington, a Civil War veteran who had been wounded in the same battle at Frayser's Farm. . . "Sgt Charles W. Edrington," findagrave.com, August 23, 2008.

The Exchange Hotel had been in operation before the war . . . John Hennessy, "The Exchange Hotel: Temporary Home for Escaped Slaves," *Fredericksburg Remembered*, September 3, 2010.

McElfresh had been part of President Lincoln's security detail in 1864 . . . *Evening Star*, Washington, D.C., July 02, 1881.

A trial was set for the following Monday, September 2 . . . *Alexandria Gazette*, August 29, 1872.

Brentsville was hardly a maximum-security facility . . . *Alexandria Gazette*, August 29, 1872; interviews with Brentsville historic site staff.

A cornshuck mattress may have been more comfortable than it sounds . . . E.A. Howland, *The New England Economical Housekeeper and Family Receipt Book*, Cincinnati: H.W. Derby, 1845, p. 51.

"I am here incarcerated." *Alexandria Gazette*, August 29, 1872.

"I am thoroughly convinced that Miss Fewell has been villainously treated, " *Alexandria Gazette*, August 29, 1872.

Thornton then grabbed Lucien . . . *Savannah* (Ga.) *Morning News*, September 4, 1872, p. 1.

Sheriff John T. Goodwin later printed a card . . . Reprinted in *Spirit of Jefferson*, Charles Town, Va., September 24, 1872.

The Civil War . . . *had led to marvelous advancements in health care* . . . F.W. Blaisdesll, "Medical Advances During the Civil War," *Archives of Surgery*, Vol. 123, No. 9, September 1988, pp. 1045–1050.

For starters, the bullet probably would have been located with certainty . . . Personal correspondence with Dr. Kim Toone, January 29, 2015.

With the benefit of modern medical knowledge . . . Correspondence with Dr. Toone.

"Clark is dead!" *Alexandria Gazette*, September 2, 1872.

"The parting with the corpse. . ." *Alexandria Gazette*, Sept. 5, 1872.

We do know that she never remarried . . . U.S. Census, 1880 and 1900; "Mary
    Elizabeth Lee Clark," findagrave.com, August 21, 2003; "Mary
    Elizabeth Lee" werelate.org, October 25, 2011.

Chapter Six: Legal Eagles

Fannie, confined to her room, had no idea James Clark was dead . . . *Evening Star*,
    Washington, D.C., October 02, 1872.

A soldier from Wisconsin . . . *slavery and freedom* . . . "April 1862:
    Correspondence of the *Sentinel;* Letter from Gen. McDowell's
    Army," *Second Wisconsin Volunteer Infantry*, undated.

Born in 1822, he was one of 11 children . . . Hunton, 1933, pp. 3–9.

*The vote in favor of secession at the convention was 88–55. The popular vote was
    128,884–32,134:* Dabney, 1971, pp. 292, 294.

Custer showed great generosity . . . Hunton, 1933, pp. 123–124.

Hunton's military medical history . . . Jack D. Welsh, *Medical Histories of
    Confederate Generals*, Kent State University Press, 1999, pp. 108–109.

"From 1865-1872, I had all the business I could attend to . . ." Hunton, 1933,
    p. 145.

*Notwithstanding the terrible condition of the country during this period of
    reconstruction* . . . Hunton, 1933, p. 150.

William Henry Fitzhugh Payne . . . Clement A. Evans, ed., *Confederate
    Military History*, Vol. III, Atlanta, Ga: Confederate Publishing
    Company, 1899, pp. 645–646.

The type of unit and the name were a topic of later conversation . . . Lewis Helm,
    Black Horse Cavalry: Defend Our Beloved Country, Higher Education
    Publications, 2004, p. 2.

During the subsequent Gettysburg Campaign . . . Stiles, 1985, p. 33.

The third member of the defense team was Henry Wirtz Thomas . . . *Bulletin of the
    Virginia State Library*, Vols. 13–14, 1920, p. 27.

Most of the residents above Cedar Run felt Lucien's actions were justified . . . Alexandria Gazette, September 7, 1872.

Newspapers around the country also varied in their judgments . . . Reprinted in the *Fredericksburg Ledger,* September 6, 1872.

"Never before have we so fully realized the full import of the words of King David . . ." Reprinted in the *Alexandria Gazette,* September 7, 1872.

Sinclair was from an established family . . . "The Infamous Fewell Trial—Part IV," *The Bell Ringer,* Vol. 1, No. 3, December 2005; "Judge Charles E Sinclair," findagrave.com, Oct 03, 2007.

. . . he nominated Eppa Hunton as brigadier general for the fifth militia . . . Journal of the House Delegates of the State of Virginia for the Session of 1855–56, Richmond, Va., 1856.

Brigham Young argued that Kinney was off base and would have "to take that back" . . . Quoted in Michael W. Homer, "The Judiciary and the Common Law in Utah Territory,1850-1861," *Dialogue: A Journal Of Mormon Thought,* 1988.

This, then, was the situation when Charles Sinclair arrived on the scene, along with Governor Alfred Cumming and fellow judges Delana R. Eccles and John Cradlebaugh in June 1858 . . . Homer, 1988.

Sinclair opened court at Salt Lake City in November 1858 . . . Orson F. Whitney, *History of Utah, Vol. I,* Salt Lake City, Utah: George Q. Cannon & Sons Co., 1892, pp. 689–710.

Sinclair responded harshly "and declared that he was now ready to do anything he could against both the church and people" . . . Homer, 1988.

While there are accounts of Sinclair being a drunk. . . Wilford Woodruff, Mormon apostle, journal entry, March 10, 1859, reprinted on *LDS Church History* blog, undated.

By October he was in California, boarding a steamer for Panama en route back to Washington . . . Daily Alta, San Francisco, California, October 22, 1859.

Midwestern newspapers questioned the judges "whining because legal process is not summary enough in Utah to suit their views" . . . Cincinnati Daily Press, Cincinnati, Ohio, March 23, 1860.

"In the general prostration of all professional pursuits. . ." Charles E. Sinclair, letter to Governor John Letcher, Prince William County papers transcripts, Prince William County Virginia website, October 28, 1861.

Sinclair's obituary credits him with working for the Confederate secret service . . . Alexandria Gazette, March 11, 1887.

In divorce papers filed by Lucy in 1867, she affirms they had not lived together for five years . . . Lucy B. Sinclair, divorce papers filed against Charles E. Sinclair, chancery papers.

On August 6, 1872, Judge Aylet Nicol appointed him to replace Jim as commonwealth's attorney . . . Alexandria Gazette, August 7, 1872.

Born in Drummondtown, Va., on December 3, 1806 . . . Craig M. Simpson, *A Good Southerner: The Life and Times of Henry Wise,* Chapel Hill, N.C.: Univ. of North Carolina Press, 1942.

"You may forgive us. . ." Joshua Lawrence Chamberlain, *The Passing of the Armies, An Account of the Final Campaign of the Army of the Potomac,* University of Nebraska Press, reprint, 1998, p. xiii.

"I am now free of responsibility for their care and comfort . . ." Simpson, 1942, p. 286.

Rounding out the prosecution was J.Y. Menifee . . . U.S. Census, 1880; Elisabeth B. & C.E. Johnson Jr., *Rappahannock County, Virginia: A History,* Walsworth Pub. Co., 1981, p. 45.

Lucien's time behind bars was reportedly taking a toll on his health . . . Evening Star, September 23, 1872; "The Infamous Fewell Trial—Part IV," 2005.

Chapter Seven: Arraigned and Elected

In 1865, Mary Harris, the 19-year-old daughter of Irish immigrants, traveled from Iowa to Washington, D.C. . . . Lee Chambers-Schiller, "Seduced, Betrayed, and Revenged," in Michael A. Bellesiles, ed., *Lethal Imagination: Violence and Brutality in American History,* New York: NYU Press, 1999, pp. 185–209.

William McKaig owned a prosperous iron operation in Cumberland, Md. . . . J. Thomas Scharf, *History of Western Maryland*, Baltimore: Regional Pub. Co., 1968, p. 423; Laura James, "The Famous Black-McKaig Trial," *CLEWS Your Home for Historic True Crime*, May 11, 2005.

Born March 11, 1822, Nicol had spent some time in Washington, D.C. . . . "Judge Aylett Nicol," findagrave.com, November 8, 2006; "The Infamous Fewell Trial—Part IV," 2005; U.S. Census, 1870.

He had also served together with James Clark on the Union Church board of trustees . . . U.S. Department of the Interior, National Register of Historic Places, Brentsville Historic District nomination, 1990.

It must also be noted that the concept of law and order in 1872 Virginia did not quite match modern perceptions of due process . . . Brett and Kate McKay, "Honor in the American South," *The Art of Manliness* blog, November 26, 2012.

For what has gone down in history as a relative non-event, the election of 1872 nonetheless had its fair share of nastiness and media backbiting . . . Gillette, 1971, pp. 1322–1323.

Those running the campaign did their homework, targeted the critical states of North Carolina, Maine, and Ohio, and hired 300 people to parse every word Greeley had ever published . . . Gillette, 1971, p. 1323.

While his output might be admirable, the results were not . . . James Parton, *The Life of Horace Greeley*, Houghton, Mifflin and Co., 1889, p. 552.

At the Yale commencement in July, Brown delivered a drunken tirade . . . Gillette, 1971, p. 1327.

A popular joke at the time revolved around a Brown gaffe from his 1870 campaign . . . Kenneth H. Winn, "Benjamin Gratz Brown," *Missouri Civil War Sesquicentennial* web page, undated.

"I am not dead but wish I were" . . . Quoted in Chip Bishop, *Lion and the Journalist: The Unlikely Friendship of Theodore Roosevelt and Joseph Bucklin Bishop*, Lanham, Md.: Rowman & Littlefield, Nov 8, 2011, p. 16.

Henry Ward Beecher, a renowned preacher and brother of abolitionist author Harriet Beecher Stowe . . . MacPherson, 2014, pp. 115, 185–186.

Chapter Eight: Opening Arguments

*Another possible reason for fewer attendees was something the papers at the time
referred to as the "horse disease," an outbreak of equine flu that was later
recognized as the Great Epizootic (animal epidemic) of 1872* . . . James
Law, *Equine Influenza Epidemic of 1872: Report of the U.S. Commissioner
of Agriculture for the year 1872*, 1873.

Chapter Nine: The Verdict

Over the weekend, the town of Boston suffered a devastating fire . . . "The
Rebuilding of Boston. One Year After the Great Fire. November
10, 1872 – November 10, 1873," reprinted on *Damrell's Fire*
website; "A Brief History of the Boston Fire Department," City of
Boston website, undated.

Isaac Ray was the leading forensic psychiatrist of the 1800s . . . U.S. National
Library of Medicine, "19th-Century Psychiatrists of Note," *Diseases
of the Mind: Highlights of American Psychiatry Through 1900*, updated
March 21, 2015.

*On November 24, 1868, Henry Rives Pollard, publisher and editor of the
Richmond, Va.,* Southern Opinion, *was shot* . . . Richard F. Hamm,
"A Good and Efficient Remedy for Libel," *Murder, Honor and Law:
Four Virginia Homicides from Reconstruction to the Great Depression*,
Charlottesville, Va.: University of Virginia Press, 2003, pp. 12–57.

*Almost exactly one year later, on November 25, 1869, Daniel McFarland walked
into the* New York Tribune *office and fatally shot Tribune editor Albert
Richardson* . . . Robert Wilhelm, "The Richardson-McFarland
Tragedy," *Murder by Gaslight* website, July 10, 2010.

Joseph Reid's place was a welcoming spot . . . *Manassas Journal*, April 27, 1910.

Epilogue: From Presidents to Pistol Johnnie

He would have received 66 electoral votes . . . "1872 Presidential Election Results," *Dave Leip's Atlas of U.S. Presidential Elections*, undated.

Woodhull and Claflin . . . MacPherson, 2014, passim.

The nation plunged into the financial Panic of 1873 . . . Charles Bracelen Flood, *Grant's Final Victory: Ulysses S. Grant's Heroic Last Year*, Boston: Da Capo Press, 2012, p. 76.

That year's Republican convention in Chicago . . . Leonard Dinnerstein, "Election of 1880," in Arthur Schlesinger, Jr., ed., *History of American Presidential Elections, 1789–2001*, Vol. IV, 1971, pp. 1494, 1496.

He went in on a project to build a railroad . . . William S. McFeeley, *Grant*, New York; W. W. Norton and Company, 2002, 486–489.

At the same time, his son was involved with some shady dealings . . . McFeeley, 2002, 488–494.

Desperate for funds, Grant wrote several articles on his Civil War campaigns . . . McFeeley, 2002, 494, 501–504.

Grant's memoir is an interesting read . . . Ulysses S. Grant, *Personal Memoirs of U. S. Grant*, New York: Charles L. Webster and Company, 1885–86.

Thousands of veterans marched with Grant's casket . . . "Grant's Funeral March," *American Experience*, undated.

The town of Manassas incorporated in 1873 . . . *Acts and Joint Resolutions Passed by the General Assembly of the State of Virginia at its Session of 1872–73*, Richmond, Va.: R.F. Walker, Superintendent of Public Printing, 1872.

An 1878 business license lists the senior Fewell as branching into commerce . . . Ronald Ray Turner, *Manassas Virginia 1870-1970 Businesses*, Prince William County, 2002a, p. 20.

Twenty years after the referendum that spelled James Clark's downfall, Manassas would finally wrest the title of county seat from Brentsville . . . "History," City of Manassas website, undated.

Brentsville had been built on a hill . . . Charles A. Grymes, "Railroad Cities," *Virginia Places*, undated.

Upon ceasing incarceration operations . . . Prince William County, "Jailhouse at Brentsville," *Historic Preservation*, undated.

The courthouse complex was featured on a 2009 episode of the SyFy channel's show Ghost Hunters . . . Keith Walker, " 'Ghost Hunters' Team Pays Visit to Brentsville," *Richmond Times Dispatch*, August 15, 2009; Hauntedplaces.org, "Brentsville Courthouse Historic Centre," web page, undated.

He and Elder Clark (who died in November 1882 after a short bout of paralysis, possibly from a stroke) were buried . . . *Spirit of Jefferson*, Charles Town, Va., November 14, 1882; Carolyn G. Lynn, "Master List of Quantico Cemeteries," undated; DiCicco, Mike, "Many of Quantico's Former Residents Remain Buried On Base," *Quantico Sentry*, Sept. 21, 2012; "Cedar Run Cemetery," undated; "Pvt. James F. Clark," findagrave.com, January 16, 2007.

Jim's older daughter, Laura, married a man named Jesse Stone . . . "Laura Lee Clark," werelate.org, October 25, 2011.

His younger daughter, Bertha, remained unwed . . . "Bertha Clark," werelate.org, October 27, 2011.

Caught up in a property dispute in 1876 . . . "Corruption in the Courts," History Engine: Tools for Collaborative Education and Research, University of Richmond, undated.

Nicol died on March 10, 1878 . . . "Judge Aylett Nicol," findagrave.com, November 8, 2006.

His son, Charles E. Nicol, followed in his footsteps . . . Paul Brandon Barringer, James Mercer Garnett, Rosewell Page, *University of Virginia: Its History, Influence, Equipment and Characteristics, with Biographical Sketches and Portraits of Founders, Benefactors, Officers and Alumni*, Vol. 2, New York: Lewis Publishing Co., 1904, p. 148.

Charles Sinclair, after stepping into Jim's spot as Commonwealth's Attorney, followed further in his footsteps a couple years later, assuming editorship of the Manassas Gazette . . . *Alexandria Gazette*, June 20, 1874.

He died of apoplexy . . . *Alexandria Gazette*, March 11, 1887; *New York Tribune*, March 12, 1887.

But after carefully cultivating a Republican reputation, he eventually soured on Grant, if not the party . . . Barton Haxall Wise, *The Life of Henry A. Wise of Virginia, 1806-1876*, Macmillan Company, 1899, p. 391.

Still, his sons John Sergeant Wise and Richard Alsop Wise both later affiliated with the Republican Party . . . Wise, 1899, passim.

Eppa Hunton continued the string of illustrious successes . . . Hunton, 1933, passim.

Eppa Hunton III also co-founded the notable Richmond law firm Hunton and Williams . . . Hunton, 1933, p. 232; Hunton and Williams; "About Us: History," undated; Richmond Legal Development Center, "Eppa Hunton VI," undated.

William Fitzhugh Payne, like his former partner, was also bitten by the politics bug . . . William Wirt Henry and Ainsworth Rand Spofford, *Eminent and Representative Men of Virginia and the District of Columbia in the Nineteenth Century*, Madison, Wis.: Brant and Fuller, 1893, pp. 549–550; Lynn Hopewell, *A Biographical Register of the Members of Fauquier County Virginia's Black Horse Cavalry, 1859-1865*, Warrenton, Va.: Black Horse Press, 2003, (unpublished), p. 18.

Henry Wirtz Thomas continued on the bench . . . Thomas William Herringshaw, ed., *Herringshaw's National Library of American Biography*, Vol. V, American Publishers' Association, 1914, p. 439.

His wife, Betty, died in 1900 . . . "Mary Elizabeth 'Bettie' Fewell Merchant," findagrave.com, December 5, 2006.

He lived out his days attending annual Confederate reunions . . . Toler, 2013, p. 34; Manassas Journal, March 21, 1913, reprinted in Morgan Breeden, *The Manassas Journal Reports of Deaths: Manassas, Virginia, 1911–1915*, Manassas, Va.: Bull Run Regional Library, November 2010, pp. 193–195.

In December 1873, he was back before the grand jury . . . Turner, 2004a, pp. 116–117.

But in July 1876, he was in jail again . . . Turner, 2004a, pp. 139–140.

In August, Lucien was on the other side of the law . . . Turner, 2004a, p. 142.

It's not until May 1877 that he's in the court records again . . . Turner, 2004a, p. 150.

In 1880, Sarah was living with her son Charles and his family . . . U.S. Census, 1880; New Mexico territorial census, 1885; interview with Mary Jane Zeltner, Fewell's great-granddaughter, June 4, 2015.

Alice Hyson recounts an 85-mile stage ride . . . Hyson, Alice, "Reminiscences of a Pioneer Plaza Missionary Who Went When a Young Girl to New Mexico," *Home Mission Monthly*, New York, Presbyterian Church in the U.S.A., Vol. 229, No. 1, November 1914, p. 8.

But by 1886, Lucien was facing another murder rap . . . New Mexico Supreme Court, "Territory V. Fewell," *Reports of Cases Determined in the Supreme Court of the Territory of New Mexico,* Vol. 5, New Mexican Printing Company, 1896, pp. 34–44.

Frank Bond, a prominent New Mexico entrepreneur, said the story ended this way . . . Frank Bond, "Memoirs of Forty Years in New Mexico," 1929, reprinted in Frank D. Reeve and Paul A. F. Walter, eds., *Historical Review, New Mexico,* Vol. 21, 1946, pp. 343–344.

A longer and even more fantastical version of this tale . . . Allen Kelly, "Juanita's Elopement," *Recreation*, American Canoe Association, Vol. 22, No. 1, 1905, pp. 295–301.

In 1900, he was working as a carpenter in Raton, New Mexico . . . U.S. Census, 1900.

Family legend has it that he died when he was trampled . . . Interview with Mary Jane Zeltner, June 4, 2015.

For all her distress at the time of the trial, she was married two years later . . . Ancestry.com. *District of Columbia, Select Marriages, 1830–1921* [database on-line]. Provo, Utah: Ancestry.com Operations, Inc, 2014.

James Trimmer appears to have suffered from nervous exhaustion . . . *Washington Herald*, November 11, 1909.

A coroner's jury declared his death was the result of pneumonia and broken ribs . . . Evening Star, November 15, 1909.

Fannie died five years later, on Aug. 31, 1914 . . . Manassas Democrat, September 3, 1914, reprinted in Ronald Ray Turner, *Prince William County Virginia: 1900–1930 Obituaries*, Prince William County, 1996, p. 362.

Bibliography

"1872 Presidential Election Results," *Dave Leip's Atlas of U.S. Presidential Elections*, undated. Retrieved June 6, 2015: http://uselectionatlas.org/RESULTS/national.php?year=1872

Acts and Joint Resolutions Passed by the General Assembly of the State of Virginia at its Session of 1871–72, Richmond, Va.: R.F. Walker, Superintendent of Public Printing, 1872.

Acts and Joint Resolutions Passed by the General Assembly of the State of Virginia at its Session of 1872–73, Richmond, Va.: R.F. Walker, Superintendent of Public Printing, 1872.

Albuquerque Daily Citizen, Albuquerque, N.M., 1900

Albuquerque Weekly Citizen, Albuquerque, N.M., 1891

Alexandria Gazette, Alexandria, Va., 1870–1872.

"Ancestors and Family History of Kevin James Devine and Etoye D. Johnson," Ancestry.com, undated. Retrieved May 21, 2015: http://freepages.genealogy.rootsweb.ancestry.com/~devinejohnsonfamhist/pafg49.htm

Arnold, S., "Business and Finance: Robert Rennert," *German Marylanders*, undated. Retrieved May 23, 2015: http://www.germanmarylanders.org/profile-index/business-finance

"April 1862: Correspondence of the *Sentinel;* Letter from Gen. McDowell's Army," *Second Wisconsin Volunteer Infantry*, undated. Retrieved May 24, 2015: http://www.secondwi.com/fromthefront/6th%20wis/1862/april_1862.htm

Backus, Bill, "William Hyden," *Brentsville Neighbors*, March 2014. Retrieved May 22, 2015: http://www.historicprincewilliam.org/brentsvilleneighbors/102_March_2014.pdf

Banks, Andrew C., "A Shocking Death!" *Brentsville Neighbors*, April 2014. Retrieved May 22, 2012: http://www.historicprincewilliam.org/brentsvilleneighbors/079%20April%202012.pdf

Barringer, Paul Brandon, James Mercer Garnett, Rosewell Page, *University of Virginia: Its History, Influence, Equipment and Characteristics, with Biographical Sketches and Portraits of Founders, Benefactors, Officers and Alumni*, Vol. 2, New York: Lewis Publishing Co., 1904, p. 148.

Beirne, Frances F., *The Amiable Baltimoreans*, Baltimore, Md.: JHU Press, 1984.

Belmont Chronicle, St. Clairsville, Ohio, 1881.

Bishop, Chip, *Lion and the Journalist: The Unlikely Friendship of Theodore Roosevelt and Joseph Bucklin Bishop*, Lanham, Md.: Rowman & Littlefield, Nov 8, 2011, p. 16.

Blaisdell, F.W., "Medical Advances During the Civil War," *Archives of Surgery*, Vol. 123, No. 9, September 1988, pp. 1045–1050.

Bond, Frank, "Memoirs of Forty Years in New Mexico," 1929, reprinted in *Historical Review, New Mexico*, Frank D. Reeve and Paul A. F. Walter, eds., Vol. 21, 1946.

Boston Chamber of Commerce, *The Boston Fire*, 1922.

Boyd, William H., *Boyd's Directory of the District of Columbia*, Washington, D.C., 1877. Retrieved May 24, 2015: http://archive.org/stream/boydsdirectoryof1877wash/boydsdirec toryof1877wash_djvu.txt

Breeden, Morgan, *The Manassas Journal Reports of Deaths: Manassas, Virginia, 1911–1915,* Manassas, Va.: Bull Run Regional Library, November 2010.

Brentsville Courthouse and Jail, Prince William County, waymarking.com, undated. Retrieved May 22, 2015: http://www.waymarking.com/waymarks/WMET78_Brentsville_ Courthouse_and_Jail_Prince_William_County_VA

"A Brief History of the Boston Fire Department," City of Boston website, undated. Retrieved May 25, 2015: http://www.cityofboston.gov/fire/about/history.asp

Bristol News, Bristol, Va., and Tenn., Sept. 10, 1872.

Browne, John, "Manassas Gap Railroad," *The Story of Ravensworth* website, undated. Retrieved September 15, 2014: http://ravensworthstory.org/landmarks/manassas-gap-rr/

Bulletin of the Virginia State Library: A List of the Portraits and Pieces of Statuary in the Virginia State Library, Richmond, Va.: Davis Bottom, Superintendent of Public Printing, 1920.

Cauble, Frank P., *Biography of Wilmer McLean, May 3, 1814-June 5, 1882*, Lynchburg, Virginia: H.E. Howard, 1987.

"Cedar Run Cemetery" *Stafford County Cemeteries and Churches* website, undated. Retrieved May 27, 2015: http://www.rootsweb.ancestry.com/~vastaffo/cemeteries/cedarr uncem.htm

Chamberlain, Joshua Lawrence. *The Passing of the Armies, An Account of the Final Campaign of the Army of the Potomac*, University of Nebraska Press, reprint, 1998.

Chambers-Schiller, Lee, "Seduced, Betrayed, and Revenged," in Michael A. Bellesiles, ed., *Lethal Imagination: Violence and Brutality in American History*, New York: NYU Press, 1999, pp. 185–209.

Chancery Records Index, Library of Virginia, Lucien Fewell & Wife vs. James R. Brawner et al., 1871. Retrieved May 21, 2015: http://www.lva.virginia.gov/chancery/case_detail.asp?CFN=153-1871-001

Chandler, Julian A.C., *The History of Suffrage in Virginia,* Baltimore, Md.: Johns Hopkins Press, 1901.

"Charles Edwin Brawner, Fan of Manassas Winters," *Brawner Bulletin,* family newsletter, Summer 1997, p. 3. Retrieved October 3, 2014: http://www.oocities.org/heartland/prairie/6614/collections/bblt n24.pdf

Charlotte Democrat, Charlotte, N.C., 1872.

Censer, Jane Turner, *The Reconstruction of White Southern Womanhood, 1865–1895*, Baton Rouge, La.: Louisiana State University Press, 2003.

Cincinnati Daily Press, Cincinnati, Ohio, March 23, 1860.

"Clark, James F., Co. A," Fourth Virginia Cavalry, muster roll, 1861–1865. Retrieved (subscription only) September 19, 2014: http://www.fold3.com/image/8120404/

Clark, John, "Discourse of Elder John Clark, upon the Subject of 'The Relation of Master and Servant,'" *The Primitive Baptist,* August 25, 1860.

————, "The Regeneration of the Soul," in *Exposure of Heresies Propagated by Some Old School Baptists*, undated. Retrieved May 27, 2015: http://www.primitivebaptist.org/index.php?option=com_content &task=view&id=1464&Itemid=36

Confederate Controllers Office, descriptive list and account of pay and clothing, November 9, 1862. Retrieved (subscription only) September 19, 2014: http://www.fold3.com/image/11640494/

Confederate States Auditor for the War Department, register of claims of deceased officers and soldiers from Virginia which were filed for settlement, January 19, 1863. Retrieved (subscription only) September 19, 2014: http://www.fold3.com/image/11640472/

Confederated Southern Memorial Association, *History of the Confederated Memorial Associations of the South*, New Orleans, La.: Graham Press, 1904. Retrieved June 7, 2014: http://books.google.com/books?id=TBFCAAAAIAAJ

Congressional Serial Set, *The Miscellaneous Documents of the House of Representatives for the First Session of the Forty-Second Congress*, Washington, D.C.: U.S. Government Printing Office, 1871.

Dabney, Virginius, *Virginia: The New Dominion, A History from 1607 to the Present*, New York: Doubleday and Company, 1971.

Daily Alta, California October 22, 1859.

Davis, Varina, *Jefferson Davis: Ex-President of the Confederate States of America, A Memoir by his Wife*, Vol. 1.

Deseret News, November 2, 1859.

DiCicco, Mike, "Many of Quantico's Former Residents Remain Buried On Base," *Quantico Sentry*, Sept. 21, 2012. Retrieved June 7, 2014: http://www.quanticosentryonline.com/news/article_f266d825-50d1-5ceb-a127-791b0c1bd2d2.html

Dinnerstein, Leonard, "Election of 1880," in Arthur Schlesinger, Jr., ed., *History of American Presidential Elections, 1789–2001*, Vol. IV, 1971.

District of Columbia, Select Marriages, 1830-1921, Ancestry.com, undated. Retrieved May 21, 2015: http://search.ancestry.com/cgi-bin/sse.dll?db=FS1DCMarriages&h=403226&indiv=try&o_vc=Record:OtherRecord&rhSource=60214

Droppa, Dennis, Piedmont Railroaders, *Norfolk Southern Railway* web page, 2002. Retrieved September 15, 2014: http://www.trainweb.org/PiedmontRR/railhst1.html

Dunn, William, Master in Chancery of the Circuit Court for Baltimore City, "Clarence M. Mitchell, Jr. Courthouse," *Explore Baltimore Heritage*, undated. Retrieved May 24, 2015: http://explore.baltimoreheritage.org/items/show/215

Evans, Clement A., ed., *Confederate Military History*, Vol. III, Atlanta, Ga: Confederate Publishing Company, 1899, pp. 645–646.

Evening Star, Washington, D.C., 1860, 1872.

Ferguson, Natalie, "A Brief History of the Dolly Varden Dress Craze," *A Frolic Through Time: Experiments in Period Dressmaking and, of Course, the Occasional Side Trip*, Saturday, August 23, 2008. Retrieved May 24, 2015: http://zipzipinkspot.blogspot.com/2008/08/brief-history-of-dolly-varden-dress.html

"Fewell, L.N., Co. H," 17th Virginia Infantry, muster rolls, 1862. Retrieved (subscription only) September 19, 2014: http://www.fold3.com/image/11640407/

"Fewell Trial Update," *The Bell Ringer*, June 2006. Retrieved May 23, 2015: http://nps-vip.net/Brentsville/newsletters/2006-06-BellRinger.pdf

"Fewell, W.H., Co. H," 17th Virginia Infantry, muster rolls, 1862. Retrieved (subscription only) September 19, 2014: http://www.fold3.com/image/11640463/

Fletcher, Carlton, "Manuel C. Causten, Prisoner of War," *Glover Park History* website, undated. Retrieved May 10, 2015: http://gloverparkhistory.com/estates-and-farms/weston/prisoner-of-war/

Flood, Charles Bracelen, *Grant's Final Victory: Ulysses S. Grant's Heroic Last Year*, Boston: Da Capo Press, 2012.

Foster, Feather Schwartz, "The Sons of Jefferson Davis," *Presidential History Blog*, May 1, 2014. Retrieved May 21, 2015: https://featherfoster.wordpress.com/2014/05/01/the-sons-of-jefferson-davis/

Fredericksburg Ledger, Fredericksburg, Va, 1868–1872.

Gilbert, Joan, "The Ringo and Tom Bass," *Saddle and Bridle*, undated. Accessed July 3, 2014: http://www.artbycrane.com/equinearticles/horsehistory/ringoandtombass.html

Gillette, William, "Election of 1872," in Arthur Schlesinger, Jr., ed., *History of American Presidential Elections, 1789–2001*, Vol. IV, 1971.

Goldsmith, Barbara, *Other Powers: The Age of Suffrage, Spiritualism, and the Scandalous Victoria Woodhull*, New York: Alfred A. Knopf, 1998, pp. 55, 58.

Grant, Ulysses S., *Personal Memoirs of U. S. Grant*, New York: Charles L. Webster and Company, 1885–86.

"Grant's Funeral March," *American Experience*, undated. Retrieved June 6, 2015:
http://www.pbs.org/wgbh/americanexperience/features/general-article/grant-funeral/

Hamm, Richard F., *Murder, Honor and Law: Four Virginia Homicides from Reconstruction to the Great Depression*, Charlottesville, Va.: University of Virginia Press, 2003.

Hauntedplaces.org, "Brentsville Courthouse Historic Centre," web page, undated.
http://www.hauntedplaces.org/item/brentsville-courthouse-historic-centre/

Headquarters Department of Virginia, Parole of Honor for James F. Clark, April 28, 1865. Retrieved (subscription only) September 19, 2014: http://www.fold3.com/image/8120440/

Heinemann, Ronald L., John G. Kolp, Anthony S Parent, Jr., William G. Shade, *Old Dominion, New Commonwealth: A History of Virginia, 1607–2007*, Charlottesville, Va.: University of Virginia Press, 2007.

Helm, Lewis, *Black Horse Cavalry: Defend Our Beloved Country*, Higher Education Publications, 2004.

Hennessy, John, "The Exchange Hotel: Temporary Home for Escaped Slaves," *Fredericksburg Remembered*, September 3, 2010. Retrieved May 24, 2015:
https://fredericksburghistory.wordpress.com/2010/09/03/the-exchange-hotel-temporary-home-for-escaped-slaves/

Henry, Alfred Judson, *Recent Practice in the Erection of Lightning Conductors*, Washington D.C.: Weather Bureau, 1906.

Henry, William Wirt, and Ainsworth Rand Spofford, *Eminent and Representative Men of Virginia and the District of Columbia in the Nineteenth Century*, Madison, Wis.: Brant and Fuller, 1893.

Herringshaw, Thomas William, ed., *Herringshaw's National Library of American Biography*, Vol. V, American Publishers' Association, 1914.

"History," City of Manassas website, undated. Retrieved June 6, 2015: http://www.manassascity.org/DocumentCenter/Home/View/3907

Homans, Benjamin, *The United States Railroad Directory for 1856*, New York: B. Homans, 1856.

Homer, Michael W., "The Judiciary and the Common Law in Utah Territory,1850-1861," *Dialogue : A Journal of Mormon Thought*, 1988. Retrieved December 26, 2014: http://66.147.244.190/~dialogu5/wp-content/uploads/sbi/articles/Dialogue_V21N01_99.pdf

Hopewell, Lynn, *A Biographical Register of the Members of Fauquier County Virginia's Black Horse Cavalry, 1859-1865*, Warrenton, Va.: Black Horse Press, 2003, (unpublished), p. 18. Retrieved June 6, 2015: http://blackhorsecavalry.org/files/roster%20august%202002%20special.pdf

Howland, E.A., *The New England Economical Housekeeper and Family Receipt Book*, Cincinnati: H.W. Derby, 1845, p. 51.

Hunton, Eppa, *Autobiography of Eppa Hunton*, Richmond Va.: William Byrd Press, 1933.

Hunton and Williams; "About Us: History," undated. Retrieved June 6, 2015: https://www.hunton.com/history/

Hyson, Alice, "Reminiscences of a Pioneer Plaza Missionary Who Went When a Young Girl to New Mexico," *Home Mission Monthly*, New York, Presbyterian Church in the U.S.A., Vol. 229, No., 1, November 1914.

"The Infamous Fewell Trial—Part IV," *The Bell Ringer*, Vol. 1, No. 3, December 2005.

James, Laura, "The Famous Black-McKaig Trial," *CLEWS Your Home for Historic True Crime*, May 11, 2005. Retrieved May 25, 2015: http://laurajames.typepad.com/clews/2005/05/the_famous_blac.html

Janney, Caroline L., *Burying the Dead but Not the Past: Ladies' Memorial Associations and the Lost Cause (Civil War America)*, University of North Carolina Press, 2008.

Johnson, Elisabeth B., and C.E. Johnson Jr., *Rappahannock County, Virginia: A History*, Walsworth Pub. Co., 1981, p. 45.

Jones, Terry L., "The Beast in the Big Easy," *New York Times*, May 18, 2012.

Journal of the House Delegates of the State of Virginia for the Session of 1855–56, Richmond, Va., 1856.

Journal of the Senate of the Commonwealth of Virginia, Richmond, Va.: R.F. Walker, Superintendent Public Printing, 1875

"Judge Aylett Nicol," findagrave.com, November 8, 2006. Retrieved May 25, 2015: http://www.findagrave.com/cgi-bin/fg.cgi?page=gr&GRid=16550893

"Judge Charles E Sinclair," findagrave.com, October 03, 2007. Retrieved May 24, 2015: http://www.findagrave.com/cgi-bin/fg.cgi?page=gr&GRid=21943825

Kelly, Allen, "Juanita's Elopement," *Recreation*, American Canoe Association, Vol. 22, No. 1, 1905, pp. 295–301.

Kelly, Jacques, "A Once-Grand Summer Resort," *Baltimore Sun,* July 9, 2010.

Kenzer, Robert, "The Uncertainty of Life: A Profile of Virginia's *Civil War Widows*," in Joan E. Cashin, *The War Was You and Me: Civilians in the American Civil War*. Princeton, N.J.: Princeton University Press, 2002.

Kneebone, John T., "Ku Klux Klan in Virginia," *Encyclopedia Virginia*, website, April 21, 2015. Retrieved May 10, 2015: http://www.encyclopediavirginia.org/Ku_Klux_Klan_in_Virginia #its1

Kosch, James R., *White Oak Primitive Baptist Church: Established 1789: History of White Oak Primitive Baptist Church, 1789-1989*, Culpeper, Va.: J.E. Alderton, 1989.

Laubach, David Charles, *American Baptist Home Mission Roots, 1824–2010*, Valley Forge, Pa.: American Baptist Home Mission Societies, 2010, p. 4. Retrieved May 10, 2015: http://www.abhms.org/docs/Roots%20booklet.pdf

"Laura Lee Clark," werelate.org, October 25, 2011. Retrieved May 27, 2015: http://www.werelate.org/wiki/Person:Laura_Clark_%2818%29

Law, James, *Equine Influenza Epidemic of 1872: Report of the U.S. Commissioner of Agriculture for the year 1872*, 1873. Retrieved May 25, 2015: http://en.wikisource.org/wiki/Equine_Influenza_Epidemic_of_1 872

Lee, Caroline Jackson, family tree, ancestry.com. Retrieved June 7, 2014: http://bit.ly/29CgYiz

"Letter from Utah," New York Times, January 15, 1859. Retrieved December 20, 2014: http://cdm15999.contentdm.oclc.org/cdm/singleitem/collection/ 19CMNI/id/10085/rec/12

Library of VA, *Literary Fund Letter Book, August 6, 1838–December 6, 1842*, SAI 29

Library of Virginia, *Reconstruction*, web page, undated. Retrieved May 20, 2015: http://www.lva.virginia.gov/public/guides/Civil-War/Reconstruction.htm

Lynn, Carolyn G., "Master List of Quantico Cemeteries," undated. Retrieved June 6, 2015: http://files.usgwarchives.net/va/princewilliam/cemeteries/quantico.txt

MacPherson, Myra, *The Scarlet Sisters: Sex, Suffrage, and Scandal in the Gilded Age*, New York: Twelve, 2014.

Manassas City Cemetery, Manassas Va.: Prince William County Genealogical Society, 1990. Retrieved May 10, 2015: http://eservice.pwcgov.org/library/digitallibrary/PDF/The%20Manassas%20City%20Cemetery.pdf

Manassas Gazette, 1869–1872.

Manassas Journal, 1910.

"Mary Elizabeth 'Bettie' Fewell Merchant," findagrave.com, December 5, 2006. Retrieved June 6, 2015: http://www.findagrave.com/cgi-bin/fg.cgi?page=gr&GRid=16918833

"Mary Elizabeth Lee" werelate.org, October 25, 2011. Retrieved May 26, 2015: http://www.werelate.org/wiki/Person:Marry_Lee_%281%29

"Mary Elizabeth Lee Clark," findagrave.com, August 21, 2003. Retrieved May 26, 2015: http://www.findagrave.com/cgi-bin/fg.cgi?page=gr&GScid=1297722&GRid=7782872&

Mathis, James R., *The Making of the Primitive Baptists: A Cultural and Intellectual History of the Antimission Movement, 1800–1840*, New York: Routledge, 2004.

Maurer, David, "Torrential Rains are Measured by the Flood of 1870," *Daily Progress*, Dec. 1, 1991.

McFeeley, William S., *Grant*, New York; W. W. Norton and Company, 2002.

McKay, Brett, and Kate McKay, "Honor in the American South," *The Art of Manliness* blog, November 26, 2012. Retrieved May 25, 2015: http://www.artofmanliness.com/2012/11/26/manly-honor-part-v-honor-in-the-american-south/

Melville, Herman, "The Lightning Rod Man," originally in *Putnam's Monthly Magazine*, August 1854. Retrieved May 21, 2015: http://www.melville.org/lrman.htm

Mohun, Arwen, "Lightning Rods and the Commodification of Risk in Nineteenth Century America," in *Playing With Fire: Histories of the Lightning Rod*, Peter Heering, Oliver Hochadel, and David J. Rhees, eds., Philadelphia, Pa.: American Philosophical Society for its *Transactions* series, Vol. 99, 2009, pp. 167–180.

Mulvaney, Kathleen, and The Manassas Museum Association, *Manassas: A Place of Passages*, Charleston, S.C.: Acadia Publishing, 1999.

Musselman, Homer, "Civil War Veterans," *Stafford County Military Information*, website, Feb. 7, 2001. Retrieved June 7, 2014: http://www.rootsweb.ancestry.com/~vastaffo/military/civilwarvets.htm

National Daily Republican, Washington, D.C. 1872

National Park Service, "Civil War," *Prince William Forest*, web page, undated-a. Retrieved May 22, 2015: http://www.nps.gov/prwi/learn/historyculture/civil-war.htm

New Mexico Supreme Court, "Territory V. Fewell," *Reports of Cases Determined in the Supreme Court of the Territory of New Mexico*, Vol. 5, New Mexican Printing Company, 1896, pp. 34–44.

New Mexico Territorial Census, 1885.

New York Herald, 1872.

New York Sun, 1872, 1894.

New York Times, 1872.

Parton, James, *The Life of Horace Greeley*, Houghton, Mifflin and Co., 1889.

Pastore, Vera, "White Oak Primitive Baptist: Noted for Its Artistic Lines and Rich History," *Free Lance-Star*, Stafford, Va., March 10, 1994.

Phin, John, *Plain Directions for the Construction and Erection of Lightning-Rods*, New York: Handicraft Publication Company, 1871. Retrieved October 9, 2014:
http://books.google.com/books?id=eutIAAAAIAAJ

Pierson, J. Fred, *Ramapo to Chancellorsville and Beyond*, Richmond, Va.: A. Scott, 2002.

Pittman, R.H., *Biographical History of Primitive or Old-School Baptist Ministers of the United States; Including a Brief Treatise on the Subject of Deacons, Their Duties, Etc., With Some Personal Mention of These Offices*, Anderson, Ind.: Herald Printing Co., 1909.

Political Arena, Fredericksburg, Va., 1828.

Poulin, Jeffrey M., "A Brief History of the Manassas and Confederate Cemeteries," in *Manassas City Cemetery*, Manassas Va.: Prince William County Genealogical Society, 1990. Retrieved May 10, 2015:
http://eservice.pwcgov.org/library/digitallibrary/PDF/The%20M anassas%20City%20Cemetery.pdf

"Primitive Baptists," *About Religion* website, undated. Retrieved May 10, 2015:
http://christianity.about.com/od/Primitive-Baptist/a/Primitive-Baptists.htm

Prince William County, *Will Book L.*, p. 90-91.

Prince William County, *Brentsville Courthouse Historic Centre*, undated-a. Retrieved May 21, 2015:
http://www.pwcgov.org/government/dept/publicworks/hp/Pag es/Brentsville-Courthouse-Historic-Centre.aspx

———, "Jailhouse at Brentsville," *Historic Preservation*, undated-b. Retrieved June 6, 2015:
http://www.pwcgov.org/government/dept/publicworks/hp/Pag es/Jailhouse-at-Brentsville.aspx

————, *The Underground Railroad Connection to Prince William County at Brentsville,* undated-c. Retrieved May 22, 2015: http://www.pwcgov.org/government/dept/publicworks/hp/Pag es/Brentsville-Link-to-the-Underground-Railroad.aspx

————, "Brentsville Historic Complex," YouTube, uploaded Jan. 10, 2011. Retrieved May 22, 2015: https://www.youtube.com/watch?v=baXazCOiXPY

Putnam, Mary Burnham, *The Baptists and Slavery: 1840–1845*, Ann Arbor, Mich.: George Wahr, 1913.

Railroad Job Descriptions, website, May 28, 2000. Retrieved May 21, 2015: http://www.usgennet.org/usa/ne/topic/railroads/job.html

Raleigh News, March 28, 1872.

"The Rebuilding of Boston. One Year After the Great Fire. November 10, 1872 – November 10, 1873," reprinted on *Damrell's Fire* website. Retrieved May 25, 2015: http://www.damrellsfire.com/article_BMJ_1_year_later.html

Reid, Christian (Frances Christine Fisher), *Mabel Lee*, Appleton, 1870.

Richmond Daily Enquirer & Examiner, Richmond, Va., 1864, 1868.

Richmond Legal Development Center, "Eppa Hunton VI," undated. Retrieved June 6, 2015: http://www.rldclaw.org/eppa-hunton-vi/

Round, George Carr, Commonwealth's Attorney for Prince William County, Virginia, letter to the House Reconstruction Committee, September 13, 1869.

————, remarks made before the House Reconstruction Committee, December 18, 1869.

————, letter to the editor, *Alexandria Daily State Journal,* September 11, 1872.

Ryland, Garnett, *The Baptists of Virginia, 1699–1926*, Richmond, Va.: Virginia Baptist Board of Missions and Education, 1955.

Savage, Lon, "Local Spas Cured Ailments Galore," *A Guide to Historic Salem,* Vol. 4, No. 2, 1998. Retrieved May 27, 2015: http://www.salemmuseum.org/guide_archives/HSV4N2.aspx

Savannah (Ga.) *Morning News*, September 4, 1872, p. 1. Retrieved May 24, 2015: http://newspapers-pdf.galileo.usg.edu/smn/smn1872/smn1872-0855.pdf

Scharf, J. Thomas, *History of Western Maryland*, Baltimore: Regional Pub. Co., 1968, p. 423.

Eugene M. Scheel, *Crossroads and Corners: A Tour of the Villages, Towns, and Post Offices of Prince William County, Virginia, Past and Present*, Prince William County, Va.: Historic Prince William Inc., 1996

Schlesinger, Arthur, Jr., ed., *History of American Presidential Elections, 1789–2001*, Vol. IV, 1971.

Scully, Jane, "The Life and Times of the Manassas Gap Railroad," *Fairfax County, Virginia* web page, undated. Retrieved September 14, 2014: http://www.fairfaxcounty.gov/parks/resource-management/archives/manassagap.htm

Sears, Stephen W., *To The Gates of Richmond: The Peninsula Campaign*, New York: Houghton Mifflin Harcourt, 2001.

"Sgt Charles W. Edrington," findagrave.com, August 23, 2008. Retrieved May 24, 2015: http://www.findagrave.com/cgi-bin/fg.cgi?page=gr&GSvcid=223366&GRid=29251548&

Siegel, Charles, *The Orange & Alexandria Railroad*, 2002–2012. Retrieved June 7, 2014: http://www.nvcc.edu/home/csiegel/

Simpson, Craig M., *A Good Southerner: The Life and Times of Henry Wise*, Chapel Hill, N.C.: Univ. of North Carolina Press, 1942.

Sinclair Charles, E., letter to Governor John Letcher, Prince William County papers transcripts, Prince William County Virginia website, October 28, 1861. Retrieved December 20, 2014: http://www.pwcvirginia.com/documents/GovernorJohnLetcher2 .pdf

Sinclair, Lucy B., divorce papers filed against Charles E. Sinclair, chancery papers. Retrieved December 20, 2014: http://www.lva.virginia.gov/chancery/full_case_detail.asp?CFN= 047-1867-018#img

Smoot, W.M., *Reminiscences of the Baptists of Virginia*, Occoquan, Va.: printed at Office of Sectarian, 1902.

Sparks, Hoyt D.F., *Primitive Baptist History*, Hoyt Sparks, 2014.

Spirit of Jefferson, Charles Town, Va., September 24, 1872.

Stewart, Peter C., *Early Professional Baseball in Hampton Roads: A History, 1884-1928*, North Carolina: McFarland, 2010.

Stiles, Kenneth L., *4th Virginia Cavalry*, The Virginia Regimental Histories Series, 2nd ed., Lynchburg, Va.: H.E. Howard, 1985.

Stoddard, Henry Luther, Horace Greeley: Printer, Editor, Crusader, G. P. Putnam's Sons, 1946, pp. 231–234.

Sweet, William Warren, *Religion on the American Frontier: Baptists, 1783–1830,* Henry Holt Publishers, 1931.

The Telescope, August 13, 1825. Reprinted in Vols. 1–2, New York: William Burnett & Company, 1824, p. 44; Retrieved May 22, 2015: http://bit.ly/29bbWZx

Thurman family website, undated. Retrieved May 10, 2015: http://www.afrigeneas.com/slavedata/Thurman-VA-1817.txt

Toler, John T., "From Captor to Prisoner: Lt. Ben Merchant, CSA, Was One of the 'Immortal 600,'" *Warrenton Lifestyle Magazine*, February 2013, pp. 28–34. Retrieved September 15, 2014: http://interactivepdf.uniflip.com/2/25656/293416/pub/

Townsend, Jan, *The Civil War in Prince William County*, Prince William County, Va.: Prince William County Historical Commission, 2011.

Turner, Ronald Ray, *Brentsville Jail Escape*, undated-a. Retrieved May 22, 2015:
http://www.pwcvirginia.com/documents/BrentsvilleJailEscape.pdf

———, *Commonwealth vs. Agnes*, undated-b. Retrieved May 22, 2015: http://www.pwcvirginia.com/documents/AGNES.pdf

———, *L.N. Fewell*, undated-c. Retrieved May 21, 2015: http://www.pwcvirginia.com/documents/F.N.Fewell.pdf

———, *Prince William County Virginia: Clerk's Loose Papers, Volume VII, Selected Transcripts 1833-1938*, Prince William County, undated-d.

———, *The Removal of the Courthouse from Brentsville to Manassas: Fraud or Sour Grapes*, Prince William County, undated-e. Retrieved May 22, 2015:
http://www.pwcvirginia.com/documents/BrentsvilleCourthouseremoval.pdf

———, *Prince William County Virginia: 1900–1930 Obituaries*, Prince William County, 1996.

———, *Manassas Virginia 1870-1970 Businesses*, Prince William County, 2002a.

———, *Prince William County Virginia: Marriages, 1854–1938*, Prince William County, 2002b.

———, *Prince William County Virginia: Clerk's Loose Papers, Vol. III: Selected Transcripts 1804–1899, Indictments, Juries, and Trials*, Prince William County, 2004a.

———, *Prince William County Virginia: Clerk's Loose Papers, Volume IV, Selected Transcripts 1811-1899, Miscellaneous Records*, Prince William County, 2004b.

———, *Prince William County Virginia: Clerk's Loose Papers, Volume VII, Selected Transcripts*, Prince William County, 2006a.

———, *Prince William County Virginia: Clerk's Loose Papers, Volume VIII, Selected Transcripts*, Prince William County, 2006b.

————, *Prince William County Virginia: Clerk's Loose Papers, Volume VIII, Selected Transcripts,* Prince William County, 2006c.

Ulman, H. Charles, *Lawyers' Record and Official Register of the United States,* New York: A.S. Barnes and Co., 1872, p. 984. Retrieved December 20, 2014: https://play.google.com/books/reader?id=54wzAQAAMAAJ&pr intsec=frontcover&output=reader&authuser=0&hl=en&pg=GBS .PA1

U.S. Census, 1810, 1850, 1860, 1870, 1880, 1900.

U.S. National Library of Medicine, "19th-Century Psychiatrists of Note," *Diseases of the Mind: Highlights of American Psychiatry Through 1900,* updated March 21, 2015. Retrieved June 15, 2015: http://www.nlm.nih.gov/hmd/diseases/note.html

U.S. National Register of Historic Places, National Park Service, *Soldiers and Sailors Database,* undated. Retrieved September 15, 2014: http://bit.ly/29ambN0

U.S. National Register of Historic Places, National Park Service, National Register of Historic Places, Manassas Historic District registration, May 10, 1988. Retrieved May 22, 2015: http://www.dhr.virginia.gov/registers/cities/manassas/155-0161_manassas_hd_1988_final_nomination.pdf

U.S. Department of the Interior, National Register of Historic Places, Brentsville Historic District nomination, 1990. Retrieved May 25, 2015: http://www.dhr.virginia.gov/registers/Counties/PrinceWilliam/0 76-0338_Brentsville_Historic_District_1990_Final_Nomination.pdf

————, Brentsville Courthouse nomination, 1989. Retrieved May 25, 2015: http://www.dhr.virginia.gov/registers/Counties/PrinceWilliam/0 76-0021_Prince_William_County_Courthouse,_Brentsville_1989_Fin al_Nomination.pdf

Virginia Herald, Fredericksburg, Va., 1867.

"VNP Acquires Pages and Pages of Page County Newspaper", *Fit to Print* blog, Virginia Newspaper Project at the Library of Virginia, October 23, 2012. Retrieved May 21, 2015: http://www.virginiamemory.com/blogs/fit-to-print/2012/10/23/vnp-acquires-pages-and-pages-of-page-county-newspapers/

Wallace, Lee A., Jr., *Seventeenth Virginia Infantry (The Virginia Regimental Histories Series)*, 1st ed., Lynchburg, Va.: H.E. Howard, 1990.

Walker, Keith, " 'Ghost Hunters' Team Pays Visit to Brentsville," *Richmond Times Dispatch*, August 15, 2009.

Warfield, Edgar, *Manassas to Appomattox: The Civil War Memoirs of Pvt. Edgar Warfield, 17th Virginia Infantry*, McLean, Va.: EPM Publications Inc., 1996 (reprint).

Warren Sentinel, Front Royal, Va., 1869–1872.

Washington Herald, 1909.

Weisberg, Barbara, *Talking to the Dead*, New York: Harper Collins, 2009.

Welsh, Jack D., *Medical Histories of Confederate Generals*, Kent State University Press, 1999, pp. 108–109.

Whitney, Orson F., *History of Utah*, Vol. I, Salt Lake City, Utah: George Q. Cannon & Sons Co., 1892, pp. 689-710.

"Who Remembers?" *Manassas Journal*, Nov. 7, 1935.

Wilhelm, Robert, "The Richardson-McFarland Tragedy," *Murder by Gaslight* website, July 10, 2010. Retrieved May 25, 2015: http://www.murderbygaslight.com/2010/07/richardson-mcfarland-tragedy.html

"William Brawner," findagrave.com, January 16, 2007. Retrieved May 27, 2015: http://www.findagrave.com/cgi-bin/fg.cgi?page=gr&GRid=17496869

Wingfield, Marshall, *A History of Caroline County, Virginia*, Baltimore, Md.: Genealogical Publishing Co., 2005.

Winn, Kenneth H., "Benjamin Gratz Brown," *Missouri Civil War Sesquicentennial* web page, undated. Retrieved May 25, 2015: http://mocivilwar150.com/history/figure/213

Wise, Barton Haxall, *The Life of Henry A. Wise of Virginia, 1806-1876,* Macmillan Company, 1899.

Wise, George, *History of the Seventeenth Virginia Infantry, C.S.A,* Baltimore: Kelly, Piet & Co., 1870.

Woodruff, Wilford, Mormon apostle, journal entry, March 10, 1859, reprinted on *LDS Church History* blog, undated. Retrieved June 4, 2015: http://lds-church-history.blogspot.com/2011/08/history-of-word-of-wisdom-jan-15-1859.html

Made in the USA
Lexington, KY
12 December 2016